Dr Richard Race, Roehampton University,
April 2012.

INSTITUTIONAL TRANSFORMATION TO ENGAGE A DIVERSE STUDENT BODY

INTERNATIONAL PERSPECTIVES ON HIGHER EDUCATION RESEARCH

Series Editor: Malcolm Tight

INTERNATIONAL PERSPECTIVES ON HIGHER
EDUCATION RESEARCH   VOLUME 6

INSTITUTIONAL TRANSFORMATION TO ENGAGE A DIVERSE STUDENT BODY

EDITED BY

LIZ THOMAS
MALCOLM TIGHT

Emerald

United Kingdom – North America – Japan
India – Malaysia – China

Emerald Group Publishing Limited
Howard House, Wagon Lane, Bingley BD16 1WA, UK

First edition 2011

Copyright © 2011 Emerald Group Publishing Limited

Reprints and permission service
Contact: booksandseries@emeraldinsight.com

British Library Cataloguing in Publication Data
A catalogue record for this book is available from the British Library

ISBN: 978-0-85724-903-6
ISSN: 1479-3628 (Series)

Emerald Group Publishing Limited, Howard House, Environmental Management System has been certified by ISOQAR to ISO 14001:2004 standards

Awarded in recognition of Emerald's production department's adherence to quality systems and processes when preparing scholarly journals for print

INVESTOR IN PEOPLE

CONTENTS

LIST OF CONTRIBUTORS

Rashidah N. Andrews	College of Liberal Arts, Temple University, Philadelphia, PA, USA
Derek Bland	School of Learning and Professional Studies, Faculty of Education, Queensland University of Technology (QUT), Brisbane, Qld, Australia
Betsy Bowerman	Widening Participation Office, University of Bristol, UK
Linda Cooper	Centre for Higher Education Development (CHED), University of Cape Town (UCT), South Africa
Glenda Crosling	Monash University Sunway Campus, Malaysia
Chris Croudace	Head of Outreach and Widening Participation, University of the West of England, UK
Blaženka Divjak	Faculty of Organization and Informatics Varazdin, University of Zagreb, Croatia
Jayne K. Drake	College of Liberal Arts, Temple University, Philadelphia, PA, USA
Vicky Duckworth	Centre for Learning and Identity Studies (CLIS), Edge Hill University, Lancashire, UK
Scott E. Evenbeck	New Community College, City University of New York (CUNY), New York, NY, USA
Kerry Ferguson	Equity and Student Services Division, La Trobe University, Melbourne, Vic., Australia

Michelle Gammo-Felton	Liverpool Institute for Performing Arts (LIPA), Liverpool, UK
Michelle Garvey	Trinity College Dublin (TCD), Ireland
Janet Graham	Supporting Professionalism in Admissions (SPA) Programme, UK
Marit Greek	Centre for Educational Research and Development, Oslo University College, Norway
Margaret Hart	The Open University (OU), UK
Sue Hatt	Aimhigher South West, University of the West of England, Bristol, UK
Sandra Hill	Business School, University of the West of Scotland, Hamilton, UK
Tony Hoare	Department of Geography, Bristol University, UK
Renata Horvatek	Faculty of Organization and Informatics Varazdin, University of Zagreb, Croatia
Amanda Ingleby	Centre for Learning Innovation and Professional Practice (CLIPP), Aston University, Birmingham, UK
Salma Ismail	Centre for Higher Education Development (CHED), University of Cape Town (UCT), South Africa
Steve Kendall	University of Bedfordshire, Luton, UK
Christopher M. Klinger	School of Communication, International Studies and Languages, University of South Australia (UniSA), Adelaide, SA, Australia
Kerri-Lee D. Krause	Griffith Institute for Higher Education, Griffith University, Brisbane, Qld, Australia
Renaud Maes	Unité de Psychologie des Organisations, Université Libre de Bruxelles, Belgium

Neil L. Murray	School of Communication, International Studies and Languages, University of South Australia (UniSA), Adelaide, SA, Australia
Tony O'Shea-Poon	The Open University (OU), UK
Frank E. Ross	University of North Texas at Dallas, USA
Sabine Severiens	Risbo, Risbo/Erasmus University Rotterdam, Rotterdam, The Netherlands
Dan Shaffer	Supporting Professionalism in Admissions (SPA) Programme, UK
Brian Spittle	Center for Access and Attainment, DePaul University, Chicago, IL, USA
Jacqueline Stevenson	Leeds Metropolitan University, UK
Michel Sylin	Université Libre de Bruxelles, Belgium
Cécile Sztalberg	Université Libre de Bruxelles, Belgium
James Tate	Aimhigher South West, University of the West of England, Bristol, UK
Liz Thomas	Widening Participation Research Centre, Edge Hill University, UK
Violeta Vidaček-Hainš	Faculty of Organization and Informatics Varazdin, University of Zagreb, Croatia
Richard Waller	Director of Lifelong Learning, Department of Education, University of the West of England, Bristol, UK
Rick Wolff	Risbo, Risbo/Erasmus University Rotterdam, Rotterdam, The Netherlands
Wâtte Zijlstra	Marketing and Research (central staff), The Hague University, The Netherlands

LIST OF INSTITUTIONAL CASE STUDIES

CHAPTER 1

INSTITUTIONAL TRANSFORMATION TO ENGAGE A DIVERSE STUDENT BODY

Liz Thomas

ABSTRACT

Purpose – *This chapter provides an overview of the book and discusses student diversity and institutional responses.*

Methodology/approach – *The chapter draws together literature and conceptual thinking about what student diversity is. It then analyses the drivers for increased diversity within higher education in the case studies in this book. Alternative approaches to diversity are presented, drawing on a synthesis of approaches identified in the literature. Finally, the chapter provides a summary of the other chapters and the associated case studies.*

Findings – *The chapter finds that diversity incorporates difference across a number of dimensions: education, personal disposition, current circumstances and cultural heritage. There are a wide range of reasons prompting institutions to recruit a diverse student population: a commitment to social justice, expansion and access to new markets, tapping the pool of talent, enhancing the student experience, national and/or regional policy, funding incentives, conforming with equality legislation, institutional research and personal commitment of staff. Institutions can respond to diversity in different ways. The idealised types are: altruistic (no institutional*

Institutional Transformation to Engage a Diverse Student Body
International Perspectives on Higher Education Research, Volume 6, 1–15
Copyright © 2011 by Emerald Group Publishing Limited
ISSN: 1479-3628/doi:10.1108/S1479-3628(2011)0000006003

change), academic (little or no change), utilitarian (special access and additional support mechanisms) and transformative (positive view of diversity resulting in institutional development).

Research limitations – *This chapter draws largely on the author's work in England and the United Kingdom and the case studies presented in this book.*

Practical implications – *This chapter is important as an introduction to the book, and providing frameworks to think about diversity.*

Social implications – *The framework for institutional change assists institutions to critically consider the response they make to a more diverse student population.*

Originality/value – *The paper provides original perspectives to conceptualising and responding to diversity.*

Keywords: Institutional responses to diversity; institutional transformation; student diversity

INTRODUCTION

This book is centred around the belief that the transformation of higher education institutions (HEIs) is necessary to engage a diverse student body, both to encourage them to enter higher education (HE) and to enable them to be successful in HE and beyond. In 1999 Maggie Woodrow said:

> To achieve a genuinely pluralistic higher education which meets the needs of students from under-represented groups, will require a shift from an ethos of selective normality to one of diversity and inclusion. (Maggie Woodrow, 8th Annual European Access Network Conference, Malta)[1]

Student engagement refers to the active involvement of students with peers, institutional staff and the institution and is necessary for students to be successful learners and graduates. To facilitate this, institutions need to proactively provide a range of opportunities for engagement, develop the capacity of staff and students to engage, and manage and co-ordinate the process. This requires institutional transformation, which includes an institutional commitment in engaging a diverse student body and changing institutional structures, processes and governance; developing an inclusive culture and altering processes of knowledge creation and knowledge transfer to be more inclusive of a diverse student body. This book examines how institutions need to transform themselves to engage a diverse student population and uses a range of institutional case studies from around the world to explore how this is happening in practice, including the enabling factors, the challenges and future developments. It is important first however to clarify what student diversity is, why the student population is becoming more diverse and to review alternative institutional responses to diversity.

STUDENT DIVERSITY

Student diversity is used in this book to refer to those students who differ from the elite student groups who have traditionally monopolised access to HE. Historically HE has been the preserve of the more privileged groups in society, and although those groups who have been largely excluded vary to some extent between countries, they also have much in common. Student diversity is also used here to refer to students from specific equality groups or with protected characteristics, currently defined in the United Kingdom as age, disability, gender reassignment, race, religion or belief, sex, sexual orientation, marriage and civil partnership, and pregnancy and maternity. Thus, student diversity can incorporate difference across a number of dimensions, namely previous education, personal disposition, current circumstances and cultural heritage, summarised with examples in Table 1 (Thomas & May, 2010).

The approach promoted in this book does not focus on specific target groups or dimensions of diversity, but rather strives towards proactively making HE accessible, relevant and engaging to all students through a mainstreamed approach to institutional transformation. This reflects commitment to an inclusive approach and recognition that individuals combine a range of diverse characteristics implying that only focusing on a particular aspect of their diversity could be meaningless.

AN INCREASINGLY DIVERSE STUDENT BODY

The most simple explanation for why the student population is becoming more diverse is expansion of the HE sector. For example, between 1983–1984 and 1993–1994, the UK HE sector grew by 77% (HEFCE, 2001a, 2001b). The growth, which was particularly accelerated between 1988–1989

Table 1. Student Diversity.

Diversity Dimensions	Examples
Educational	Level/type of entry qualifications, skills, ability, knowledge, educational experience, life and work experience, learning approaches
Dispositional	Identity, self-esteem, confidence, motivation, aspirations, expectations, preferences, attitudes, assumptions, beliefs, emotional intelligence, maturity, learning styles perspectives, interests, self-awareness, gender, sexuality
Circumstantial	Age, disability, paid/voluntary employment, caring responsibilities, geographical location, access to IT and transport services, flexibility, time available, entitlements, financial background and means, marital status
Cultural	Language, values, cultural capital, religion and belief, country of origin/residence, ethnicity/race, social background

Source: From Thomas and May (2010).

and 1993–1994, included expansion in full-time undergraduate study, especially at newer 'post-1992 HEIs'[2] and expansion of full- and part-time postgraduate study. This level of growth has inevitably resulted in some increases in student diversity, especially as the expansion was, in part, due to more women and more mature students entering the system. The expansion of HE systems is a trend seen in many countries, there are however a range of drivers internationally, nationally, institutionally and at the individual level that are driving change towards a more diverse student population. It is largely driven by economic concerns about the higher level skills of the population in the context of post-industrialisation and the continued growth of the knowledge economy (Thomas, 2001). For example, Ferguson (in this volume) notes that Australia is now 9th of 30 in the Organisation for Economic and Development (OECD) for the proportion of the population aged 25–34 years with higher degree qualifications, down from 7th a decade ago. Currently in Australia 29% of 25–34-year olds have degree-level qualifications. Current HE reforms emanating from the Bradley Review of Higher Education (2008) have set specific targets to be met, specifically that 40% of 25–34-year olds will have attained at least a bachelor-level qualification by 2020, an increase of 11%.

Research in the United Kingdom (Shaw, Brain, Bridger, Foreman, & Reid, 2007) identified a range of reasons why HEIs want to increase student diversity, and many of the case studies in this book identify institutional reasons why they have undertaken institutional change. The drivers identified include the policy drivers noted earlier, but extend beyond this to include student recruitment and access to new markets, improving learning and teaching and institutional social responsibility. These drivers and the potential benefits identified by Shaw et al. have been amended and extended by drawing on the case studies in this book. This synthesised summary is presented in Table 2. It should be noted that the third column is derived from the drivers expressed or implied in the case studies, and in reality there may be more.

Archer (2007) critically summarises the UK 'widening participation' (WP) policy context as embracing both economic and social rationales:

> as a means for revitalising national and local economies, and boosting individual and collective wealth ... as part of a 'civilising' mission within society ... and as a means for fostering greater social equality through the inclusion ... of 'disadvantaged' social groups into higher education. (Archer, 2007, p. 636)

These dual drivers are also embedded into the Australian government-commissioned Bradley Review of higher education (Bradley, 2008), which was translated into a national target that, by 2020, 20% of undergraduate students should come from lower socio-economic groups. HEIs are therefore required to be both educational establishments and agents of social change.

Despite widespread concern in the United Kingdom about the lack of impact of various WP interventions and strategies (NAO, 2008; Gorard et al., 2006), the most recent data paints a positive picture about the participation of students from historically underrepresented groups (HEFCE, 2010). This study reports the expansion of young participation in England from 30% in the mid-1990s to 46% at the end of the 2000s. Today, young people from disadvantaged areas are substantially more likely to enter HE than they were 15 + years ago (although much of this change has been since the mid-2000s). Thus, the proportion of young people living in the most disadvantaged areas (defined by participation rates, parental education, occupation or income) who enter HE has increased by around +30% over the past five years, and by +50% over the past 15 years. This is shown in Chart 1.

Thus, over the past 8–12 years the diversity of the student population has increased. This has not affected all institutions universally, as much of the increase in diversity has been into certain types of HE, and particular institutions. Expansion in HE is unlikely to continue over the next decade as it occurred in the previous one; however, the economic imperatives and the social justice demands still hold true and are only being fully recognised by

Table 2. Institutional Drivers and Benefits for Increasing Student
Diversity.

Driver	Potential Benefits	Case Studies Identifying This Driver
Institutional commitment to social justice, often related to institutional history, place and identity	Demonstrated commitment to institutional mission Contributing to local, regional or national social and economic regeneration	Aston University De Paul University Edge Hill University La Trobe University Leeds Metropolitan University The Open University Oslo University College University of Bedfordshire University of Southern Australia
Increasing student numbers and/or providing access to new student markets or establishing a niche market	Access to new student groups Financial viability of courses, departments or institution Reduced reliance on Funding Council grants	De Paul University Edge Hill University Monash University Malaysia Oslo University College Université libre de Bruxelles University of Bedfordshire University of the West of England
Tapping the pool of talent	Attracting a larger pool of highly qualified applicants to enhance reputation and/ or maintain high academic standards	De Paul University Liverpool Institute for the Performing Arts (LIPA) University of Bristol
To improve the student experience, including the quality of learning and teaching, to improve student retention and to improve progression in the labour market	Improved learning outcomes for all students Improved social experience for all students Improved student retention Improved progression into the labour market and employment of graduates	Aston University Edge Hill University Monash University Malaysia The Open University Oslo University College Temple University Trinity College Dublin University of Southern Australia University of the West of Scotland University of Zagreb

Table 2. (*Continued*)

Driver	Potential Benefits	Case Studies Identifying This Driver
National or regional policy promoting equity, social justice and/or economic development	Comply with policy and avoid sanctions Good performance with respect to national/regional targets Access to additional funding	Aston University Dutch institutions in urban areas La Trobe University The Open University Trinity College Dublin Université libre de Bruxelles University of Bristol University of Cape Town University of West of England
Providing access to funding streams	Additional support for institutional strategic aims or to ensure financial viability	Aston University La Trobe University University of Bristol University of West of England
Antidiscrimination and equality legislation	Comply with legislative requirement Avoidance of litigation	La Trobe University The Open University University of Zagreb
To improve institutional performance in response to research findings	To improve access or student experience and enhance institution	Aston University Leeds Metropolitan Trinity College Dublin University of Bristol University of Zagreb
Personal commitment by staff	Satisfaction and opportunity to improve social justice within the institution	Aston University Leeds Metropolitan Monash University Malaysia Oslo University College Queensland University of Technology University of Bristol University of Cape Town University of the West of Scotland University of Zagreb

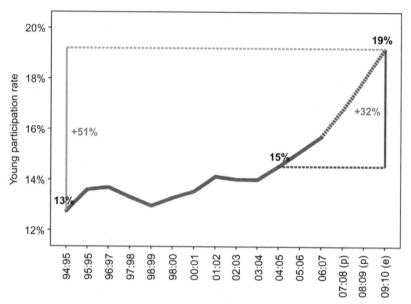

Chart 1. Trends in young participation for the most disadvantaged areas determined by HE participation rates (POLAR2 classification, adjusted). *Source*: HEFCE, 2010, p. 7.

some countries now. Ironically, the weak financial climate coupled with the persistent need for a more skilled workforce is now driving institutional transformation towards potentially radical models of employer engagement and work-based and work-related higher learning.

INSTITUTIONAL RESPONSES TO DIVERSITY

In response to the multiple, and possibly conflicting (Archer, 2007, p. 637) drivers identified earlier, institutions have developed a range of approaches to encourage, or accommodate, an increasingly diverse student population. The underlying philosophy and the type of changes made are influenced by issues such as history and mission, institutional self-identify, leadership, location, regionality and sense of place and market position (Shaw et al., 2007; Thomas et al., 2010a, 2010b). The following discussion aims to identify and model 'ideal types' of WP. Ideal types are a means to lever the scholar into practical research by orienting him or her more precisely to the aspect of social reality that they want to investigate, allowing them to acquire 'a "purchase" upon empirical reality by means of its "simplification"' (Kalberg, 1994, p. 85). The following discussion draws on and extends the typologies developed by Jones and Thomas (2005) and analysis of institutional responses to WP reported in Thomas et al. (2005).

Thomas et al. (2005) identified a split between institutions engaging in WP to help them meet institutional priorities (such as increased recruitment, greater student diversity, and/or meeting the needs of the local community and economy), and those engaging in WP outreach activities for broadly social justice reasons (and in response to national policy incentives). The latter approach can be described as *altruistic*. If an institution adopts an altruistic approach to WP, they are likely to undertake activities to promote wider participation in HE, but this is not related to an interest in, or commitment to admit students to the institution. The WP activities may therefore not have any impact on the institution undertaking them and are likely to only be undertaken while there is external funding to support the work. The altruistic approach can look positive on the surface, as it is not tarnished by marketing and recruitment activities, but it is underpinned by a lack of commitment to admit the students targeted, and it is unlikely to be sustainable (Thomas et al., 2005, p. 173).

Beyond this approach to WP, Jones and Thomas (2005) identified three further institutional responses or ideal types: academic, utilitarian and transformative. Briefly, the former refers to the need to raise aspirations among underrepresented groups, and in particular 'gifted and talented' (G&T) pupils from non-traditional backgrounds who are slipping through the net by not applying to study in HE. Institutions engaging in academic approaches are interested in the recruitment of these anomalous students from target groups, but do not have to adjust admissions process, or make any adjustments for these students once they are in HE. The problem from this perspective is viewed as attitudinal on the part of students and does not necessitate any institutional adaptation.

The utilitarian approach views students as lacking both suitable aspirations and prior academic achievement (entry qualifications). This approach therefore requires institutions to work to raise students awareness and knowledge of HE, and either to increase their academic achievements or to create special admissions processes to admit students from the target groups (e.g., lowering entry requirements, recognising a wider range of pre-entry qualifications and experiences or through compacts or other special arrangements). This approach therefore necessitates institutional change to support new types of students to enter and also to progress successfully through HE.

The transformative approach to WP understands the need to engage with potential students from communities and groups who are not participating in HE (Billingham, 2009, 2010) to create a new and more relevant HE experience. Such an approach is rooted in the assumption that HEIs need to undergo far-reaching structural and cultural change to learn and value from the difference and diversity that a genuinely representative student body would bring (in contrast to the homogenising drivers underpinning the earlier models). As discussed later in the text, it would involve changes to admissions processes, learning and teaching contents and delivery, and organisational and governance issues to promote student engagement and change.

Drawing on these four ideal types it is possible to construct a continuum of institutional responses to diversity (Fig. 1), with the altruistic response, involving no institutional change at one end, and the transformative approach, involving substantial change, at the other.

This extended model of ideal types could give the impression that the four approaches are relatively self-contained interpretations of 'widening parti- cipation' or responses to student diversity. Indeed, Jones and Thomas (2005) were criticised by Shaw et al. (2007) for the implication that HEIs 'fit' one of these categories – instead they noted that institutions may embrace more than one approach to diversity. However, Shaw et al.'s solution – to replace 'utilitarian' with 'mixed' or 'differential' while retaining the academic and transformative models – muddies the waters and misses the point of models or 'ideal types'. Their own empirical work suggests that *all* HEIs are mixed and differential. This is of course because 'HEIs are culturally complex organisations with different approaches to widening participation existing **within** institutions' (Greenbank, 2007, p. 212, emphasis added), and many of the responses to student diversity occur at the programme, departmental or

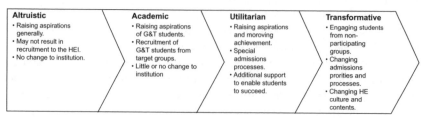

Fig. 1. Continuum of Institutional Responses to Student Diversity.

faculty level. Thus, the 'real world' is much more complex and messy, but it is still valuable to identify and differentiate conceptual models of WP and institutional responses to diversity, without expecting them to be translated perfectly into reality.

The next chapter examines the reasons why institutions are being encouraged or are choosing to move towards a more transformative approach to engage students in their HE experience, and the following chapter explores what a transformed institution looks like.

ABOUT THIS BOOK

This chapter has provided an overview of the issues of student diversity and institutional responses to WP. Some of these issues of diversity and institutional responses are then illustrated by case studies from The Open University in the United Kingdom (Hart and O'Shea-Poon) and the University of Cape Town in South Africa (Ismail and Cooper). While both case studies explore how the institutions have responded to external drivers for greater social justice in HE, their responses have been different. The Open University's commitment to inclusion lies at the heart of its founding mission. Change has taken place to widen participation and improve equality across the student lifecycle with a central focus on the student experience, the quality of learning, teaching and support and maximising the engagement and involvement of students. This institution has therefore adopted a transformative approach, enabled by strengthening governance frameworks and supported practitioner networks. Colleagues in the Higher and Adult Education Studies Development Unit at the University of Cape Town discuss how staff on the periphery have worked to widen access to historically excluded adult learners, but the institution has taken a more utilitarian approach. Ismail and Cooper argue however that it is essential that changes to provide access to learning and to curriculum contents and pedagogy are accompanied by wider transformation impacting on the institutional culture.

The next chapter draws on research from the United States, Australia and the United Kingdom, including a current programme in England to explore the importance of student engagement to improve student retention and success. Institutions that seek to enhance student retention through greater engagement will need to undertake transformative change, as it requires staff to operate in different ways. The role of engagement is illustrated through two case studies. First Derek Bland discusses the transformative value of engaging Australian school students who have little interest in education and progression to HE in researching their peers' perspectives of factors relating to low aspiration for and access to HE. On the basis of their findings, the students created an informative DVD to address student needs, became re-engaged with education themselves and this had a positive impact on the school culture resulting in many more young people progressing to HE. Andrews and Drake present evidence of an initiative from Temple University in the United States designed to improve student retention. It is based on knowing your students better so being able to identify those at risk of withdrawal and on the provision of one-to-one engagement sessions. This intervention improve the retention rate for this group of students by nearly 7% to bring them in line with the rest of the university population.

Chapter 3 further develops the notion of institutional transformation. In particular it draws from work in the United Kingdom and Europe to develop a framework identifying the types of changes that institutions need to make to mainstream their approach to student diversity. Drawing on analysis of 129 Widening Participation Strategic Assessments from English HEIs the chapter explores the extent to which these institutions are taking a transformative approach to WP. Two case studies from England and Australia provide in-depth examples of how they have implemented transformational change. Aston University in the United Kingdom (Ingleby) has adopted a whole institution approach to change across the student lifecycle including a focus on learning and teaching and employability; the case study reflects on the institutional journey and identifies the importance of senior management support and an evidence-informed approach. Similarly, La Trobe University in Australia (Ferguson) has sought to diversify its student population, and the character of its provision to enable these students to be successful. This is led by a senior member of staff and identifies the wider benefits of institutional development and change.

Chapter 4 by Sue Hatt and James Tate examines the importance of engaging students pre-entry and into HE, and how this must be integrated into the core work of the institution rather than divorced from it. This includes work to engage both young people and adults, and the link between engaging new student cohorts and the need for institutional change in anticipation of new interests and expectations. These issues are then explored through institutional case studies from Australia, the Netherlands and the United Kingdom. The University of Bedfordshire (Kendall) in the United Kingdom is a university with a very strong commitment to WP even during a period when there are pressures on all institutions to be more 'selective' about the students they recruit. The University has developed systemic partnerships with schools and colleges to engage young people to bring them into HE and then support them to be successful. Similarly, the University of Southern Australia (Klinger and Murray) has a strategic commitment to social inclusion, and has a well-established programme to enable adults without entry qualifications to prepare for HE and be successful within mainstream provision. A study based in three HEIs in the Netherlands (Severiens et al.) considers progression to vocational HE, which is particularly favoured by ethnic minority groups. It finds that too often the emphasis is on expecting students to change to fit into HE, rather than a more transformative approach in which institutions are changed.

Chapter 5 by Janet Graham and Dan Shaffer discusses the relationships between pre-entry interventions, admissions processes and student transition, and the associated need for institutional development to create an integrated approach. The case study about Liverpool Institute for the Performing Arts (Gammo-Felton) demonstrates the challenges related to WP that are faced by an institution that has a very high demand for a small number of places, and for which middle-class students are significantly more likely to have the necessary social and cultural capital to gain a place. De Paul University in the United States (Spittle) has used Strategic Enrolment Management to balance its commitment to social justice, its strong market position and associated demand for places and its need for student fee income. The case study from the Université libre de Bruxelles in Belgium (Maes et al.) discusses how the acknowledgment or recognition of prior experiential learning (APEL) is used to widen participation, but how this also requires institutions to change to be able to enable these students to be successful in HE, including pedagogical and culture change.

Chapter 6 by Kerri-Lee Krause argues for transformative learning to engage students from diverse backgrounds, exploring how learning, teaching, curricula and academic support can be transformed to engage students in their learning and beyond. These themes are developed in a series of case studies that explore how institutions have sought to transform the student learning experience to make it more engaging and inclusive. Trinity College Dublin has used a student survey about learning and teaching to develop an audit tool to facilitate academic members of staff to develop more inclusive curricular that are engaging to a more diverse student population. In contrast Scott E. Evenbeck and Frank E. Ross develop student learning communities to promote peer interaction and engagement in learning, and Vidaček-Hainš et al. explore strategies for engaging staff in delivering more learning through a blended approach to improve the learning experience and retention of students in the Faculty of Organisation and Informatics at the University of Zagreb in Croatia. Glenda Crosling discusses how local staff in an Australian University campus in Malaysia are gaining confidence to develop more relevant curricula to in-country and regional international students to provide a more relevant and engaging learning experience.

Chapter 7 argues that institutions must also address the progression of their students beyond HE into employment and further learning, including postgraduate study. It argues that institutions need to embed learning about employability and progression to further learning into their core learning and teaching experience, otherwise students from underrepresented and equality groups are likely to be disadvantaged when they move on from their undergraduate study. This is illustrated by analysis of how some English HEIs are addressing employability and access to postgraduate study, and a strategic approach to WP, progression and success is proposed. An example of how students can be supported to develop skills that help them both in their studying and as they progress into the labour market is provided from the University of the West of Scotland by Sandra Hill. In particular, the case study explores how pedagogy can be used to develop the social capital of first-generation undergraduates in a business school, and how this contributes to the development of employability skills and attributes to support their progression beyond HE.

Chapter 8 draws on the evidence presented in the chapters and case studies to identify the essential and desirable conditions for institutional transformation to engage a diverse student population. These include:

i. Commitment to a transformational approach;
ii. Sharing understanding and meaning;
iii. Institutional strategy for change: senior leadership, policy alignment, creating a facilitating infrastructure across the student lifecycle and co-ordinating change;
iv. Engaging staff and creating an inclusive culture;
v. Taking an evidence-informed approach;
vi. Linking change to other institutional priorities and developments and
vii. An enabling policy and funding context.

These features are further illustrated by the final case studies in the book. Stevenson reflects on the process of change at Leeds Metropolitan University in the United Kingdom and demonstrates the importance of developing a shared understanding of WP. Greek describes a bottom up strategy to engage staff in a more inclusive approach to learning and teaching. Duckworth then explores how staff engagement and an enabling management approach contributes to creating an inclusive culture at Edge Hill University in the United Kingdom. The final case study by Hoare et al. charts the mainstreaming and embedding of WP at two very different universities in Bristol in the United Kingdom – the University of Bristol and the University of the West of England. Both institutions have adapted and changed to engage a more diverse student body. They have developed clear institutional strategies and made extensive use of data and research to inform the process, plus they also recognise the value of strong senior leadership.

NOTES

1. http://www.ean-edu.org/index.php?option=com_content&view=category&layout=blog&id=39&Itemid=75

2. Thirty-five post-1992 universities were created from former polytechnics as result of the 1992 Further and Higher Education Act, which abolished the binary line.

CHAPTER 1.1

INSTITUTIONAL TRANSFORMATION TO ENGAGE A DIVERSE STUDENT BODY AT THE OPEN UNIVERSITY

Margaret Hart and Tony O'Shea-Poon

ABSTRACT

This case study focuses on the experience of The Open University in creating educational opportunities and social justice for all since its inception over 40 years ago. Setting developments over the past few years in the context of the University's mission, history and model of supported open learning, the case study identifies institutional transformation as an ongoing, organic process of innovation and embedding of learning that needs to respond to a constantly changing internal and external environment. Increasing student diversity has been achieved through ongoing developments in strategy, governance and practice, underpinned by a developing evidence base that explicitly seeks out the student voice. Whilst the case study is unique, the learning it highlights is transferrable to a wide range of institutions, particularly at a time when the demand for part-time and flexible higher education is on the rise.

Keywords: Diversity; engagement; opportunity; student; widening participation

Institutional Transformation to Engage a Diverse Student Body
International Perspectives on Higher Education Research, Volume 6, 17–28
Copyright © 2011 by Emerald Group Publishing Limited
All rights of reproduction in any form reserved
ISSN: 1479-3628/doi:10.1108/S1479-3628(2011)0000006004

INTRODUCTION

The Open University's (OU) commitment to inclusion lies at the heart of its founding mission, which remains central today.

> The Open University is open to people, places, methods and ideas. It promotes educational opportunity and social justice by providing high-quality university education to all who wish to realise their ambitions and fulfil their potential.

The University's open access policy, which allows anyone to register for an undergraduate course without prior qualifications or entry requirements, was a radical and defining feature at the outset and continues to be a critical factor in enabling participation by non-traditional students today. The entire ethos of the University was therefore geared towards *widening participation* long before this phrase entered UK national education policy.

Within this mission, the OU's understanding of inclusion, equity and opportunity has been continuously refocused over time in response to an ever-shifting external environment. This case study therefore starts from the premise that educational institutions must redefine models and approaches to student participation, engagement and success in an ongoing process of institutional transformation.

In particular, we discuss institutional change at the OU over the past decade in response to environmental factors that have included:

- the former UK Labour government's commitment to a target of 50% of young people participating in higher education by 2010;
- the introduction of public sector equality duties, requiring universities to demonstrate how they promote equality of opportunity and
- technological change enabling innovation and new approaches to learning and teaching, while at the same time creating potential barriers for some learners.

Success has been achieved through a student lifecycle approach to widening participation and equity with a central focus on the student experience, the quality of learning, teaching and support and maximising engagement and involvement of students. This approach has been enabled by strengthening governance frameworks and supported practitioner networks.

Our reflection summarises key principles that have supported the OU's continuous transformation as an organisation that values institutional learning through student engagement. As we approach an uncertain new era that will be significantly shaped by the priorities of the 2010 Conservative/

Liberal coalition government, we suggest ways in which continuing progress in widening participation and equity can best be assured.

INSTITUTIONAL CONTEXT

Established in 1969, the OU represented a bold educational experiment that has subsequently been replicated in many parts of the world, bringing access to higher education to countless people who had previously been excluded from the chance to participate.

The OU is the United Kingdom's only university dedicated to distance education. Through a model of supported open learning, students learn in their own time and place by accessing high-quality print and multimedia teaching materials, supplemented by personalised tuition, learning feedback, formal assessment and access to a range of online and regional and national support services.

The OU is the largest academic institution in the United Kingdom and Europe, with 14 core subjects, more than 200 qualifications and around 600 modules being studied by around 200,000 undergraduate and postgraduate students in the United Kingdom, Europe and beyond.

Nearly all the University's students study part-time and 70% are in full-time employment. Over time, the UK student population has become increasingly diverse, now closely mirroring the socioeconomic composition of the United Kingdom's population as a whole, and with around 11% ethnic minority students, more than 11,000 (6.5%) disabled students and an estimated 15,000 students (around 8%) for whom English is not their first language.

STRATEGY, GOVERNANCE AND PRACTICE

Strategy

OU Futures 2010–2013, the University's highest level strategy, continues to reinforce a commitment to social justice and equity, and is complemented by the specific concerns of the Equality Scheme and the Widening Participation Strategy. These strategies together have a sandwiching effect on other strategies that influence the policies and practices across the institution as demonstrated in Boxes 1 and 2.

The University's Widening Participation Strategy focuses resource and effort towards addressing two particular challenges within the UK higher

Box 1. Open University Core Strategies

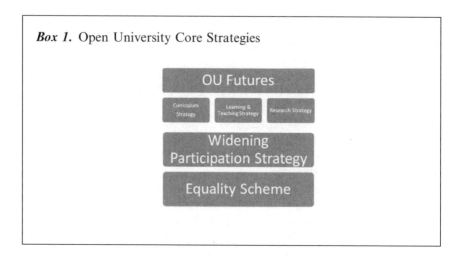

education sector: bridging the social class gap and reducing the ethnicity academic attainment gap. It adopts a student lifecycle approach, recognising the importance of recruitment, completion and academic attainment, with targets and indicators to measure progress across these different stages of the student journey. The strategy brings together and drives a range of new developments in recruitment, curriculum, pedagogy, student support and research, straddling many University functions and embedding the themes of opportunity, engagement and success.

Likewise, the Equality Scheme 2009–2012 sets out specific objectives, performance indicators and actions to support the creation of an inclusive environment. These straddle the entire institution, along with a set of cross-institutional enabling activities that include staff development, staff responsibilities and an agreed set of behaviours that are valued by the institution. The development of the Equality Scheme in 2009 is an example of meaningful engagement, which went well beyond statutory equality involvement and consultation requirements to engage a very large number of staff and students in determining priorities.

Governance

These strategies and approaches have been supported by the development of a more responsive governance and management structure, including a dedicated Widening Participation Management Group and an Equality and Diversity

---

Box 2. Embedding Equity and Widening Participation in Core Strategies: A Case Study

The Learning and Teaching Strategy 2009 builds on the University's continued drive towards e-learning and will influence the direction and approaches taken across the University in developing pedagogy over the next few years. The strategy recognises the tensions between a focus on e-learning and achieving an accessible and inclusive offer to students and embeds accessibility, widening participation and equality as underpinning principles:

- Accessibility – The OU needs to ensure that its diverse population of students is given the support it needs to enable access to our high-quality learning materials in different formats. Rather than providing alternatives to technology, we enable students to cross the digital divide to benefit from technology enhanced learning experiences.
- Widening participation and equality – New approaches to course design and the processes that support production and presentation will need to be assessed for their impacts on different groups of students, particularly those at entry level, so that the efficiencies, enhancements and transformations we make support recruitment, retention and progression of students from diverse backgrounds.

Management Group, both of which involve senior representatives from across the institution. These groups feed into committees responsible for the curriculum, learning and teaching, student support and research, each of which furthers student engagement through formally appointed representatives.

These high-level decision-making forums are complemented by a range of informal, but supported and resourced, networks, including a Faculty Equality and Diversity Implementation Network and a Widening Participation Network that bring together academic, academic-related and support staff, tutors and student representatives, providing further coherence to a wide and complex inclusion agenda.

Practice

The University's lifecycle approach to student participation, engagement and success, aims to ensure that the student experience is central in the services and support it offers.

Recruitment

The recruitment of students from low socio-economic groups is achieved through a range of approaches including marketing activity, workplace partnerships and a highly targeted Community Partnerships Programme. Through this programme, regionally based staff work in long-term partnerships with local community organisations such as extended schools, children's centres and voluntary sector groups to recruit and support students living in the most disadvantaged communities (Box 3).

Recruitment depends on the provision of a curriculum offer that is both relevant and accessible. In the year 2000, the OU launched its *Openings Programme* designed specifically to build confidence for students new to HE study (Box 4). Subsequent developments include an increasing number of Foundation Degrees and the embedding of widening participation as a key principle in the overall Curriculum Strategy.

Box 3. Reaching Students through Community Partnerships

'It was a parent and existing OU student who pressed a business card into my hand one morning in the playground and urged me to ring the number on it. So began our adventure with the OU's Community Partnership Manager in our area.

The first "drop-in" session at Home Farm Primary, squeezing onto chairs from Key Stage 1, huddled round knee high tables in a noisy corridor, did not immediately conjure images of ivory towers and seats of learning. Yet it was symbolic of our new Community University as our OU colleague spent two hours talking in detail with a dozen interested parents. The sessions were repeated at two other primary schools and again in these wonderfully DIY settings as our pool of intrigued, nervous, hesitant and excited prospective students grew.

A dozen parents registered to begin "Openings" courses in September 2007. And so we were off. Fortnightly study sessions at Hollingwood Primary. Word of mouth and more interested students ....

The celebration night with a packed room of students, children, parents, grandparents, food, uncles, drink, cousins .... You name it we were all there to applaud the first graduates of our new Community University'.

Matt Hannam, Extended Schools Project Manager, Bradford

Box 4. Curriculum Response: The Openings Programme

The programme consists of short, 10 credits, introductory level modules, which span the curriculum and introduce subject knowledge while building confidence and teaching core study skills. Modules run for 20 weeks, and tuition is provided through study materials and one-to-one support by telephone. There are no exams. Fees are kept as low as possible, and there is generous financial support.

Over 100,000 students have taken Openings modules to date. Analysis shows that Openings students are more likely to complete and pass their next course compared to students who did not start with an Openings course, and this pattern is even more marked for students who came to the University with low previous educational qualifications.

Retention

Support for students is provided both through named individual tutors and through an established *Learner Support Framework*, which identifies nine key activities at points in the student journey that have been shown to make a difference to outcomes (Table 1).

The tension between widening participation and e-learning highlighted in the Learning and Teaching Strategy is being addressed through a programme of activity to 'bridge the digital divide'. This focuses on providing support in accessing and building information and computing skills across the student journey. In some cases this can include support in the purchase of computers. A new development in the Openings Programme is the integration of an additional five credits of study building the computing and technology skills necessary for progression to 30- and 60-point modules.

A particular challenge for the OU is how best to balance a diversity of student goals and the wide choices offered by a modular curriculum, with the benefits, both to students and to the institution, of progression to further modules. Progression is identified as a key focus area in *OU Futures*, and the development of clear pathways through the curriculum, with more integrated academic and student support, is receiving much attention.

Academic Attainment

Interventions to support retention also have a direct impact on attainment. Various indicators such as prior qualifications help to predict those students

Table 1. Open University Learner Support Framework.

Student Journey	Key Activities	Examples
Exploration Consideration Decision	1. Module and programme information, advice and guidance	Respond to enquiries to enable learners to make informed decisions about their study aims and plans for their course/ programme of study
Orientation	2. Pre-course support	Offer reactive advice and support to all students and welcome new students 'at risk' by telephone or email
Preparation	3. Development of generic studentship skills	Respond to electronic enquiries, signpost students to learning skills resources and arrange additional individual support where required
Study	4. Study support	Provide proactive and reactive support to students at critical points in courses and programmes of study
	5. Support for assignments	Respond to enquiries, signpost to online support and encourage students to consider options available in relation to assessment strategies
	6. Mid-module support	Send out and respond to mid-course e-message to encourage students to maintain momentum in their studies
	7. Careers information, advice and guidance	Respond to enquiries and empower students to recognise their potential and achieve their goals
Consolidation	8. Examination and end of course assessment support	Send out exam e-message and encourage students to take/ submit exams/end of course assessments and revise effectively
Reflection Completion	9. Support for progression	Respond to enquiries and assist students in reflecting on their study aims and registering for next course of study if appropriate

at greatest risk of under-achieving, and these students are prioritised for additional contact to support progress.

The attainment of students living in areas of multiple-deprivation and of black and minority ethnic students have specific targets within the Widening

Participation Strategy and the University has a programme of research and action to raise attainment (Box 5).

EVIDENCE OF EFFECTIVENESS

The changing profile of the student population provides both the clearest evidence of the impact of institutional change and a key driver towards ongoing transformation.

In the decade between academic years 1999–2000 and 2009–2010, the OU

- increased the intake of students with educational qualifications below two A' Levels (the standard required for typical higher education entry), from 39% to over 50%;
- increased the intake of students from the lowest socio-economic quintile from 15.3% to 17.8% and reduced those in the highest socio-economic quintile from 23.5% to 21%, thereby achieving a student demographic

---

Box 5. Addressing the Ethnicity Academic Attainment Gap

Across the UK HE sector, ethnicity is a strong predictor for academic attainment and White students outperform all other ethnic groups. The OU ethnicity and attainment project draws together a wide range of research and action developed across the University and through participation in the Higher Education Academy and Equality Challenge Unit programme, which aims to reduce the ethnicity attainment gap.

OU-led research projects have focused on assessment mechanisms, language and conceptions of learning. These findings have influenced further activity including significant awareness raising, the development of an institution-wide action plan addressing student support, tutor support and curriculum development and new initiatives such as the development of language support resources for tutors. Institutional learning has been captured in a reflective paper, submitted at the end of the HEA/ECU summit programme.

Closing the ethnicity attainment gap continues to be a priority in the Widening Participation Strategy and the Equality Scheme and trends are monitored regularly.

---

profile that is more reflective of the population of the United Kingdom as a whole;

- more than doubled the proportion of new ethnic minority undergraduate students, from 5% to 11%;
- more than doubled the proportion of students aged under 21, from 4.2% to 9%; and
- improved retention rates for disabled students.

Much work is taking place to embed the learning from specific initiatives. For example, all faculties are currently developing Widening Participation Action Plans, which will draw on the lessons learned through the Openings Programme. The marketing function is drawing on images and lessons from the community partnerships work to inform its wider campaigns. And the quality and robustness of equality action plans across faculties has improved as a result of greater engagement achieved through informal networks discussed earlier.

This process of embedding is complemented by the development of capacity more rigorously to measure the impact of specific developments. For example, the digital divide programme was underpinned by a qualitative student research project that sought feedback from students from low socio-economic groups about the barriers they experienced in relation to e-learning. The Community Partnerships Programme is supported by a dedicated programme of evaluation, which has demonstrated the importance of locally based, face to face support in enhancing the completion and attainment rates of students from our widening participation target groups. Research into the ethnicity attainment gap has led to evidence-based action focusing primarily in the area of English language development. The University is investing significantly in the development of a widening participation research hub, which will enhance our knowledge more widely and enable us more effectively and efficiently to transfer learning into practice.

REFLECTION

Engaging a diverse student body is an organic process that changes over time in response to both internal and external environmental factors. The OU was a participant in the Higher Education Academy's 2007 programme on embedding inclusion and concurs with May and Bridger's (2010) analysis of the internal factors which support transformation: change is required at both institutional and individual level, it is essential to build an evidence base from which to bring about change and a multi-method, tailored approach is necessary involving different stakeholder groups and functions across the university.

A particular challenge in the OU is the size and complexity of the institution, which is reflected in widely distributed responsibilities. For example, building a shared understanding of what is meant by widening participation in the OU context, and of the appropriate balance between outreach and inreach, is time consuming and can extend the timescales required to bring about change. The same is true of balancing the need for clarity of roles whilst implementing a co-ordinated and integrated agenda. Considerable progress has been made in promoting student engagement, for example in the development of the Equality Scheme and the Community Partnerships Programme, but elsewhere, mainstreaming this beyond the involvement of representative students on formal groups and committees continues to be a challenge.

In addition to these considerations, external factors including legislative and government requirements and funding streams have a strong influence on approaches and outcomes. For example, within a broad culture of equality and inclusion, the OU's widening participation targets have become increasingly tightly focused in response to national agendas.

The overriding importance of funding arrangements cannot be over-emphasised, particularly at a time of squeezing of budgets across the higher education sector. For example, the HEFCE widening participation premium for recruitment of students from disadvantaged communities actively supports targeted activity such as the Openings and Community Partnerships Programmes. The formation of the new Conservative/Liberal government in the United Kingdom in May 2010 can be expected to mark the start of a new era in policies and funding, with public expenditure cuts inevitable. And, in coming years, the outcome of the 2010 Independent Review of Higher Education Funding and Student Finance, which is likely to recommend an increase in student fees, may overshadow action taken by any individual institution. Ensuring that the diversity of the student body is maintained and that universities are responsive to an increasingly complex array of needs will be dependent on careful analysis of the impact of proposed cuts in expenditure. It will be particularly important to undertake assessment of the differential impact of proposed changes across different groups, as emphasised by the Equality and Human Rights Commission for Great Britain in guidance issued to the sector in 2010. Equality law already requires this for disability, gender and race and the expected extension to other individual characteristics in the future is to be welcomed. The risk of

unintended consequences of changes driven by the need to save costs is high
and must be anticipated and where possible forestalled.

In the longer term, progress will best be assured through a shift of mindset
from safeguarding progress that has already been made to building the
business case for increasing diversity. As the OU's Vice-Chancellor states in
the introduction to the Equality Scheme, 2009–2012, 'In these more
challenging economic times, our actions will need to demonstrate our
commitment to the University's equality and diversity vision, enabling us to
utilise the enormous strength that diversity brings'. Defining and quantify-
ing this strength more clearly at institutional, sector and government levels
will be key in enabling the OU to continue to be a transformative institution.

CHAPTER 1.2

'RESISTANCE FROM THE PERIPHERY?' A CASE STUDY OF ATTEMPTS TO WIDEN ACCESS TO ADULT LEARNERS AT A SOUTH AFRICAN UNIVERSITY ☆

Salma Ismail and Linda Cooper

ABSTRACT

This chapter focuses on a case study of attempts at one South African university to widen access to adult learners from diverse race, class and gender backgrounds. It locates the education of adults within a post-apartheid policy framework aimed at transforming higher education on the one hand and pressures on universities brought about by changes in the global economy on the other. It then outlines the history of adult education programmes at the University of Cape Town, an institution that has an elite, colonial history and that privileges research over teaching. The chapter then considers the results of a 2008 survey of adult learners' experiences of the institutional culture and institution's systems, and the ways in which these present barriers to adult learners. It critically assesses three strategies adopted by staff on the 'periphery' of the institution to widen access to adult learners; these focus on:

☆ Phrase taken from Weiler (1984).

Institutional Transformation to Engage a Diverse Student Body
International Perspectives on Higher Education Research, Volume 6, 29–40
Copyright © 2011 by Emerald Group Publishing Limited
All rights of reproduction in any form reserved
ISSN: 1479-3628/doi:10.1108/S1479-3628(2011)0000006005

changing the institutional culture, developing policies and processes of recognition of prior learning (RPL) and transforming the curriculum. The chapter concludes that programme innovations have been possible with the aim of ensuring that curriculum is responsive to adult learners; however, widening access and increasing participation for adult learners also needs to be accompanied by significant changes in how the university is administered and run and that while alternative access routes into the university are theoretically possible, practical and political barriers remain.

Keywords: Adult learners; institutional culture; recognition of prior learning; transforming curricula; post apartheid policies

INTRODUCTION

South Africa's transition to democracy has ushered in new higher education policies aimed at broadening the base of, and increasing the general participation rate in, public higher education. These are linked to the longer-term goals of facilitating lifelong learning, developing the skills base of the country and redressing historical inequities in the provision of education. A key feature of the projected new system is that it will reflect a broadening of the social base in terms of race, class, gender, age and disability. One way of widening access is by recruiting increasing numbers of 'non-traditional' learners, identified as workers, mature adults, women and disabled people.

This chapter focuses on a case study of efforts at one South African university to widen access to adult learners from diverse race, class and gender backgrounds. It starts by looking at the backdrop of higher education policies aimed at transforming the profile of university students more broadly, and locating the education of adults within this policy framework. It then explores a case study of resistance by staff from the 'periphery' of one university to the institution's marginalisation of adult education. It examines their attempts to diversify the student body by widening access to adult learners through three strategies: changing the institutional culture, developing policies and processes of recognition of prior learning (RPL) and transforming the curriculum.

HIGHER EDUCATION AND WIDENING ACCESS TO A MORE DIVERSE STUDENT BODY

Policy provisions since 1994 have required South African universities to address issues of redress and equity in terms of race, class, gender, age and disability both as a political and as a economic project. There have been a range of policy and institutional changes at universities aimed at widening access to young black students from diverse backgrounds who were excluded from higher education under apartheid (black includes all racial groups disenfranchised during apartheid). Increased numbers of black students have been admitted through writing alternative admissions tests, through target setting, school recruitment policies and varying entry requirements for different racial groups. At UCT, the increased admission of black students has also been supported by academic development programmes, extended or revised curricula and state financial aid in the forms of scholarships and low interest rate loans.

There has been a growing debate however around the fact that success and participation rates of black students remain low in comparison with those of white students (Jansen, 2010; Scott, 2010; Yeld, 2010). The completion rate of black students nationally is approximately 33% and the participation rate is about 50% while those for white students are approximately 66% and 80% respectively (Scott, 2010, p. 234). It is generally agreed that the low success rates of black students can mainly be accounted for by a dysfunctional schooling system. Additional factors are the need for curricular reform (Scott, 2010) and the high costs of university education that lead to high student drop-out rates (see Letseka, 2009).

Some argue however that the basic source of the problem is that redress and equity issues have been progressively de-prioritised as South Africa's economy has become more enmeshed with the global economy. For example, du Toit (2010) argues that from 2000 the higher education discourse on equity through redress shifted to a discourse dominated by 'efficiency' and alignment with a macro economic growth plan that stressed human resource development and responsiveness of higher education to the labour market. By 2005, the state began capping students numbers and (in line with global trends), reducing funding for higher education, and placing emphasis on 'efficiency' and student 'throughput' (du Toit, 2010, p. 97). These shifts have been accompanied by moves towards a more managerial culture and the foregrounding of science and technology at the expense of the humanities.

These changes are interpreted by du Toit (2010, p. 103) as part of a broader shift by the African National Congress (ANC) government under President Thabo Mbeki from 'backward-looking equity-as-redress' to 'forward-looking equity-in-development'. This is explained by du Toit as a shift from a national concern for 'dealing with the past' (as associated with the Truth and Reconciliation Commission) to a more forward-looking language of economic development. In this process the post-apartheid system of higher education has been de-racialised, but remains an elite system, with privilege increasingly being based on class rather than 'race' (du Toit, 2010, p. 104).

What are the implications of these trends for the widening of access to higher education on the part of adult learners?

WIDENING ACCESS TO ADULT LEARNERS

Buchler, Castle, Osman, and Walters (2004, p. 152) have argued that: 'the education of adults in a society such as South Africa is a political, moral, historical and economic issue – and it is not merely one of these, but all of them'. Nevertheless, in the processes of restructuring higher education, adult education and training has not been a priority. Life-long opportunities for learning for older workers in colleges, technikons and universities are largely absent, and the post-school education and training sector has not massified nor modernised compared to other systems in the world (HSRC, 2003). In the 1990s, responsibility for adult education and training was relegated to the Department of Labour (rather than the Education ministry) to link it more directly to labour market needs. Echoing global discourses, responsibility for adult education is also increasing being shifted to the individual adult learner who is portrayed as needing to take responsibility for their own learning (Edwards & Usher, 2000).

Most of the literature in South Africa on widening access to higher education has concerned itself with increasing the provision of higher education generally for people previously disadvantaged under apartheid (Featherman, Hall, & Krislov, 2010). Adult learners have not been singled out as a group that requires special consideration. There is very little research on the extent to which tertiary institutions are widening access to adult learners, nor on alternative access methods or the curricular, pedagogical or institutional changes necessary to increase retention and pass rates of adult learners. Walters (2004, p. 38) argues that there is no serious intent to widen access to adult learners in a context where equity in relation to race and gender enjoys priority and that the state has to move from symbolic to substantive policy and provide the material resources necessary for implementing measures to widen access for adult learners. She further argues that organised labour – which was at the forefront of arguing for widening access for adult learners in the early 1990s – does not see increasing access of workers to higher education as a priority in the context of massive unemployment and low growth rates.

The next part of the chapter focuses on a case study of efforts by staff at one South African university to widen access to adult learners from diverse race, class and gender backgrounds. For the purposes of this chapter, we have defined adult learners according to 'life situation' rather than age, as students who have significant life and work experience, who usually combine study and work and who also carry significant family responsibilities. The section begins by locating the adult education teaching programmes within the institutional history of the University of Cape Town (UCT). It then goes on to consider three dimensions of the efforts to widen access to adult learners: changing the institutional culture, developing policies and processes of RPL and transforming curriculum.

ADULT EDUCATION TEACHING AT THE UNIVERSITY OF CAPE TOWN

The UCT is South Africa's oldest university, founded in the early 19th century as a teaching institution modelled on the 'Oxbridge' model, attracting young white men of the settler class (Saunders, 2010, p. 259). UCT was theoretically open to all races until 1959, but the number of black people who enrolled was very small. In 1959 the apartheid government declared UCT a 'white university' to be reserved for whites only. Over the next three decades, tiny numbers of black students were admitted under restrictive conditions until the 1990s when the university finally opened its doors to admit all students irrespective of race. The current student profile of UCT is 42% black and 22% white while the remainder comprises international students (18%) and those who choose not classify themselves (UCT, 2010). Despite widening access to black students, the historical legacy of the institution remains: its colonial, Eurocentric origins, its focus on recruiting young, relatively privileged, school-leaving learners, and its conservative and very traditional views on what constitutes knowledge, and on where and how knowledge is produced and acquired.

This elite, colonial history is reflected in the origins of the Department of Adult Education and Extra-Mural studies in a Summer School, a non-formal, liberal-arts programme that has run annually for over 60 years, and has always attracted largely a middle-class audience of white, middle-aged South Africans. During the 1980s however, as the struggle against apartheid began to grow, the department's Summer School was supplemented by a formal offering – the Advanced Diploma for Educators of Adults – as well as a range of non-formal short courses aimed at community-based activists as well as a programme of research focusing on adult literacy. In the 1990s, the department added a two-year, entry-level diploma as well as a Master's programme in Adult Education. These initiatives focused on building the capacity of an adult education sector that consisted largely of trade union educators, community activists, literacy practitioners and leaders and managers of progressive anti-apartheid non-governmental organisations and civic bodies. The undergraduate adult students were largely black and predominantly women who had lost the opportunity of higher education because of apartheid education policies.

As noted earlier, the post-apartheid state implemented a number of new policies to restructure higher education. In part these aimed to implement institutional redress, but they have been criticised as also bringing universities in line with a neo-liberal economy and a shift to a managerial culture (Higgins, 2007, pp. 117–121). As part of these changes, there was a widespread restructuring of faculties and departments.

In 1999 the Adult Education department at UCT was 'merged' into the School of Education; then in 2000, most adult education staff were moved into the new Centre for Higher Education Development (CHED), while the adult education programmes continued to be offered through the School of Education. In this way, adult education staff were shifted to a newly established faculty that had multiple roles in institutional development and did not have its own disciplinary authority, while adult education teaching programmes occupied a peripheral space in the School of Education. This restructuring sent out a signal that adult learners were not the university's first priority.

Despite this marginalisation, adult education programmes at the university have continued to attract increasing numbers of students (although taught by fewer staff). In addition adult education staff have taken initiatives to widen access more broadly to adult learners across UCT through an institution-wide body, the Adult Learners Working Group (ALWG) established in 2004.

CHANGING INSTITUTIONAL CULTURE AND PRACTICES

Institutional support for adult learners has in part been dependent on the advocacy and lobbying work of the ALWG. One of the issues that this group has focused on is the institutional environment that is unsupportive of adult learners in a number of respects. A survey of adult learners at UCT, focusing on adult learners' experiences of the institution's systems and institutional culture, found that adult learners experience a range of institutional barriers to studying at UCT (Cooper, Majepelo, & Pottier, 2008).

Institutional Culture

Institutional culture is understood to mean traditions and practices, often deep-rooted and operating at both social and professional levels, which have become the established norm in an institution. Institutional culture is reflected in both the physical and administrative arrangements and includes how people interact with each other, individuals' perception of their working environment, language, academic culture, ceremonies, attitudes of tolerance as well as outreach and extension services (Ismail, 2007, p. 85).

The ALWG survey found that many adult learners do not feel 'at home' at UCT. Hall (2010, p. 355) argues that UCT is a complex institution that holds the contradictions of the old and the tensions of the new. For example, in graduation ceremonies students graduate along with ululation, the blowing of vuvuzelas (air horns) and diverse dress codes, but Gaudeamus is still sung, and faculty in academic gowns still proceed in rank order leading the vice chancellor to convene the assembly. Like other students, adult students experience the contradictions of this complex institutional culture as well as feeling marginalised in terms of language, class background and age. However the main concerns of adult learners that emerged from the survey were the institution's practical workings in terms of its administration systems, access to student facilities and fees policy.

Institutional Workings

UCT is set up for undergraduate study and is geared mainly towards full-time students. Its administrative offices and student facilities such as computer services, canteens and writing centre are not easily accessible to working adults after hours. Extending the hours of opening of offices and access to facilities remains a major challenge for the ALWG.

The university has a fees policy whereby students have to pay most of their fee up front at the beginning of the year before registration. Students are meant to access this information online, but many adult learners from poorer communities do not have access to the Internet to check on fees and fees policy. For those who have family responsibilities and school fees to pay at the beginning of the year this fee arrangement is punitive. Despite efforts to change this on the part of the ALWG, the university's administration claims that its computer systems cannot accommodate special categories of students like adult learners.

Another issue taken up by members of the ALWG has been that of financial support. Up until 2008 the university and the state did not provide financial support for working adults or easy access to low-interest loans. The survey identified financial distress as a common factor deterring adults from applying to study or leading to drop out from programmes (Cooper et al., 2008). Members of the ALWG have had only limited success in getting the university to agree to make financial aid available to a small number of adult students.

RECOGNITION OF PRIOR LEARNING

In 2004, along with other higher education institutions, UCT was required by new statutory regulations to adopt an institution-wide policy on RPL (UCT, 2004). An attempt was made to incorporate into the policy the most progressive principles that had been evolved internationally. The policy commits UCT to 'redressing inequities and supporting lifelong learning through widening access to adult learners' based on a belief that 'there are able people with valuable knowledge and experience in workplaces and communities who could benefit from university study' (UCT, 2004, p. 2). It emphasises that 'RPL is based on a developmental model, not a deficit model of adult learning; it builds on knowledge and skills that adults have already acquired', and that 'RPL is part of UCT's broader commitment to be socially responsive to key social needs, and to significant constituencies in government and civil society' (UCT, 2004, p. 4). It foregrounds the value of the knowledge that adult learners can bring into the academy: 'The knowledge and skills reflected in successful applications for RPL contribute to the fund of human knowledge and thus inform and enrich the curricular, pedagogical, and critical practices of the academy' (UCT, 2004, p. 9).

Despite progressive policy being in place, access through RPL has remained a tiny proportion of admissions at UCT, particularly at under-graduate level. The majority of successful RPL applicants have been into postgraduate programmes, often in more applied fields. In the few sites that RPL has been established on an ongoing basis, some innovative practices have evolved. However, the team responsible for processing RPL applications has encountered a range of obstacles. First, faculty gate-keepers often demand rigid comparisons, rather than general equivalence between 'knowledges'. For example, to gain access at post-graduate level, RPL candidates are expected to demonstrate that they have prior research experience which they are unlikely to have gained through typical 'learning-on-the-job'; meanwhile candidates' other skills, knowledge and experience are barely considered. A further obstacle is the 'second guessing' of RPL assessors' judgment: in some cases, although academics have carried out a lengthy RPL assessment process and submitted a detailed report, their recommendations are turned down-wholly or in part. This happens also in a context where there is a lack of explicit criteria, and a general unwillingness to define access criteria for what constitutes 'post-graduateness'. Another problem is that lecturers who are asked to assess an RPL candidate sometimes struggle to articulate their judgement in the meta-language required to make an argument about general conceptual ability and academic 'literacies'. Finally there is a serious lack of resources to do what it is a time-consuming task.

Academic resistance to RPL draws for its intellectual justification on some cogent critiques of RPL. One strand of these critiques emphasises the differentiation of knowledge and seriously questions whether knowledge gained experientially and which is embedded in specific contexts, is transferable across contexts – particularly into an academic context (Young, 2008). Another is that the humanistic, developmental model of RPL renders invisible the academic assessment criteria that will – sooner or later – inevitably be brought to bear in assessing the RPL student (Shalem & Steinberg, 2006). A third strand of critique of RPL stems from the argument that not all knowledge is equally valid or worthy – to argue otherwise leads us into relativism – and that there are codified bodies of knowledge that our society relies on that must form the basis of higher education curricula (Muller, 2000). These kinds of arguments are often cited by leading academics at UCT, and UCT RPL staff have had to seek a way of engaging with these critiques while maintaining the position that experiential, work- and community-based knowledge is an important category of knowledge that provides adult learners with the potential to succeed in academic study and that 'everyday' knowledge can also act to enrich the academic knowledge archive.

TRANSFORMING CURRICULUM

The UCT has been resistant to global trends towards more interdisciplinary higher education programmes and greater social responsiveness of higher education curricula. These trends are viewed by some as undermining academic standards and academic autonomy, while others are critical of them for being part of what they see as the increased marketisation of higher education (Muller, 2000; Ensor, 2003).

There is however a particular kind of curriculum responsiveness in the form of tailoring of curriculum to adult learners' needs that has evolved in some of UCT's adult learner-focused programmes. One such model is the Diploma in (Adult) Education. This programme originated as a non-formal programme for community activists in the 1980s; it was formalised in 1995 into a two-year part-time programme and 15 years later, it continues to take in a bi-annual cohort of adult educators from diverse fields. Its curriculum has been adapted over successive years in response to a number of specific constituencies:

- Textile and telecommunication industry trainers, where the curriculum has fore grounded a critical look at South Africa's skills development policy, the impact of the global economy on work and learning, as well as strategies for education practitioners to bring about changes in the workplace;
- Trade union educators, where the curriculum has been adapted to incorporate a focus on the long, varied and rich history of trade union education, learning in social action contexts, the relationship between education and ideology and education and organising; and traditions of radical pedagogy; and
- A current cohort of trade union gender activists, where feminist theory and feminist pedagogy is threaded throughout the curriculum and where there is a central focus on changing gendered organisational practices and power relationships.

Another example of how curriculum responsiveness has been enacted in relation to adult learners at UCT is the Disability Studies MPhil Programme. The programme's main constituency is people who have been activists and policy advocates in the disability rights movement nationally and on the African continent. Their experiential knowledge is valued by lecturers because it is seen as providing insights uniquely available to those who are directly affected by disability, and as something that can complement and enrich formal academic knowledge. From the outset the programme has also worked in partnership with disability rights organisations that have constituted an active social movement in South Africa since the closing decade of apartheid, to negotiate the aims of the programme and to develop curriculum. Disability movement leaders and activists have been drawn into the programme not only as students but also as guest lecturers, with the programme being viewed as a site for dialogue between academics and social movement activists (Cooper, 2011).

Despite its innovative approach, or possibly because of it, this programme has also encountered obstacles: attempts to sustain its interdisciplinary structure were thwarted, and it was forced to relocate to the Health Sciences Faculty; support of academically under-prepared adult learners has proved to be very resource demanding, with programme leaders coming under pressure to 'economise' and streamline the allocation of resources; and questions have been raised about its academic status and about whether it meets 'academic standards'.

CONCLUSION

This chapter has shown that within teaching programmes, where academic staff still remain relatively autonomous in terms of curriculum design, innovations have been possible with the aim of ensuring that curriculum is responsive to adult learners. In other words, student access at an epistemological level can be facilitated through creative approaches and strategies.

However, the chapter has argued that widening access and increasing participation for adult learners also needs to be accompanied by significant changes in how the university is administered and run: for example in the opening hours of administrative offices and student facilities, and in systems of financial support and payment of fees. Even more intractable is the challenge of changing the broader institutional culture and creating a symbolic environment, traditions and practices that will allow adult learners to feel 'at home'.

Finally, the chapter has shown that while access to the university through RPL is theoretically possible, enormous practical and political barriers remain. These include the lack of resourcing for what is a time-consuming process, as well as academics' resistance to students coming in through an alternative access route. It has been shown that in admitting adult learners through RPL the team responsible for processing applications has come into conflict with the conventional standards of social science and with arguments for the superiority of disciplinary knowledge over experiential knowledge.

Some of the challenges to conventional notions of 'academic standards' have long-since been posed by black academics and feminists (e.g. Jansen,

1991; Lather, 1986; Harding, 1986) as well as by postmodern writers (e.g. Scott, 2004). In addition, in South Africa there have been moves towards Africanisation of the curriculum and exploring how indigenous knowledge systems might link with global systems of knowledge production and transmission. Despite these developments, those in power have shown that they continue to have the ability to define knowledge and on this basis exclude students whom they determine as not having the required knowledge and competencies for university study. In meeting these challenges, the strategy of 'resistance from the periphery' has been to argue for the continued value of experiential, work, community and political knowledge as important categories of knowledge in themselves, as well as providing a basis for adult students to succeed in academic study.

CHAPTER 2

ENGAGING STUDENTS TO IMPROVE RETENTION AND SUCCESS

Liz Thomas

ABSTRACT

Purpose – *This chapter identifies the reasons why institutions need to undertake transformation to engage a diverse student population: it presents a model of student retention and success, which centres on student engagement pre- and post-entry.*

Methodology/approach – *The chapter overviews the literature on student retention and success and utilises emerging findings from the meta-analysis of the What works? Student retention and success programme.*

Findings – *The emerging model puts student engagement at the heart of student retention and success. Institutions should promote engagement by*

- *Provision of a range of opportunities for student engagement of different types, at different levels, across the institution in different sites (academic sphere, social sphere and professional services sphere), throughout the student lifecycle.*
- *Developing students to recognise the importance of engagement and to have the capacity to engage in a range of opportunities.*

Institutional Transformation to Engage a Diverse Student Body
International Perspectives on Higher Education Research, Volume 6, 41–55
Copyright © 2011 by Emerald Group Publishing Limited
All rights of reproduction in any form reserved
ISSN: 1479-3628/doi:10.1108/S1479-3628(2011)0000006006

- *Developing staff responsibility for and capacity to provide effective engagement opportunities.*
- *Taking responsibility for engagement, including monitoring engagement and acting when there are indicators of lower levels of engagement.*
- *Creating a partnership between students and institutions towards a shared outcome of successful learners and graduates.*

Research limitations – *This chapter draws on emergent findings from the What works? programme.*

Practical implications – *This chapter assists institutions to improve student retention and success by focusing on engagement and institutional culture.*

Social implications – *The model assists institutions to critically consider transformation to engage a diverse student population and improve retention and success.*

Originality/value – *The chapter pre-views original research about engagement, retention and success, which are international concerns.*

Keywords: Student engagement; retention; success; institutional transformation

INTRODUCTION

The previous chapter discussed the national and institutional drivers to engage a more diverse student body and possible institutional responses. Chapters 4 and 5 develop these themes in terms of engaging students through pre-entry work and the admissions process, to enable students from a wide range of backgrounds, particularly those traditionally excluded from higher education (HE), to participate. This chapter focuses on the need to engage students across the student lifecycle (including pre-entry) to enhance student retention and success. These themes are further developed in Chapters 6 and 7, which focus on transforming the learning experience to engage a diverse student body and progression beyond the first degree, respectively.

This chapter identifies the reasons why institutions need to undertake transformation to engage a diverse student population to improve student retention and success. This can be contrasted with alternative responses to diversity outlined in Chapter 1, including making no changes or simply bolting on additional services to support students from non-traditional backgrounds to be successful. The chapter presents a model of student retention and success, which centres on student engagement and is being developed as part of the What works? Student retention and success programme in England (see www.actiononaccess.org/retention).

CONCERN ABOUT RETENTION AND STUDENT SUCCESS

This book is based on the premise that institutions need to change to enable students from under-represented and equality groups to gain entry to HE and also to enable them be successful. There are range of economic and ethical arguments as to why institutions should be concerned about student retention and success.

In terms of economics, when a student leaves an institution before completion of their target award, this represents lost income for the institution, which cannot easily be replaced. The lost income includes tuition fees paid directly by students or by the government, plus additional fees, such as those associated with student accommodation. For example, currently in England (2010–2011), an institution receives the following funding per student per year: student fees of £3,290, and a Higher Education Funding Council for England (HEFCE) teaching grant ranging between £3,964 and £15,856 (with different rates being paid for different subjects, which are divided into four bands), although £1,285 is deducted from each amount in recognition of student fee payments. Additional HEFCE fee income may also accrue in the form of widening participation and disability premiums linked to student characteristics. Other income may include accommodation costs; at my own institution catered accommodation costs are a little over £3,300 per year (the rate varies between institutions depending on the type of accommodation, services provided and location of the institution). This makes the total income per student over the course of a three-year degree programme in excess of £20,000 (excluding additional payments).

From 2012, student fees in England will increase, ranging from £6,000 to £9,000 per year, plus the institution will receive a small payment from the state per student for each year of study (which is likely to start at about £600). Thus, from 2012 even at the lowest end, a non-residential student will generate a minimum income of about £19,800 and a residential student an income £28,800 over the course of a three-year degree programme.

The economic argument for student retention and completion operates at the national level too. The National Audit Office in the United Kingdom has undertaken two reviews about student retention (NAO, 2002, 2007) intended to ensure value for money for the tax payer. The tenor of each of these reports, and the subsequent Public Accounts Committee reports (e.g. House of Commons Public Accounts Committee, 2008) has been that institutions should step up their efforts to improve student retention and completion, even though in the international context the United Kingdom has high rates of success at about 90% (although there are significant variations between institutions, disciplines and student characteristics such as age and entry qualifications).

In terms of ethics and social responsibility, it seems reasonable to argue that if an institution admits students to HE, it has an obligation to take reasonable steps to enable them to be successful. In Europe, the Bologna process designed to create a European Higher Education Area asserts that 'Access into higher education should be widened by fostering the potential of students from underrepresented groups and by providing adequate conditions for the completion of their studies' (Conference of European Ministers responsible for higher education, 2009). Speaking in this context, Bamber and Tett (2001, p. 15) suggest that 'Higher education must accept that the implications of offering access to non-traditional students do not end, but rather begin, at the point of entry'. Furthermore, in the words of Vincent Tinto (2008), access without support is not opportunity. Success can be understood as a less institutionally oriented and more student-centred concept and may not equate to retention and completion. Success may extend beyond the HE experience (e.g. be defined in terms of securing good employment or being happy) or may include starting in HE and deciding it is not the right pathway (Quinn et al., 2005a, 2005b).

The compelling economic arguments for focusing on student retention and the associated ethical concerns about student success beg the question of how institutions can improve the retention and success of students in HE. Although these arguments have centred on the English context, student retention, completion and success is a matter of international concern (see, e.g., Thomas & Quinn, 2006; van Stolk, Tiessen, Clift, & Levitt, 2007).

STUDENT ENGAGEMENT, RETENTION AND SUCCESS

Previous work on student retention and withdrawal has identified the need for students to adjust and integrate to HE to be successful (Harvey & Drew,

2006). This can be particularly challenging for students from 'non-traditional groups', who are less likely to feel like they belong and more likely to feel like outsiders (Leathwood & O'Connell, 2003; Read, Archer, & Leathwood, 2003; Thomas, 2002a, 2002b). This has been conceptualised through the use of Bourdieu's work on 'habitus' and 'cultural capital'. 'Habitus' refers to the norms and practices, or dispositions, of particular social classes or groups (Bourdieu & Passeron, 1977). These are created or shaped by people's experiences and the norms of the people around them, and thus upbringing and family are particularly influential. The ways of doing things (the habitus) of the dominant classes in HE have to a large extent become the norm for HE organisations and those who work and learn in them, and this can be considered as the institutional habitus (Reay, David, & Ball, 2001). Those who are from the same social, cultural and educational backgrounds have intimate understanding of these practices and ways of being, and this is termed 'cultural capital'. In other words, their upbringing has endowed them with cultural capital that allows them to fit into HE more easily than for students who have different family backgrounds – which may be related to social class, race, education, family values and so on. A student from the dominant social groups 'encounters a social world of which it is a product, it is like a "fish in water": it does not feel the weight of the water and it takes the world about itself for granted' (Bourdieu & Wacquant, 1992, p. 127). Conversely, a student from a non-traditional background may therefore feel like "a fish out of water", and thus withdraw early from HE.

WHAT WORKS? STUDENT RETENTION AND SUCCESS PROGRAMME

This three-year programme, which is funded by the Paul Hamlyn Foundation and HEFCE, aims to generate robust evidence about the most effective strategies to ensure high continuation and completion rates within HE. Primary data collection is through seven funded projects involving 22 higher education institutions (HEIs) in England and beyond. As the director of the support and co-ordination team, I have worked with project teams to influence and guide the process of data collection and analysis and undertaken programme-level meta-analysis of project findings. The meta-analysis is currently informing a conceptual model of student retention and success (Thomas & May, forthcoming). The initial model (Thomas et al., 2009) was informed by literature from the United Kingdom. This has been revised and updated in response to feedback from practitioners, researchers and experts across the HE sector and by drawing on US literature and emerging empirical data.

LINKING STUDENT ENGAGEMENT TO RETENTION AND SUCCESS

Our analysis of the interim project reports points to the centrality of student engagement to enhance retention and success in HE (Thomas & May, forthcoming). This echoes research work in the United States and Australia, which is emphasising the importance of student engagement to improve student persistence in HE (Kuh, Kinzie, Schuh, Whitt, & Associates, 2005; James, Krause, & Jennings, 2010). Very simply, the evidence suggests that if students are able to engage with peers, institutional staff and the institution per se, then they are less likely to feel like outsiders. They are able to build an identity that incorporates their HE experience, and their habitus (or way of doing things) is subtly moulded to become more aligned with the institutional habitus. Simultaneously, the institutional habitus can be informed (albeit in a limited way) by the norms, values and practices of new student groups. Thus, institutions need to provide opportunities for student engagement across the institution – in the academic, social and professional service spheres. For many students from diverse backgrounds, the academic sphere is particularly important as a site for all forms of engagement, as many of these students spend less time on campus to engage in the social and professional service spheres than students from more traditional backgrounds due to employment, family and community commitments and often living in the family home rather than in HE accommodation with fellow students (Thomas, 2006). Our model puts student engagement at the centre of student retention and success:

> Student engagement lies at the heart of retention and success and therefore offers institutions the answer to their improvement. Essentially institutions need to attend to not just the number and range of interventions or services they provide, but the quality and extent of the students' interactions with those as well as the institution more broadly. Successful higher education depends on a partnership between a student and the institution they attend. (Thomas & May, forthcoming).

ACADEMIC ENGAGEMENT

Academic engagement puts students at the heart of their learning experience and gives them a more proactive role. Kuh (2009, p. 683) has defined student engagement as 'the time and effort students devote to activities that are empirically linked to desired outcomes of college *and* what institutions do to induce students to participate in these activities (Kuh, 2001, 2008, 2009)' (emphasis in the original). According to Huba and Freed (2000), student engagement entails a move from a teacher-centred paradigm to a learner-centred paradigm, in which students construct knowledge through a more active and authentic learning process facilitated by academic staff, rather than relying on the transmission of knowledge from teacher to student. This constructivist learning paradigm has implications for pedagogy, including group learning, engaging activities, feedback and formative assessment (see Crosling, Thomas and Heagney, 2008). Indeed, Chickering and Gamson (1987) outline 'seven effective educational practices' to improve student engagement, which include contact between students and academic members of staff; encouraging reciprocity and cooperation among students; facilitating active learning; providing prompt feedback; devoting time to learning activities; communicating high expectations and respecting diverse talents and ways of learning. Krause (in Chapter 6 of this publication) extends the notion of academic engagement by arguing that

> Learning occurs in a range of settings, both within and beyond the formal curriculum. It involves developing connections within the university as well as building on prior learning, along with learning that takes place in the workplace and community settings.

Academic engagement is related to 'effective learning' and may be synonymous with or necessary for 'deep' (as opposed to surface) learning (Ramsden, 2003, p. 97). Engagement in the academic sphere is central to effective learning, which contributes to persistence and academic success. This is illustrated by the case study by Andrews and Drake, which provides evidence about the impact on retention of increased interaction between staff and students.

SOCIAL ENGAGEMENT

Engagement however can take place beyond the academic domain, in other spheres of the institution, and can have a positive impact on students' retention and success too. Vincent Tinto's influential work points to the importance not just of academic interaction but also of social engagement (Tinto, 1993), and this is supported by research in the United Kingdom (Thomas, 2002; Wilcox, Winn, & Fyvie-Gauld, 2005).

The emerging empirical evidence reinforces the vital role of friendship to many students, especially when they face difficulties. But it is also clear that the academic sphere can play a central role in facilitating students to develop these friendships, especially for those who spend less time on campus because they live at home or have work and family commitments. In addition, technology has been successfully used to facilitate social networking between students, especially those who are not based on campus – both pre- and post-entry.

ENGAGEMENT IN PROFESSIONAL SERVICES

UK universities provide a range of 'professional services', which are designed to attract and recruit students to the institution, provide pastoral support, and develop academic, personal and professional capacities, and these services are also sites where students can interact with each other and institutional staff and develop and nurture their student and graduate identities. Emerging empirical evidence (Thomas & May, forthcoming) demonstrates that professional services make an important contribution to the development of students' knowledge, confidence and identity as successful HE learners, both pre- and post-entry. This includes, for example, enabling students to make informed choices about institutions, subjects and courses and to have realistic expectations of HE study (see Thomas, forthcoming). Many professional services, however, are most effective when they are delivered through the academic sphere, rather than relying on students accessing these services autonomously, due to constraints of time on campus. This is exemplified in relation to employability: increasingly institutions are embedding activities designed to increase graduate employ-ability into the core curriculum in partnership with careers professionals, rather than delivering services separately through a central careers centre (see Chapter 7 in this volume). In the pre-entry arena, we know that aspiration raising and the provision of information, advice and guidance about HE is most effective when it is aligned to students' school/college learning (Action on Access, 2008).

ENGAGEMENT THROUGHOUT THE INSTITUTION

The need to engage students in the academic, social and professional services spheres is shown in Fig. 1. However, the academic sphere is a key

Fig. 1. Institutional Spheres of Engagement.

site for enabling and promoting engagement not just in academic matters but also with peers and professional services.

ENGAGEMENT ACROSS THE STUDENT LIFECYCLE

Engagement should take place throughout the student lifecycle (HEFCE, 2001a, 2001b). It begins early with institutional outreach interventions and extends throughout the process of preparing for and entering HE, time spent in HE and includes progression beyond HE into employment or further learning. This is summarised in Fig. 2.

The importance of engaging students pre-entry to increase the progression of students from non-traditional backgrounds is discussed in Chapter 4 of this volume. It is also illustrated in the case study by Bland about the transformational effect engaging disaffected young people in an HE outreach programme has on them and their school culture.

Pre-entry engagement also contributes to student retention and success in HE (Thomas, forthcoming). There is rarely a single reason why students leave HE, but rather they leave for a combination of inter-related factors. Jones (2008b) identifies the following categories of reasons why students withdraw from HE: poor preparation for HE; weak institutional or course match, resulting in poor fit and lack of commitment; unsatisfactory academic experience; lack of social integration; financial issues and personal circumstances. Engagement through pre-entry interventions can make a difference to the first three of these reasons, in particular, decision-making

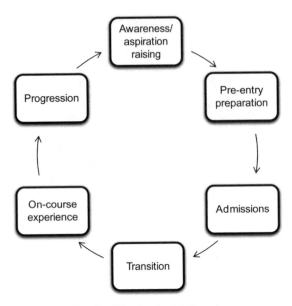

Fig. 2.   The Student Lifecycle.

about progression to HE, and expectations, academic preparation and experiences in HE. The evidence of the impact of pre-entry interventions on student retention and success is thin, but an analysis of the reasons for student withdrawal, the types of activities pre-entry interventions undertake and the available impact 'strongly suggests ... that pre-entry activities ... *ought* to have an impact on choices and decisions prior to entry, and expectations, academic preparation and experiences in HE, and thus have a positive impact on student retention' (Thomas, forthcoming).

A PARTNERSHIP: DEVELOPING STUDENTS' AND STAFF CAPACITY TO ENGAGE

The empirical work being undertaken as part of the What works? programme demonstrates that institutions should work with students to develop their capacity to engage effectively in their HE experience. This includes developing students' knowledge and understanding about the benefits of engaging across the different institutional spheres and expanding their skills to do so. Project research with part-time, mature and local students has identified a highly instrumental approach to HE, which corresponds with a devaluing of social aspects of an HE experience, reflected in comments about 'not needing more friends'. Various other studies suggest that students from 'non-traditional' backgrounds are less likely to engage with student services (Dodgson & Bolam, 2002) and with careers services (Hills, 2003). Although individuals will need different levels of engagement in the different spheres to achieve success in their own terms, 'for the majority ... the most important support seemed to derive from a special sense of community ... from reciprocal acts of recognition and confirmation' (Perry, 1999, p. 238). This implies that students need to be educated about the value of widespread engagement in their HE experience and encouraged and facilitated to engage in appropriate opportunities and given the necessary skills. This may, for example, include the provision of capacity-building modules in the core academic curriculum or through the induction process.

Institutions must also be aware of the heterogeneity of the student body, and thus the need to engage in different ways. This requires institutions to provide a range of opportunities for engagement across the institution. This includes recognising that there are differing degrees of engagement that students feel comfortable with, different levels within the institution where students may prefer to engage (e.g. module, course, department, faculty and institution) and a range of sites of engagement, as discussed earlier. A uniform approach to encouraging engagement may create pressure for conformation and result in alienation and disengagement (Mann, 2005).

Developing engagement opportunities throughout the institution and across the student lifecycle requires all staff to be involved, as it is not a task that can be left to a few committed individuals. The notion of engagement should be embedded into the institutional vision and reflected in key policy documents, and this must be actively endorsed by senior managers. Thus, the institution must consider how policies and procedures can ensure staff responsibility, accountability, development, and recognition and reward are in place in relation to engagement to enable all staff to fulfil their obligations. This may include reviewing staff recruitment (e.g. to ensure that responsibility for providing opportunities for engagement are embedded into job descriptions and selection processes); updating induction and training for new staff and continuing professional development; the provision of resources, guidance and other support; ensuring that institutional procedures require staff to engage with students (e.g. through validation processes) and that staff performance and impact are monitored and reviewed (e.g. through the annual review process) and providing mechanisms to recognise and reward staff who excel at engaging students and offer them appropriate progression opportunities. In the empirical research, some staff report that colleagues undertaking research and publication receive much greater recognition and reward within the institution that those who make efforts to improve the student experience. This differential recognition and reward of HE work needs to be embedded if staff are to be enabled to provide engaging opportunities to students.

MANAGING ENGAGEMENT: INSTITUTIONAL RESPONSIBILITY

At the senior level, the institution must take responsibility for managing and promoting student engagement to enhance retention and success. This includes building engagement into the corporate mission, vision and plan and aligning institutional policies towards this priority; providing leadership that explicitly values student engagement throughout the whole institution and across the student lifecycle and promotes whole staff responsibility for engagement and the development of a co-ordinated, evidence-informed strategy with explicit indicators and measures of success. In summary, managing engagement involves:

- Provision of a range of opportunities for engagement of different types, at different levels, across the institution in different sites, throughout the student lifecycle.
- Developing students to recognise the importance of engagement and to have the capacity to engage in a range of opportunities.
- Developing staff responsibility for and capacity to provide effective engagement opportunities.
- Taking responsibility for engagement, including monitoring engagement and acting when there are indicators of lower levels of engagement.
- Creating a partnership between students and institutions towards a shared outcome of successful learners and graduates.

The emerging model of student engagement to improve student retention and success is shown in Fig. 3. It is however still in development, and a further iteration will be published in 2011 (Thomas & May forthcoming).

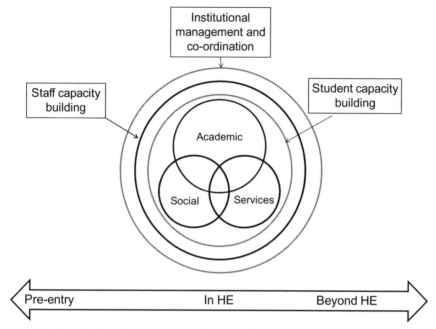

Fig. 3.   Student Engagement to Improve Student Retention and Success.

IMPLICATIONS FOR INSTITUTIONS

What the discussion earlier suggests is that HEIs should proactively provide
a range of opportunities for students to engage with peers, academic staff,
professional staff and broader constituencies (such as communities and
employers), throughout their student journey. The empirical evidence suggests that engagement in the academic sphere is particularly important, but
that this should not be at the expense of developing supportive friendship
networks and helping students to access information, skills, opportunities
and support to achieve their goals (whether this is with regard to entry into
HE, success in HE or progression into employment or further learning).
The 'overlaps' between academic and social, and academic and professional
services, are vital as this is where non-academic engagement is embedded into
the academic sphere and made accessible to a more diverse student cohort.

The research teams have been investigating the effectiveness of a range
of interventions which institutions can implement to provide engagement

opportunities across the institution. Examples include peer mentoring, personal tutoring, study advisers, student services, field trips, welcome lunch and information, extended induction, social networking, project-based learning, early feedback and so on. The empirical research is starting to suggest that the exact type of engagement opportunity is less important than the way it is offered and its intended outcomes. Thus, we suggest (Thomas & May, forthcoming) that in all spheres, engagement activities should be planned and informed by the following principles:

i.   *Proactive*: Activities should proactively seek to engage students, rather than waiting for a crisis to occur, or the more motivated students to take up opportunities.

ii.   *Inclusive*: Activities should be aimed at engaging all students, this may mean thinking about the circumstances that constrain some individuals to engage in some activities throughout the institution.

iii. *Flexible*: Activities need to be delivered sufficiently flexibly to facilitate the participation of all students, this will include consideration of timing and time commitment, as well as location and accessibility.

iv.   *Transparent*: The ways in which students are expected or able to engage in an activity should be transparent, and the potential benefits of engaging should be explicit.

v.   *Ongoing*: Activities tend to benefit from taking place over time, rather than one-off opportunities, as engagement takes time (e.g. to develop skills and build relationships).

vi.   *Timely*: Activities should be available at appropriate times, for example, students' needs for engagement in the social and service activities will change over time.

vii. *Relevant*: Activities need to be relevant to students' interests and aspirations.

viii. *Integrated*: As least some opportunities for engagement in all spheres should be integrated into core activities that students are required to do, that is, in the academic sphere.

ix.   *Collaborative*: Activities should encourage collaboration and engagement with fellow students and members of staff.

x.   *Monitored*: The extent and quality of student's engagement should be monitored, and where there is evidence of low levels of engagement, follow-up action should be taken.

We have observed that the specific activities that are being evaluated have frequently occurring outcomes. Thus, we suggest that the exact nature of an intervention is less important than the fact that it is aiming to achieve some or all of the following outcomes. Institutions should select activities or interventions that are likely to achieve the highest number of these outcomes, or for which they have particularly strong evidence that these outcomes will be achieved.

i. Nurturing supportive *peer* relations.
ii. Fostering meaningful *interaction between staff and students.*
iii. Developing students' *knowledge, confidence and identity* as successful HE learners.
iv. Providing an HE experience, which is *relevant to students' interests and future goals.*
v. Engendering a sense of entitlement and belonging in HE.

To achieve these outcomes, institutions need to encourage and facilitate partnerships between staff and students, which are based on a shared understanding of and responsibility for engagement and success. This will involve winning hearts and minds of staff and students and creating an appropriate institutional infrastructure. These themes are explored further in Chapter 8.

CHAPTER 2.1

FROM CLASSROOM RESISTANCE TO SCHOOL REFORM

Derek Bland

ABSTRACT

Purpose – *In the project described in this chapter, a group of educationally disengaged students investigated their peers' perspectives of factors relating to low aspiration for and access to university. On the basis of their findings, they created an informative DVD to address the student needs.*

Methodology/approach – *Action research processes were employed in this 'students-as-researchers' project. The research component was carried out through surveys, while the action component was the creation of the DVD.*

Findings – *The student researchers found that many of their peers had unrealistic concepts of university. A lack of role models and low teacher expectations appear to lead to low tertiary aspiration, awareness and access.*

Research limitations/ implications (if applicable) – *The DVD had a profound impact on the participants and their school, and within a few years progression to university grew to exceed the State average.*

Practical implications (if applicable) – *The student researchers provided their reasons for engagement in the project that have implications for*

Institutional Transformation to Engage a Diverse Student Body
International Perspectives on Higher Education Research, Volume 6, 57–65
Copyright © 2011 by Emerald Group Publishing Limited
ISSN: 1479-3628/doi:10.1108/S1479-3628(2011)0000006007

pedagogy and attempts to re-engage marginalised students with main-stream education.

Social implications – *The transformation of the school's culture shows that high expectations of all students, combined with creative opportunities to demonstrate their potential, can assist in increasing educational opportunities for students from low socio-economic backgrounds.*

Originality/value of paper – *The main value of the chapter is in the students' rationale for their own engagement in the project, which can inform strategies to engage marginalised students.*

Keywords: Students-as-researchers; educational disadvantage; categorisation: case study

INTRODUCTION

When Lynne Rogers became principal of Southpoint High School,[1] academic performance was poor, student drop out at year 10 (15–16 years old) was normal, and progression to university was low. Five years later, the picture is very different. The school now claims higher than average university entrance for the region and there are strong ties with a local university that include academic collaboration with teachers and students in the final years of schooling (years 11 and 12). Indeed, a 2009 survey reported that 'The most common study destination was university' (Department of Education and Training, 2009).

Although not claiming that one project was responsible for this change, the introduction of a students-as-researchers (SaR) project, aimed at maintaining the educational engagement of a group of marginalised students at the school, was a significant factor and something of a catalyst for cultural change. This chapter considers the role played by that project in making education meaningful for the student participants and the transforming influence they then had on the culture of the school.

THE SCHOOL AND CONTEXT

Southpoint High School, located in a coastal area near one of Australia's major cities, has a little over 1,000 students from years 8 to 12 (approximately 12–17 years of age) from a low socio-economic community. Around 5–10% of the school's students identify as indigenous, and there is a significant number of Pacific Islander students. There is also a high level of transience among local families. Statistically, one quarter of the school population received suspensions in 2006 and 2007.

Despite national increases in the number of students from low socio-economic status (SES) backgrounds attending university, their relative representation has remained at 15% (Department of Education, Employment and Workplace Relations, 2009a, 2009b). Universities Australia (2008), using a postcode analysis of SES recognises low SES representation in the broader community as 25%. Compounding the issue of low university representation, according to a 2009 report by the Australian Bureau of Statistics (2009), is the low proportion of the Queensland population with a bachelor's degree (13.2%) compared with most other Australian States (e.g. neighbouring New South Wales: 17.8%; the Australian Capital Territory: 25%).

THE SAR PROJECT

It was in this context that a SaR project was developed as a university and schools collaboration through which students in a number of low SES schools undertook action research to investigate local factors influencing tertiary awareness, aspiration and access. It is in keeping with a conviction that social justice requires schools to listen specifically to the voices of those who are the most at risk and the least likely to be heard on issues that directly affect their educational outcomes (Thomson, 2004). The project invites participants, generally drawn from years 9 to 11, to the university campus for basic training in research methods and discussion of social influences on educational opportunities. At the end of this workshop, each student group has an action plan ready to commence research in their schools and communities. School-level activity continues through surveys and other inquiries with the support of a facilitating teacher and the university's project coordinators. The groups then develop specific action to address issues arising from their research.

The process employed by the project encourages participants to imagine how things could be different (Noone & Cartwright, 2005) and reflects a socially just education that enables students 'to have more control of their lives ... to inquire, act and reflect on the issues that are of concern to them and to positively transform situations where they see disadvantage or unfairness in their own and other's lives' (Zyngier, 2003, p. 43).

It was the involvement of a teacher in the SaR project at a previous school that led to it being introduced to Southpoint High School. Her participation in the project provided an understanding of its potential to engage a particular group of disaffected students. The new principal, Lynne, who held positive beliefs about listening to student voices, readily agreed to the project being implemented in the school.

THE STUDENTS

The initial group of six year 9 and 10 students (1 female and 5 males) who participated in the SaR project were considered to be classroom resistors. According to the support teacher, they were disengaged, exhibited poor literacy due to various combinations of lack of attendance, poor behaviour, lack of direction and confidence, were unused to building and maintaining effective relationships, and lacked goals and plans for the future (Smith & Woodward, 2007). Attending a 'last chance' program attached to the school helped them to bide their time before reaching the minimum legal age to leave school.

Year 10 student, Kev, the most outspoken of the group, appeared to enjoy his 'outcast' status. His stated intention at the time of joining the project was 'to leave school at the end of the year'. Kev attributed his disruptive classroom behaviour to being 'with the wrong friends' and simply not enjoying school. By his own admission, he became labelled as a 'problem student' and 'class clown', seeming to enjoy these descriptors, and he had very poor relationships with staff. As noted by Graham (2007), such labels can become self-fulfilling prophecies. Students may also contribute to their own stigmatisation, believing that their abilities are fixed and using avoidance techniques to 'avoid being labelled "dumb"' (McInerney & McInerney, 2006, p. 239). Kev's ambition was to be a construction labourer, believing he had no other choice. His friend, Mick, was simply bored with school and became involved in the project at a later stage but played a key role in both the project and its influence on the school's culture. These two students became the drivers of the project and later were identified as the most influential members of the group. Other members expressed boredom with school and saw no benefit in attending regular classes. The principal's solution was to attempt to maintain their attendance through an alternative program attached to the school and it was here that the SaR project was implemented.

ENGAGING THE STUDENTS

Like most of the student group, Kev conceded that he initially agreed to become involved in the project because it would give him 'time away from school, and it sounded like it might be fun'. He added that he 'didn't think it would be useful, but could be more fun' than the school work he was otherwise expected to carry out. Apart from boredom, Mick stated that he became involved out of friendship when the group was looking for someone with particular characteristics to feature in a film and he thought it would be 'pretty cool'.

Together with small groups of students from three other schools, the Southpoint group attended the university's on-campus SaR workshop, attracted, according to Kev, by the offer of free pizza. Their high level of engagement in the discussions was a surprise to their support teacher and they responded well to questioning from the rest of the students regarding their identified issues and proposed action plan. Those issues, raised during a visually based 'brainstorming' activity, included a lack of role models (i.e. parents or other family members with university experience), peer pressure to avoid academic engagement and limited encouragement to consider university as a viable educational pathway. These initial perceptions were confirmed in their subsequent research at the school, through which they discovered very limited knowledge of university among students in years 8, 9 and 10, with many having no realistic concept of university. With very few role models to provide this information, and with teacher expectations that the students would be more interested in vocational opportunities, there was a profound lack of knowledge of matters such as how to travel to a university campus, what courses could be studied, what academic achievements were required for entry and how applications were made.

The research group decided to answer these questions through creating a DVD. Although none of them had relevant knowledge or training in filmmaking, they possessed great confidence that they could achieve something worthwhile and set about finding a staff member with some basic knowledge of the technical issues and appropriate software. Having seconded a teacher with some basic skills, they drew up a storyboard, learned how to operate video cameras and editing software and approached the university for help in identifying current students from relevant backgrounds willing to be interviewed about their passage to and experiences of university.

In developing the storyboard, the young researchers agreed that humour was to be a major component of the DVD and that it would be appropriate for it to portray 'young people passing on information to young people' (Smith & Woodward, 2007, p. 4). They also determined that it should include university students with backgrounds similar to their own and 'who had overcome obstacles to succeed at University'. These featured 'faces' were to include a variety of cultures and levels of academic ability to make the production as authentic as possible.

The result was a 20-minute production that was directly relevant to the schools' student cohort, highly informative, and engaging through its comedic style in which Kev demonstrated a role for his talent that was acceptable to his teachers. The success of the DVD took the team by surprise; shortly after it was launched at a SaR conference at the university, it won two awards. At a film industry award presentation, the young students 'rubbed shoulders with Queensland's biggies in the film industry' and other independent filmmakers; Kev and Mick were invited to be guest speakers at three subsequent education conferences with their support teacher reporting that they were 'becoming old hands at public speaking', and an educational association requested permission to publish a paper presented by them at an interstate conference.

Asked what kept him engaged in the project, Kev said,

> it was a challenge and I like challenges-I got some good friends through it and it was fun. You learnt new things each week – it wasn't the same boring stuff. I'd never done anything like it.

During the course of the DVD production project, the students did not view their participation as 'work'. As stated in a report of the project:

> Towards the end of 2006 (nine months into the project), in response to a comment on the considerable literacies he had learnt, one of the researchers replied, "I don't like English, this isn't English. We are having fun!". While engaged and having fun, they were experiencing multi-literacy learning in the context of real life, authentic tasks. They explored ways of thinking and learning, applying technology and other strategies and applications and practised and contextualized multi-literacies. (Smith & Woodward, 2007, p. 13)

Kev stated he had 'learned things in the project that led to me thinking of things I want to be a part of'. He reported a conversation with one of his peers who had told him that 'after watching your DVD I realized you can go without having to pay up money straight away'. Kev said that made him 'happy to think the video changed someone's mind'. He added that he had developed:

> great relationships with staff members-because my attitude has changed and I'm not so much of a problem student as some teachers might call you – they see me as someone they can have a friendship with. I'll show them respect, they show me respect – they help me when I need help because they know that I want to succeed.

To the surprise of many school staff, Kev and Mick decided to stay on at school. Kev wanted 'to become more of a leader in classes – help other people in class, try to be a role model for other students'. In year 12, he was elected school captain and, in this position, his former notoriety and the local fame achieved as the main face of the DVD, became a positive influence for changing attitudes among the students and the staff. The DVD became influential in the school, encouraging others to investigate tertiary options, and, as its reputation grew, new respect was generated for its creators among school staff and relationships between the teachers and the students improved across the school.

INFLUENCE ON THE SCHOOL

As stated earlier, the school's tertiary application rate and successful entry to university has increased dramatically since the making of the DVD and with the continuation of the project. The 2009 tertiary entrance rate increased to over 28% with further 3.4% deferring a tertiary offer (Department of Education and Training, 2009). A strong relationship now exists between the school and the university with further innovative collaborations being introduced more recently. The change in relationships between students and staff has been quite profound, with high expectations and increased mutual respect forming a more positive learning environment.

In providing advice to other schools, SaR project participants have identified the following key elements of the project as those that engaged them and helped them to develop new skills and knowledge, regardless of previous experience, in a project of educational significance (Bland, 2008). It was suggested by the research group that these features should inform curriculum delivery across the school syllabus:

- a scaffolded process, through which students work in collaboration with and alongside teachers, peers and university researchers: this was a new experience for the teachers as well as the students and it provided opportunities to revise opinions and expectations;

- a sense of belonging and purpose: the students rapidly developed ownership of the physical space in which project meetings were held, which led, in time, to decreased feelings of alienation from the school;
- mutual respect for the particular skills and knowledge that each participant brings to the research process: the students' local and cultural knowledge were of equal importance to the professional knowledge of the researchers and teachers;
- real life, relevant problems: the students were experiencing multi-literacy learning in the context of real life, authentic tasks (Smith & Woodward, 2007);
- ownership of the process and the outcomes: while guided, the research, data analysis and subsequent action increasingly came under the control of the students;
- the ability to make decisions that affect their environment and help others: knowing that the outcomes would benefit others was a key motivating factor for the students;
- the workshop process of consciousness-raising: this event was identified as a key moment in 'awakening' the students' awareness of the socio-political contexts of education; and
- risk-taking and learning from mistakes: being able to trial ideas and to see mistakes as learning was a novel experience for the students.

The DVD was made by and for students, using appropriate media and language. Although the SaR project has promoted student voice through a number of innovative and creative media, including performance and creative art work, the DVD is the most powerful example of how student voice expressed through creative visual means can transform a school culture. The aim of the DVD was to answer the students' questions about university access, student life and tertiary study, but it also illustrated to the school that by listening to the voices of these marginalised students, they could provide educational opportunities that were engaging and relevant. Furthermore, a critical viewing of the content of the DVD highlighted deficiencies in the careers and education guidance that impacted negatively on the group and, it appeared, on a great number of their peers. The students, for example, appeared to believe that there was a general paucity of information about tertiary studies and that they received limited encouragement from teachers to aim for university. This perception is in accord with the Universities Australia (2008) report, participation and equity, that found that low SES students were much less likely to believe they were encouraged by teachers to aim for university (44% of students) than higher SES students (58%).

The change in the academic culture of the school cannot be attributed solely to the one project. It did, however, provide the opportunity for the principal to demonstrate and vindicate her belief in the students' abilities. It was a chance to show, in practical terms, how 'disengagement can be reversed if students feel that significant others in the school are able to see and acknowledge some of their strengths' (Rudduck & Flutter, 2004, p. 70).

NOTE

1. Statements by students and staff were made in focus groups and individual interviews unless otherwise indicated. School and participant names are pseudonyms.

CHAPTER 2.2

PROJECT 2013: A MODEL FOR INCREASING FIRST-YEAR AT-RISK STUDENT RETENTION RATES

Rashidah N. Andrews and Jayne K. Drake

ABSTRACT

Purpose – *Through a description of changes in institutional approaches to academic advising, this case study provides strategies for improving retention rates of first-year students deemed 'at-risk' of leaving university before second-year enrolment.*

Methodology/approach – *The study targets first-years who have been identified as 'at-risk' in the College of Liberal Arts (CLA) at Temple University in Philadelphia, Pennsylvania. Temple is a large public research institution in the United States, home to approximately 35,000 full-time equivalent (FTE) students, of whom, 6,000 are enrolled in the CLA. The current case study focuses on the systematic and intentional processes developed by academic advisors or tutors in CLA to ensure students' progression from their first to second year. Project 2013, named for the intended graduation year of the initial target population, is a proactive retention initiative, and this study delineates the evolution of the innovation, development of the target group, project objectives, implementation of retention strategies, outcomes of the project, successes, limitations and future considerations.*

Institutional Transformation to Engage a Diverse Student Body
International Perspectives on Higher Education Research, Volume 6, 67–75
ISSN: 1479-3628/doi:10.1108/S1479-3628(2011)0000006008

Findings – *Through sustained highly personalised interventions with first-year 'at-risk' students, the retention rate for this population improved by nearly 7% over the University's average for similar students and met the overall retention rate of the University's general student population.*

Practical implications – *The outcomes of this project suggest that with careful, strategic planning, clear execution by facilitators and ongoing assessment of such interventions, student retention and, by extension, persistence to graduation should improve significantly enough to warrant strong, ongoing institutional commitment.*

Keywords: Academic advising; retention strategies; persistence to graduation; at-risk students; first-year students

INTRODUCTION

Researchers on student retention in higher education (HE) are all clear on one critical point – among the most powerful predictors of students' overall satisfaction with their undergraduate experience is the sense of belonging and connection to the institution (Tinto, 1993; Engle & O'Brien, 2007). The vast majority of new students do find their way: sometimes on their own, sometimes with the help of new-found friends, sometimes with advice from family and other relatives and sometimes with the assistance of an academic or faculty advisor. Often, advisors or tutors are the first institutional representatives whom students meet on their journey into university. As such, advisors play a key role in helping students navigate the sometimes rocky shoals of institutional policies, procedures, customs and requirements. Advisors are often encouraged to become proactive in reaching out to students before they get into academic difficulties, especially in reaching out to 'at-risk' students, who may have particular difficulty in navigating these shoals. In recent years, colleges and universities around the world have concluded that effective retention programs have academic advising at the heart of their efforts to educate and retain students (Tinto, 1993).

In their own efforts to address retention of students most 'at-risk' of dropout, the College of Liberal Arts (CLA) Academic Advising Centre at Temple University (a large public research institution in the United States), developed and implemented systematic strategies intended to improve the retention numbers of this cohort to match the retention rate of the College's and University's general first-year population. 'At-risk' first-years – defined in this case as students most likely to leave the institution for various reasons before their second year – were targeted based on predictive factors, which will be described in more detail. The case was premised on research suggesting that specific advising interventions, faculty engagement and other direct contact strategies are key approaches to improving retention rates at large, urban institutions (Muraskin & Lee, 2004; Tinto, 2004; Engle & O'Brien, 2007).

CLA's retention intervention, also known as Project 2013, began to take shape during an annual Advising Centre staff retreat in summer 2009. During that retreat, the Centre's Director formed a Retention Work Group (RWG) to look at possible retention interventions for its first-generation students (students whose parents have not completed an undergraduate degree). Throughout that summer and into the early fall, the RWG undertook a literature review, researched best practices and reviewed possible retention strategies. Other schools and colleges within Temple University were asked to focus on retaining students at risk of leaving before the second year, but CLA developed its own strategies that included this retention concept along with long-term options to sustain a cohort through to graduation. The CLA RWG posited the following: 'while targeting specific populations is critical, every student has the potential to become "at-risk" over time; therefore, every retention strategy should consider efficient practices with possible benefit for all students'. This premise informed project planning and implementation processes, and the alignment of these objectives with those of the larger university ensured continued institutional investment.

THE TARGET GROUP

The grade point average (GPA) of first-year students is among the best early predictors of student persistence to graduation (Tinto, 2004; Engle & O'Brien, 2007). With this understanding, the University's Measurement and Research Centre (MARC) used data collected over three years to identify predictive factors for attrition, including first-year GPA. Eighty-seven incoming CLA freshmen were determined most 'at-risk' based on a predicted first-year GPA in the lowest 20% of the entering class. A combination of academic variables was used to estimate this risk factor including high school GPA, high school attended, entrance exam scores, mathematics and English placement test scores and subsequent placement into lower level math and writing courses. The impact of non-academic risk factors was also considered. The predictive risk model developed as a result, included responses to the following high-attrition questions and statements on a new student questionnaire completed by all entering first-year students:

- Intention to work full time while attending university;
- Consideration of transfer to another university before graduation;
- Disagreement with the statement 'I am organised and have good study habits' and
- Importance of wanting to get away from home as a reason to go to college.

Narrowing down factors most likely to impact retention and focusing on students demonstrating the highest risk of attrition allowed identification of students most in need of direct intervention.

IMPLEMENTATION

A six-member RWG served as primary managers of the CLA Project 2013. In advance of the launch of the program, the team of academic advisors and the director of the CLA Academic Advising Centre met several times a month to discuss the parameters of the project and to report to each other and external audiences as appropriate. Members of the group introduced the initiative to the CLA deans, faculty chairs and directors, professional advisors from across the University and delivered a formal presentation of the Project at a 2010 National Academic Advising Association (NACADA) Regional Conference. The implementation plans for the CLA retention interventions were strategically planned to ensure they produced optimal impact on student behaviour, sense of belonging and decision-making. Interventions were also structured to be sensitive to advisors' student workloads and critical policy deadlines during the academic year.

SPECIFIC INTERVENTIONS

Fall 2009

Seven academic advisors were assigned 12–13 students each in the target group. The target students were unaware of their selection as 'at-risk' first-years to minimise stigmatisation. Each student initially met with their appointed advisors for a one-hour highly personalised developmental advising appointment at the beginning of the term and then again at midterm. These extended advising appointments represented a significant shift in practice over the more standard half-hour appointments CLA students generally received to address academic progress-to-date, course registration, personal development concerns and so on. Project 2013 students were not just encouraged to maintain contact with their assigned advisors, but also encouraged to seek additional support from multiple resource centres on campus, including the writing and math and science resource centres. At midterm, advisors contacted students through email and phone based on the results of the University's academic progress reports and again at the end of the term when fall grades were posted.

Spring 2010

At the beginning of the spring term, advisors invited students in the target group to meet individually for half-hour developmental advising appointments, and, as in the fall term, advisors contacted students to discuss the results of the midterm academic progress reports and to review fall 2010 rosters. The frequent contacts throughout the year were meant to establish continuity of care, improve student engagement and support a sense of belonging in their first year.

OUTCOMES

On the basis of research and planning, the RWG anticipated six primary outcomes of Project 2013. First, students in the interventions group would be retained at rates similar to or higher than the retention rates of the University's and the CLA' first-year students. Second, the target cohort, as well as the larger CLA freshmen population, would have an enhanced advising experience encouraging them to continue accessing advising resources and key campus support services introduced in their first year. By doing so, the team anticipated meaningful engagement in the total University experience and increased likelihood of persistence to a four-year undergraduate degree at Temple. Third, if the retention data culled from this project should prove to be promising, Project 2013 would follow the freshmen at-risk students throughout their time at the University, with advisors intervening at appropriate intervals. Fourth, it would ensure a new class of students identified as 'at-risk' every fall term be selected and remain in the program until the total number of students from the first to fourth years reaches approximately 350–400 students. Fifth, strategies employed in this project and the anticipated positive results would serve as a model for other schools and colleges at Temple University to replicate for their 'at-risk' students. Sixth, and finally, the group hoped this project would positively influence the University's aims to improve student retention campus-wide and build the expertise, knowledge and understanding among faculty, administrators and staff of at-risk student issues. Listed below are the quantitative results for the Project 2013 interventions.

RETENTION RATES FOR CLA PROJECT 2013, ACADEMIC YEAR 2009–2010

86.4%   Temple University's overall freshman retention rate from first to second year

79.3%   Temple's overall retention rate for those identified as 'at-risk'

86.2%   Project 2013 freshman retention rate, which represents an improved retention rate of 6.9% above the University's retention rate for 'at-risk' students and level with the University's overall retention rate

	$n = 87$	%
Fall '09 to fall '10 retention (year-to-year)	75	86
Fall '09 to spring '10 retention (term-to-term)	80	92
Attended one-on-one advising appointments	77	88
No response	10	12
Attended first-year seminar in fall '09	17	20
Did not register for spring '10 (attrition)	7	9

Although the numbers tell us how many were retained and lost, it does not offer a full picture of the target group's attrition behaviour. As the predictive model included at-risk factors that extended beyond academics, the RWG also collected qualitative data to determine possible attrition factors. Below are reasons cited by our first- to second-term students for their lack of progression from fall '10 to spring '10:

- Three had outstanding tuition balances from the previous term triggering holds on their student accounts. These holds automatically prevent students from registering for the second term;
- One chose to pursue full-time employment to assist with family financial struggles;
- Another chose to pursue a real estate licence to facilitate quicker entry into the job market;
- One intended to pursue an apprenticeship as a tattoo artist and
- The seventh decided to enter a rehab program to address medical and mental health issues.

The students listed above demonstrated legitimate concerns, but it was the RWG's ability to identify these reasons for leaving the institution that has been a major strength of this project. Identifying triggers for student departure is invaluable to retention and support service interventions.

SUCCESSES & LIMITATIONS

As a result of this Project, advisors were able to engage almost 90% of target students and provide ongoing follow-up support to ease campus transitions and begin fostering a sense of belonging to the institution. Students were also encouraged to develop agency in initiating contact with advisors, which contributed to their sense of autonomy and self-advocacy. Finally, flexibility in planning and implementation of the Project facilitated a 'continuous improvement' approach, which led to a more dynamic student–advisor relationship.

Limitations include the ability to attribute results solely to the work of academic advisors. Although outcomes demonstrate significant impacts of the intensive advising provided, the RWG acknowledges and continually investigates the possibility of additional variables affecting reported retention rates. Another limitation of the Project is the college-wide student-to-advisor ratio. Innovative approaches to balancing this quality vs. quantity dilemma are currently under review.

FUTURE CONSIDERATIONS

Moving forward, the CLA Academic Advising Centre has launched Project 2014 or Year 2 of its retention initiatives for the next cohort of freshmen. The RWG continues to enhance and explore ways to address academic and personal progress issues relevant to each student group. Ongoing programmatic concerns include the following:

- *Risk is not static.* The RWG understands the need to work with the University's MARC to review current risk models and to explore shifting factors that define 'at-risk' students. Future iterations of the program will assess the role of both 'risk' and potential 'protective' – or positive factors – to broaden understanding of characteristics that combine to increase the likelihood of retention at Temple.
- *Sustainability.* As the 'at-risk' students participating in Project 2013 and beyond move through the institution, the RWG is committed to analyse and modify data-driven strategies while it addresses the changing needs of students and maintaining consistent, quality advising support for all students.

TOP TIPS FOR PLANNING AND DELIVERY OF FIRST-YEAR 'AT-RISK' STUDENT RETENTION STRATEGIES

- Access retention literature appropriate to your institution's size and mission. Resources may include selected authors cited in this case.
- Establish a relationship with your Office of Institutional Research or if such an office is unavailable, consider collaborating with qualifying agencies to determine predictive factors for your potential 'at-risk' cohorts.
- Designate a work group within your office to manage project planning, implementation and assessment to avoid duplication of effort and secure buy-in.
- Provide targeted student cohorts with highly personalised academic advising or tutoring and actively encourage and support referrals to other campus resources.
- Mid-term academic reports are critical to the intervention process. Build a rapport with faculty members to encourage compliance and provide your

retention team with useful formative assessments to personalise student follow-up.

- Timing is everything! Calculate retention rates (first-to-second year enrolments) after the institutional deadline for adding and dropping classes in a given term.
- Keep central administration apprised of all projects and link individual goals with institutional goals.
- Document. Document. Document. Document the progress of planning and implementation of the interventions and record each advising contact with the 'at-risk' students.
- At every step of the process, assess the impact of the retention interventions and be willing to adjust strategies as necessary.

CHAPTER 3

INSTITUTIONAL TRANSFORMATION TO MAINSTREAM DIVERSITY

Liz Thomas

ABSTRACT

Purpose – *This chapter answers the question 'what does a transformed institution look like' by presenting a framework for institutional transformation to mainstream diversity. It exemplifies the framework by assessing how well English higher education institutions (HEIs) are doing with respect to mainstreaming. Relevant examples of change from the case studies are identified.*

Methodology/approach – *Reports from two institutional change programmes in the United Kingdom and the European Universities Charter on Lifelong Learning are synthesised to create a framework for change to mainstream diversity. The framework is used to assess the progress of English HEIs. This analysis is based on data from a thematic review of the Widening Participation Strategic Assessments (WPSAs) prepared by each of the 129 English HEIs. Each WPSA was coded up. Query reports were read and re-read to identify common approaches and themes.*

Findings – *The 12 item framework for mainstreaming diversity demonstrates that institutions need to attend to both infrastructure (policies, processes and procedures) and the institutional culture (the*

Institutional Transformation to Engage a Diverse Student Body
International Perspectives on Higher Education Research, Volume 6, 77–96
Copyright © 2011 by Emerald Group Publishing Limited
All rights of reproduction in any form reserved
ISSN: 1479-3628/doi:10.1108/S1479-3628(2011)0000006009

understandings and implementation of a strategy). The analysis suggests that English HEIs are making good progress towards this challenging agenda of change.

Research limitations – *The WPSAs are a subjective account of WP, and claims have not been checked. Furthermore, WPSAs were written at a specific time and so only provide a snap-shot of institutional approaches to diversity.*

Practical implications – *This chapter assists institutions to think about, plan and evaluate institutional transformation.*

Social implications – *This approach puts diversity at the centre of HEIs.*

Originality/value – *The chapter provides an original framework to assist institutions to assess their progress with regard to institutional transformation to engage a diverse student body.*

Keywords: Institutional transformation; mainstreaming diversity

INTRODUCTION

The previous chapter focused on student engagement, and made the case for institutional transformation to engage a diverse student body to succeed in higher education (HE). This chapter examines institutional transformation in more detail. This first part of the chapter provides an overview of institutional transformation, and draws on two programmes aimed at mainstreaming and embedding widening participation (WP), equality and diversity in UK institutions, the European Universities Association (EUA) Charter on Lifelong Learning, and the analysis of English Widening Participation Strategic Assessments (WPSAs) to consider what institutions should do to mainstream diversity. The chapter then goes on to consider how well English higher education institutions (HEIs) are doing with respect to mainstreaming. This latter section draws on data drawn from the 129 WPSAs submitted by English HEIs in June 2009 (HEFCE, 2009; Thomas et al., 2010b). Following the chapter there are case studies from Aston University in the United Kingdom and La Trobe University in Australia, discussing how they have undertaken whole institution approaches to mainstreaming diversity.

WHAT DOES A TRANSFORMED INSTITUTION LOOK LIKE?

It is increasingly widely accepted that institutional change is necessary to engage a diverse student body, both to encourage them to enter higher education and to enable them to be successful in HE. For example, Geoff Layer noted in 2002 that:

> There is always a risk that single item approaches become marginalised within a university as being the responsibility of a particular interest group. This development has been in response to Government direction, [and] has the potential to shape and change institutions so that they become more inclusive. (p. 3)

Institutional transformation refers to the process of shifting diversity, widening participation (WP) and equality 'from the margins to the mainstream' (Thomas et al., 2005) and making it central to all activities and functions that the institution undertakes. Thus everyone has responsibility for widening access and ensuring that all students are successful. Mainstreaming requires institutions to implement 'cultural change' and 'organisation, management and leadership changes' (HEFCE, 2006a). This view is expanded in the English context:

> Embedding widening participation means making it a core strategic issue for all higher education institutions. Widening participation is a responsibility for the whole HE sector, which institutions will develop and deliver in ways that are consistent with their own mission... Our strategy for widening participation will be sustainable because it will be embedded in HEIs' policy and practice, becoming part of the norm for the sector. (p. 82)

In the European context the concept of lifelong learning is closely aligned with widening participation and increasing student diversity. The Leuven Communiqué following the 2009 meeting of European Union ministers with responsibility for higher education makes an explicit link between widening participation and lifelong learning:

> Widening participation shall also be achieved through lifelong learning as an integral part of our education systems ... Lifelong learning involves obtaining qualifications, extending knowledge and understanding, gaining new skills and competences or enriching personal growth. Lifelong learning implies that qualifications may be obtained through flexible learning paths, including part-time studies, as well as work-based routes. (Conference of European Ministers responsible for higher education, 2009, para. 10)

Furthermore, the Leuven Communiqué states that effective implementation of lifelong learning is dependent on institutional changes to infrastructure and practices:

> Successful policies for lifelong learning will include basic principles and procedures for recognition of prior learning on the basis of learning outcomes regardless of whether the knowledge, skills and competences were acquired through formal, non-formal, or informal learning paths. Lifelong learning will be supported by adequate organisational structures and funding. Lifelong learning encouraged by national policies should inform the practice of higher education institutions. (Conference of European Ministers responsible for higher education, 2009, para. 11)

The view taken in this chapter is that in a transformed, inclusive higher education institution:

> equity considerations [are] embedded within all functions of the institution and treated as an ongoing process of quality enhancement. Making a shift of such magnitude requires cultural and systemic change at both the policy and practice levels. (May & Bridger, 2010, p. 6)

The Action on Access Programme

In 2008, Action on Access, the English national widening participation co-ordination team (www.actiononaccess.org), developed and implemented a programme to assist HEIs in England and Northern Ireland to 'mainstream and sustain' WP. The programme facilitated institutional teams (including senior staff) to:

- Review their institutional approach to mainstreaming and sustaining WP.
- Identify the strengths and limitations of their approach.
- Develop, implement and evaluate institutional policies and practice to overcome gaps in their current strategic approach to WP.
- Draft plans for the future to further integrate and sustain WP.

The various outputs of this programme were analysed to develop the idea of what an HEI that has mainstreamed WP would look like, which is described as a "socially inclusive university" (Thomas, 2009b). Table 1 summarises the areas for institutional change that were identified, and the types of activities that were undertaken by participating institutions.

Table 1. Areas for Change and Institutional Activities to Create a Socially Inclusive University.

Areas for Change	Types of Institutional Activities
Understanding the current situation and defining institutional priorities	• Examining the meaning, philosophy and implementation of WP within the institution • Identifying and reviewing WP activities • Identifying champions or people with responsibility for the access and success of students from under-represented groups in departments and faculties • Initiating dialogue across the institution
Developing the strategic framework	• Developing a new WP strategy and/or action plan. • Preparing a WP evaluation plan. • Amending other institutional strategies, including human resources, retention and learning and teaching to take account of student diversity. • Requiring consideration of WP issues (learning, teaching, assessment, curriculum contents, student support, etc.) in the development of new awards via the validation process • Making strategic recommendations for the institution
Embedding mechanisms to engage staff	• Working with the HR department to ensure WP responsibilities are detailed in job descriptions, contracts, etc. • Ensuring that WP principles (diverse needs) are recognised, e.g. in timetabling formula and relief from teaching, career progression promotion, etc. • Requiring course teams to report on WP activities and indicators via the annual review process • Implementing transparent funding mechanisms to support WP • Creating/improving links with academic departments • Effective communication strategy • Convening a cross institutional working group or similar

Table 1. (*Continued*)

Areas for Change	Types of Institutional Activities
Using data, evaluation and research to underpin the process	• Collection and use of institutional data at different levels within the HEI • Use of external data, including participation data • Using institutional and other research to inform practice and challenge myths about WP students • Sharing effective practice across the institution • Increased research and evaluation of interventions and approaches • Extending responsibility and accountability for WP to more people, e.g. departments, schools, faculties, etc., within the HEI

Source: Thomas (2009b).

A Framework for Institutional Change to Mainstream Diversity

An outcome of the Action on Access 'Mainstreaming and sustaining WP in institutions' programme was a reflective review checklist, which was designed to help institutions to understand what mainstreaming WP entails, and thus to identify specific changes that they need to make. The checklist, which is available from: http://www.actiononaccess.org/index.php?p = 11_2_3, covers the following topics:

- Institution-wide understanding and ownership of WP.
- Visible commitment to WP which influences strategic decision-making.
- Effective processes and structures to avoid reliance on committed individuals.
- Inclusive culture reflecting staff engagement across the institution and throughout the student lifecycle.
- Inclusive learning, teaching, assessment and curriculum approaches.
- Integrated outreach and admission processes.
- Use of data, monitoring, evaluation and research to improve practice and inform decision-making.
- Effective funding for widening participation.

May and Bridger (2010) drew on the Academy's 'Embedding inclusive policy and practice' programme and identified six key steps that need to be undertaken to bring about cultural change (listed below). They also stress the need for change to take place at the institutional level, in terms of policy, structures, processes and environmental issues, and at the individual level to attitudes, behaviour and practices.

- Ensure a shared vision and inclusive philosophy.
- Provide leadership for inclusion.
- Be systematic, holistic and proactive.
- Build and tailor an evidence base.
- Engage stakeholders through a range of methods.
- Provide opportunities for dialogue and debate.

The EUA (2008) identified steps that HEIs need to take to embed lifelong learning in universities:

- Embed the concepts of widening access and lifelong learning into institutional strategies.
- Provide education and learning to a diversified student population.
- Adapt learning programmes to ensure they are designed to widen participation and attract returning adult learners.
- Provide guidance and counselling services to support all potential students to access HE.
- Recognise prior learning to facilitate entry to HE.
- Integrate lifelong learning into the institutional quality culture, including the provision of appropriate support services for diverse learners.
- Strengthen the relationship between research, teaching and innovation in relation to lifelong learning, including developing an evidence base about lifelong learning issues.
- Use HE system and institutional reforms to create more flexible and suitable learning environment and pathways for all students.
- Develop local, regional, national and international partnerships to provide attractive and relevant programmes for learners.
- Act as role models of lifelong learning institutions by providing opportunities for all staff and lobbying for coherent local and national policy development.

These three lists have striking similarities, and have been further supplemented by emerging evidence from the analysis of English WPSAs (Thomas et al., 2010b). Taken together and synthesised a framework for mainstreaming diversity has been developed, including the following features:

i. Systematic approach to mainstreaming diversity, including embedding diversity into institutional strategies.

ii. Strategic and operational understanding of 'diversity', including identification and monitoring of specific target groups.

iii. Institutional priority, commitment and leadership to promote diversity.

iv. Staff engagement in diversity, including overt responsibility, developmental opportunities, accountability and reward.

v. Early engagement with potential learners and other partners to encourage diverse students to enter HE, provide appropriate information, advice and guidance and prepare them for success in HE.

vi. Admissions policies, processes and practices are informed by the characteristics of a diverse student population, including the provision of alternative entry mechanisms.

vii. Partnership with community groups, employers, professional bodies and others to provide relevant and engaging programmes of study in a sufficiently flexible way.

viii. Learning is student-centred and inclusive to improve the engagement, retention and achievement of all students. This should include review of induction processes, curriculum contents and delivery, student academic development and student welfare services.

ix. Progression to employability and further learning is integrated into core learning to enhance the progression of all students.

x. Commitment to student diversity extends beyond the first degree, to include master programmes and postgraduate research.

xi. The outcomes of diversity policies and interventions are monitored, e.g. via equality and quality assurance processes, tracking students, staff annual review, use of institutional data and undertaking research.

xii. National and institutional data and research are used to inform strategic and operational decision-making throughout the institution.

These are shown in Fig. 1. Institutions need to attend to both the institutional infrastructure – policies, processes and so forth, and the institutional culture – the understandings and implementation of a strategy. Thus the policy as it espoused is important, but so too is the way it is enacted and experienced by staff and students. This reinforces the need for

Fig. 1. Mainstreaming Diversity.

quality assurance, data collection and research to explore and enable these three aspects of institutional development.

AN ASSESSMENT OF PROGRESS OF ENGLISH HEIS TOWARDS MAINSTREAMING DIVERSITY

This section of the chapter draws on the framework above to assess the progress of English HEIs towards the goal of mainstreaming diversity. The process is designed to illuminate the meanings of the features identified in the mainstreaming framework.

Widening Participation Strategic Assessments

The analysis is based on the data presented in a thematic review of the WPSAs (Thomas et al., 2010b). An evidence-informed framework was developed covering strategic approaches, activities and measures, which was supplemented by emerging themes from the WPSAs. The framework was used to code up the WPSAs in a systematic way, by a single researcher, with the aid of NVivo software. Queries were then run in relation to key topics, generated through the coding and keyword searching. Each query report was read and re-read, and themes or alternative approaches were identified and grouped. The limitations of this method should be acknowledged. First, each WPSA was not, in general, read as a whole document. Second, and perhaps more significantly, the WPSAs are a subjective account of WP, in the sense that they are limited to what an individual or group of people within an institution decided to report and say about WP at a specific point in time. The data has not been triangulated, and in reality there may be additional information that institutions have not reported, and furthermore implementation may not necessarily be the same as stated. In addition, the WPSAs were written at a specific time and so will always only provide a snap-shot of widening participation work in the sector. However, WPSAs are formal institutional documents, which were intended to provide insight into what the HE sector is doing, and therefore it is legitimate to examine and interrogate them in this way.

The guidance for the production of WPSAs (HEFCE, 2009) was not highly prescriptive, but it did identify the importance of mainstreaming WP to impact upon institutional policies and practices:

> An important driver behind our request for an assessment of institutional commitment to WP is the evidence it will provide of how WP has become an integral part of the policies, processes and cultures in many institutions ... The additional evidence that we will gather from the process outlined below will enable us to illustrate robustly how the commitment to WP is manifest within institutions and how this contributes to the development of diversity in student bodies. (HEFCE, 2009, $14)

Progress in Relation to the Framework

i. *Systematic approach to mainstreaming diversity, including embedding diversity into institutional strategies.*

There is evidence that institutions are working across the student lifecycle and mainstreaming WP into institutional policies and strategies. For example:

- All of the WPSAs make reference to links with schools, primarily in the context of outreach work to improve progression of young people who would not usually consider HE.
- 115 institutions (89%) make an explicit link between admissions and WP.
- 78 institutions (60%) mention induction and 58 institutions (45%) provide detail about their induction processes.
- 117 HEIs (91%) discuss approaches to improving student retention and achievement.
- 68 (53%) institutions explicitly refer to their learning and teaching (L&T) strategy.
- The majority of institutions (112 or 87%) mention employability although only 76 (59%) provide detail about it. Others simply refer to their careers service, or identify employability as the final stage of the student lifecycle but do not provide additional information.

Furthermore, WP is increasingly connected to other institutional policies and priorities, as illustrated in Table 2.

Table 2. Links between WPSA and Other Institutional Strategies, Policies and Priorities.

Strategy/Policy/Priority	Number of Institutions	Percentage of Institutions
Access agreement	122	95
Widening participation strategy	119	92
Admissions	117	91
Retention in general[a]	117	91
Equality and diversity strategy	68	53
Learning, teaching and assessment strategy	68	53
Mission statement or corporate plan	67	52
Other strategies	30	23
Retention strategy[a]	19	15
Estates strategy	12	9
Human resources	9	7

[a]Nineteen institutions (15%) refer to an institutional retention strategy, but 117 institutions (91%) discuss retention as a priority in their WPSAs. It is not always explicit whether or not there is a formal, institution-wide retention (or similarly named) strategy.
Source: Thomas et al., 2010b.

The case studies from Aston (Ingleby) and La Trobe (Ferguson) discuss how student diversity informs a wide range of institutional policies, and strategic policy alignment is discussed in more detail in Chapter 8.

ii. *Strategic and operational understanding of diversity, including identification of specific target groups.*

Many WPSAs do not provide an overt statement of their WP definition or institutional vision, although strong commitment to WP is expressed by reference to mission statements and other corporate policies. The lack of national or institutional clarity about the identification of target groups is reflected in the large numbers of groups targeted (Table 3), many of which overlap.

The evidence about targeting, especially lower socio-economic groups (NS-SEC 4-7), shows that some institutions use a range of target groups, and

Table 3. WP Target Groups – Institutional Frequency and Percentage[a].

WP Target Groups	Frequency	Percentage
Disabled students	127	98
Black and Minority Ethnic groups (BME)	109	84
Gifted and Talented	101	78
Part-time or flexible learning	92	71
Young people NS-SEC 4-7[b]	88	68
Vocational Progression	87	67
From State Schools	85	66
From a care background	80	62
Gender	70	54
Mature learners (e.g. from the community)	69	53
Work-based learners	56	43
E-Learning or Distance learning	53	41
Primary school aged children	49	38
First generation entrants	42	33
Low participation neighbourhoods	33	26
Apprentices	31	24
Special Educational Needs	29	22
Index of Multiple Deprivation (IMD)	20	16
Lesbian, gay, bi-sexual and transsexual	16	12
Traveller Communities	3	2

[a]These figures were arrived at via two different ways. Initially, the documents were coded for these groups, and then a secondary series of text searches were conducted to ensure that all statements about these groups were covered.
[b]National Statistics Socio-economic Classification, groups 4–7 (lower socio-economic groups).
Source: Thomas et al., 2010b.

some have not fully aligned their work to national priorities. Furthermore, although 98% of institutions cite disabled students as a WP target group, only 11% set targets in relation to disabled students. It is thus possible that different parts of a single institution are working towards different WP visions, and data collection is not connected to strategic and operational planning.

The issue of institutional vision and clarity is discussed more fully in Chapter 8, and explored in the institutional case study from Leeds Metropolitan University (Stevenson).

iii. *Institutional priority, commitment and leadership to promote diversity.*

WP is increasingly being linked to other institutional policies (Table 2 above), reflecting its increasing institutional priority. Institutional commitment to WP can also be illustrated by an examining the strategic organisation of WP. Three types of organisational culture were examined: a centralised WP team or unit taking responsibility for WP; WP dispersed or mainstreamed into academic or service functions; or hybrid arrangements, with shared responsibilities for WP and a central co-ordinating function (Thomas et al., 2005). Table 4 shows the breakdown of how institutions organise their WP work.

This analysis suggests 81 HEIs (63%) have an organisational model that promotes institutional commitment to WP across the institution, rather than keeping it within a single central unit. This has the added value of promoting the engagement of more staff across the institution in WP work. It is less clear however the extent to which senior managers are involved in promoting WP and taking it forward at a strategic level.

Table 4. Institutional Organisation of WP.

Organisation of WP	Number of Institutions	Percentage of Institutions
Dispersed or mainstreamed into academic and service functions	48	37
Hybrid shared responsibilities co-ordinated centrally	33	26
Unclear	27	21
Central WP unit	17	13
Total[a]	125	97

[a]The remaining 4 institutions (3%) made no reference to how their WP work is organised.
Source: Thomas et al., 2010b.

A number of the case studies in this book point to the importance of institutional priority, commitment and leadership, including the two case studies following this chapter. This issue is also discussed in Chapter 8.

iv. *Staff engagement, including overt responsibility, developmental opportunities, accountability and reward related to diversity.*

The commitment to organisational models that require a wider cross section of staff to engage in WP is encouraging (Table 4). In addition, HEIs are undertaking a range of activities to engage staff and influence their attitudes and practices in relation to student diversity and institutional flexibility. 54 institutions (42%) identified staff training and development activities to support WP, and 22 institutions (17%) discussed sharing and promoting good practice across the institution. There is less evidence of a systematic, institution-wide approach to engaging staff through their policy infrastructure as only 9 (7%) institutions made a link between their WPSA and their human resources policy (which could integrate staff responsibility, accountability and reward for engaging in WP into institutional policy).

Staff engagement is repeatedly identified as a challenge in developmental work with institutions (e.g. Thomas & May, 2010), and it is identified as challenging in some case studies in this book (see e.g. Cooper and Ismail, Maes, Vidacek-Hains et al, Stevenson and Greek). Case studies also discuss strategies for engaging staff (see Garvey, Crosling and Duckworth, as well as Vidacek-Hains et al, Stevenson and Greek), and this topic is drawn together in Chapter 8.

v. *Early engagement with potential learners and other partners to encourage diverse students to enter HE, provide appropriate information, advice and guidance (IAG) and prepare them for success in HE.*

All English HEIs work with schools pre-entry to support progression to HE, and 101 (78%) work with further education colleges, reaching both young people and older learners. 92 institutions (71%) provide details of more formal partnerships with schools, and 49 institutions (38%) have extended their engagement into the primary sector to work with younger children to develop early awareness and understanding of HE. The majority of institutions (108 or 84%) work with at least one Aimhigher[1] partnership, a key role of which is to provide IAG, and a significant number work with Lifelong Learning Networks which develop vocational and work-based routes into HE. There is however still a need to provide better IAG for adults wanting to enter HE in most geographical areas (see also Fuller & Heath, 2010).

The process of engaging learners early has been discussed in the previous chapter (2) and is explored in more detail in the next chapter (4). It is exemplified in a number of case studies including Bland and Kendall.

vi. *Admissions policies, processes and practices are informed by the characteristics of a diverse student population, including development of alternative entry mechanisms.*

WPSA guidance required institutions to make an explicit link between WP and admissions, and 115 institutions (89%) refer to their undergraduate admissions processes. Institutions are concerned to ensure 'fair access', (a current UK concern discussed more fully in Chapter 5) although this is understood and implemented differently in the WPSAs: (i) treating everyone in exactly the same way 'regardless of background'; (ii) recognising that some students are disadvantaged by the selection process itself; and/or (iii) recognising the different circumstances in which students gained their pre-entry qualifications. Institutions describe a range of approaches to ensure fair access, including:

- use of personal and school contextual data to inform admissions decisions;
- reviewing the fairness of the interview process for target groups;
- monitoring the outcome of admission tests;
- seeking parity for students with vocational entry qualifications;
- accepting alternative forms of evidence of ability;
- providing additional support for students from targeted groups;
- taking a personalised approach to admissions;
- operating 'compact schemes' for specific students; and
- identifying alternative entry programmes for under-qualified and insufficiently experienced applicants.

These approaches to fair access in the selection process are underpinned by staff development and training, and monitoring of the admissions process.

Seventy-nine HEIs (61%) have compact schemes, which facilitate entry of students from target groups, including support with the application process and special consideration in the admissions process. However, only 5 institutions (4%) mention the use of APEL (the accreditation of prior experiential learning) to facilitate the admission of students without formal entry qualifications. There is scope for institutions to make stronger links between diversity and admissions.

Chapter 5 explores the admissions element of the student lifecycle, and the importance of engaging students through this process, and the need for institutional change. The case study from Liverpool Institute for the Performing Arts (Gammo-Felton) explores the challenges of embedding diversity into the admissions process, whereas the case study from DePaul discusses how one US institution has taken a strategic approach to balancing equity concerns with financial viability ones. The Foundation Studies programme at the University of South Australia provides an excellent example of an alternative entry route for adult learners without the formal entry requirements. The case study from Université libre de Bruxelles explores the challenges of alternative the admissions route if this is not accompanied by other institutional changes.

vii. *Partnership with community groups, employers, professional bodies and others to provide relevant and engaging programmes of study in a sufficiently flexible way.*

English HEIs are working with many partners in the context of widening participation and lifelong learning, however, many of these collaborations are focused on bringing people into HE, rather than providing a different type of HE learning experience. In summary:

- Nearly 80% of HEIs (101) refer to work with further education colleges (FECs) to improve progression from FE (level 3) to HE, and collaborative provision (i.e. delivery of HE programmes in FE colleges).
- There is evidence in some institutions of growing local community engagement, often through existing community, voluntary and faith groups. Twenty-nine institutions (22%) link widening participation to local or regional economic and/or social regeneration.
- Forty-six institutions (37%) talk about strong employer partnerships, but the link between employer engagement and diversity is not always explicit, and much of the work is in the early stages of development. A more limited number of HEIs have well established and effective models of employer engagement. These HEIs are offering learning from pre-entry to post-graduate levels, including learning from work and learning in work. Types of provision include negotiated work-based learning; tailor-made pro-grammes for individual employers; enterprise development and support; accreditation of training and other professional training for employers and continuing professional development for staff. Sometimes this is delivered in short 'bite-sized' modules, but often the delivery appears relatively

traditional (e.g. degree programmes rather than modules). Employer links span private, public and voluntary sectors.

- Eighty-three institutions (64%) make explicit reference to Foundation Degrees, which are shorter (2 year full-time equivalent) work-based and vocational qualifications delivered in partnership with employers.
- Eighty-one institutions (63%) refer to their part-time provision in relation to WP.
- Fifty institutions (39%) talk about their electronic learning resources and 24 institutions (19%) talk about distance learning.

In Chapter 4 Hatt and Tate discuss the role of partnerships in bringing new types of students into HE. In Chapter 6 Krause makes the case for engagement once students are in HE with community groups, employers and professional bodies. The case study from the University of the West of Scotland (Hill) describes how this has been done in the business school to improve the progression of first generation entrants in to the labour market.

viii. *Ensure learning is student-centred and inclusive to improve the retention and achievement of all students.*

There is encouraging evidence about the ways in which some institutions are linking diversity in L&T and implementing more inclusive practices to improve the student experience, and promote student retention and success. Indeed, 117 HEIs (91%) discuss retention issues in their WPSA (covering induction, L&T, identification of 'at risk students' and retention and achievement differentials between student groups), and there is growing awareness of the need to use institutional data to improve retention.

There is a strong recognition of the challenges of transition to higher education for all students and students from non-traditional backgrounds in particular. Seventy-eight institutions (60%) make reference to induction and 58 institutions (45%) provide details about their induction arrangements. Institutions are taking a more strategic approach to induction, and recognising it as a process rather than an event. Some institutions use the induction period to try to identify the students who are at risk, or target support at particular student groups.

There is growing awareness of the link between diversity and L&T. Sixty-eight institutions (53%) explicitly referred to their L&T strategy in the WPSA. Diversity and L&T are interacting in relation to:

- increased organisational flexibility;
- embedding study skills;

- changes to assessment strategies;
- more student-centred learning;
- curriculum development and review and
- renewed emphasis on personal tutoring, especially to identify and/or following up students who are 'at risk' of failing and/or withdrawing.

There is growing awareness of the retention and achievement of specific equity groups, and institutions are developing interventions to address the differentials, in particular for BME students (57 or 44% of HEIs).

Student engagement is discussed in Chapter 2 and engaging students in through L&T is explored in more detail in Chapter 6. It is illustrated in case studies from a number of institutions, including Bland, Andrews and Drake, Evenbeck and Ross and Crosling.

ix. *Progression to employability and further learning is integrated into core learning to enhance the progression of all students*

There is a widespread commitment to ensuring that WP spans the full student lifecycle, and most institutions (112 or 87%) mention employability, and 76 (59%) provide details. The approaches used vary however, and many are not integrated into the core curriculum, although there are more examples of this than were identified in previous studies (Thomas & Jones, 2007). There is some monitoring of differential experiences in the labour market by target groups, and this could be adopted more widely. Some institutions are responding to national or institutional data and providing additional activities for specific student groups. There is far less consideration of further learning, including postgraduate study, and where it is recognised policies and interventions are at an early stage of development.

Progression beyond the first degree is discussed in more detail in Chapter 7, which draws further on the evidence from the English WPSAs. The case study from the University of the West of Scotland (Hill) provides an example of using the academic sphere to develop students' skills to support their progression into the labour market. The case study from Aston University (Ingleby) also shows on its WP strategy embraces employability.

x. *Commitment to student diversity extends beyond the first degree, to include master programmes and postgraduate research.*

There is currently very little recognition of the concept of widening participation with regard to postgraduate study, and where it is recognised policies and interventions are at an early stage of development. The majority of institutions (over 85%) do not refer to postgraduate access or the postgraduate learning experience in their WPSA. Twenty-seven HEIs (21%) make reference to postgraduate activities, but only 18 (14%) of these references are specifically about widening participation to postgraduate study. Widening access to postgraduate study is in the early stages of development and institutions are often not explicit whether they are focusing on taught programmes or research programmes or both. At the moment a number of potential target groups have been mentioned, but there is a lack of evidence of robust targeting of these groups, and interventions are embryonic. In relation to the 'acknowledgment of prior experiential learning' (APEL) at the Université libre de Bruxelles Maes reports however that:

> The vast majority of candidates decided to follow the master's programme in 'Labour Sciences', a multidisciplinary study programme, offering four different specialisations. This master's programme was selected by the ROCEP as a key-programme to increase employability of APEL candidates. Moreover, two specialisations are organised as out-of-hours study programmes, allowing daytime workers to follow the courses. This contributes to explaining the huge success of this study programme.

Expanding diversity in postgraduate study is an area of growing concern in a number of countries, including the United Kingdom, Australia and South Africa (see McCulloch & Thomas, 2011 forthcoming).

xi. *The outcomes of diversity policies and interventions are monitored, e.g. via equality and quality assurance processes, tracking students, staff annual review, use of institutional data and undertaking research.*

The WPSAs demonstrate that generally institutions have sufficient data about the volume of activity taking place, but are less clear about the expected outcomes of policies and interventions in relation to specific target groups, and they are poor at setting targets and identifying methods of measurement to gauge the success or otherwise of their work. This has previously been identified as a shortcoming of WP in England (see e.g. NAO, 2008; Gorard et al., 2006).

xii. *National and institutional data and research are used to inform strategic and operational decision-making throughout the institution.*

In addition to institutions not having data about the outcomes of interventions, there is evidence that when institutions do have data about the access, retention, and achievement progression of WP target groups it is often not being used to inform decision-making at either a strategic or an operational level.

Some of the case studies demonstrate the value of evidence in making a case for change, and integrating it into decision-making across the university (see e.g. Hart and O'Shea-Poon, Ingleby and Hoare et al.). Other case studies present robust evidence about effectiveness, which has the potential to influence change (e.g. Bland, Andrews and Drake and Evershed and Ross). The issue of collecting and using data and research is discussed in Chapter 8.

CONCLUSIONS

This chapter presents a framework for institutional change to engage a diverse student body, and develops this framework by exploring what English HEIs are doing in relation to the 12 features of the framework. This is a broad and challenging agenda to engage with fully, and should perhaps be viewed as an ideal towards which institutions should orient themselves. This overview of institutional transformation indicates the topics that are explored in subsequent chapters and case studies in the book.

NOTE

1. Aimhigher is a nationally funded partnership programme which works at a local level to raise awareness, aspirations and attainment among young people from under-represented groups; further details are provided in Chapter 4.

CHAPTER 3.1

MAINSTREAMING WIDENING PARTICIPATION: INSTITUTIONAL TRANSFORMATION FROM SMALL BEGINNINGS

Amanda Ingleby

ABSTRACT

Purpose – *This case study outlines, and critically reflects upon, Aston University's 10 year journey towards mainstreaming widening participation. It begins in 1999 when the institution had no Widening Participation Strategy or infrastructure, working towards the current position of a strategic and institution-wide focus on student diversity and inclusion. Critical reflection on this journey details key enabling factors, challenges faced and suggestions for practice.*

Methodology/approach – *The case study outlines the underlying principles of Aston's approach to widening participation. Key principles include a full student life cycle and evidence-based practice approach, inclusive practice for all, and staff development. These principles are illustrated through examples of practice such as the Student Peer Mentoring Programme, the Learning Development Centre and the Postgraduate Certificate in Professional Practice.*

Institutional Transformation to Engage a Diverse Student Body
International Perspectives on Higher Education Research, Volume 6, 97–106
Copyright © 2011 by Emerald Group Publishing Limited
All rights of reproduction in any form reserved
ISSN: 1479-3628/doi:10.1108/S1479-3628(2011)0000006010

Findings – *Practice has been informed through seeking to better understand the changing needs of an increasingly diverse student profile. Diversity goes beyond the student groups targeted through widening participation programmes.*

Practical implications – *The case study reflects on challenges and enabling factors for the management of change, and suggests practice which may be transferable to other HE institutions.*

Originality/value of paper – *Aston has adopted a full student-life cycle from outreach work with primary schools, through to pre-entry and transition support, learner development, and on to graduation and employment. This is in contrast to the more predominant focus within the HE sector, upon the early stages of the student life cycle. Aston University has also embedded widening participation within strategies for learning and teaching, and for employability.*

Keywords: mainstreaming widening participation; inclusive practice; learning and teaching strategy; employability strategy; student life cycle

INSTITUTIONAL CONTEXT

Aston University is a single campus institution with 10,000 students, situated in the centre of Birmingham in the United Kingdom. It was founded in 1895 and became a University in 1966. It is research-led with high-quality teaching, strong industrial links with the majority of students taking up a placement year as part of their studies, and a rich student profile. Aston performs well against access benchmarks, with more than 90% of the students coming from state schools and 37% from lower socio-economic groups. In 2008–2009, 58% of home students were from an ethnic minority group, making Aston one of the most ethnically diverse student populations in the country (UUK, 2009). The School of Life and Health Sciences (including Pharmacy and Optometry programmes) is particularly diverse, along with students recruited from the West Midlands region (over two-thirds of students from the region are from an ethnic minority group). The student profile is also internationally diverse drawing overseas students from over 100 countries. In addition to meeting access benchmarks the University is successful in retaining its students, with an over 94% continuation rate. Furthermore, 82% of graduates enter employment 6 months after graduation.

MAINSTREAMING WIDENING PARTICIPATION

An Outline of the Journey

At Aston, widening participation is embedded within the University Corporate Plan, the Learning and Teaching Strategy and the Employability Strategy. Strategically, community engagement is on an equal footing with teaching and research, and the principles of widening participation, equity and inclusion are core institutional values.

This journey starts with the set up of a Widening Participation Task Group and preparation of the University's first Widening Participation Statement in 1999. At this stage there was no infrastructure for widening participation and there were no staff employed with a widening participation remit.

From the inception of the Higher Education Funding Council for England's (HEFCE) widening participation allocation (HEFCE, 1999b) the University established a rigorous internal bidding programme which resulted in the set up of small widening participation projects and pilots. Early project activity at Aston was predominantly focused on outreach with schools and colleges, and in 2002 expanded to include institutional research to better understand the needs of students from under-represented groups. Such research was critical to informing institutional practice, for example, it established a case for funding key interventions to support transition and learner development for Aston students.

During this period there was a proliferation of widening participation projects across the University, peaking at 25 projects, involving 20 staff. Provision was delivered across a range of administrative departments, the four academic Schools and Combined Honours. The key School disciplines include business, science, engineering and languages. The administrative departments include Schools and Colleges Liaison, Careers, Registry and Planning, the Students' Guild, Student Support. Activity ranged from outreach activities organised by the School of Languages and Social Sciences, to careers support for students from under-represented groups.

Strategic leadership and co-ordination of activity was provided through the Pro-Vice-Chancellor for External Liaison and the Head of Outreach and Widening Participation. A collaborative approach to widening participation activity enabled project staff to work to a shared vision, rather than in isolation. It also enabled joint working which avoided duplication and created new opportunities to further enhance provision.

Although small-scale projects provided useful pilots, and in some cases acted as a catalyst for more extensive and embedded activity, there was concern about the proliferation of projects across the University and how best to maintain coherence and effectiveness. In 2005, three 'Widening Participation Hubs' were established to address this concern. These were designed to embrace a more strategic and cross-institution approach to provision, rather than the earlier project-driven approach. The Hubs focused on three areas of the student life cycle: Outreach, Learning and Support, Placement and Employability. They provided the infrastructure which later played a key part in enabling the mainstreaming of Widening Participation strategy and practice.

In 2008, led by the Pro-Vice-Chancellor for Learning Innovation, the Widening Participation Strategy was embedded within the Learning and Teaching and Employability Strategies. At this point the hubs became operational working groups with a broadened remit to include an institutional focus on diversity, inclusive practice for all, student success and preparing students for the global workplace.

The Outreach and Community Engagement Working Group covers pre-entry, access and early student transition agendas. The Curriculum and Learner Development Working Group (previously the Learning and Support Hub) is concerned with the curriculum; teaching, learning and assessment; and learner development from first to final year. And the Employability Working Group (previously the Placement and Employability Hub) relates to the industrial placement year and transition of final year students into the graduate labour market.

One of the key objectives of the Learning and Teaching Strategy is 'creative and innovative curriculum design and delivery to support the needs of a diverse student population and their employment needs'. Specific priorities relating to supporting the needs of a diverse student population in the context of employability, include promoting the value of mentoring programmes, extending placement preparation support and targeted careers management support.

Research-Informed Practice

Early investigation into the needs of students from under-represented groups proved critical to the success of Widening Participation at Aston. The research was conducted with a genuine interest in understanding how best to support students and direct funding to the most appropriate interventions. Up until this point the University did not have a clear understanding of the possible implications of having an increasingly diverse profile.

Research examples include a longitudinal study which followed a cohort of students from Low Participation Neighbourhoods from first to final year (Hartley, 2006), a study of the mature student experience (Ulrich, 2005), and an investigation into the degree to which University facilities and access policies were appropriate for the range of students' living arrangements (Arya & Smith, 2005).

The institution started to build up a picture of the student experience and how it could be enhanced. The research was critical to the shaping of provision, including identifying the need for study skills support, more social and study space, dedicated support for mature students, and fostering group cohesion among new students. On this basis the case was established for initiatives such as the Student Peer Mentoring programme and the Maths Support Centre.

The research tradition has continued through the work of the Widening Participation Strategic Adviser, now based in Learning and Teaching Research within the Centre for Learning Innovation and Professional Practice (CLIPP). This role includes monitoring the demographic make-up of the student body and analysis of continuation and achievement data to identify and address any local performance issues.

Inclusive Practice for All

Although the institutional widening participation research focused on specific student groups, the proposed interventions were considered to be good practice for all students. For example, initial consideration was given to Peer Mentoring to aid the transition of specific groups such as mature students and students living at home. This was rejected on the basis that this could be seen as a deficit-model approach in which students groups might be perceived as receiving 'special' treatment. Also it would have excluded other students who could benefit from the provision. A decision was made to make the support available to all students who wanted a mentor. The first small-scale pilot within Combined Honours was later extended to selected disciplines in each School to add value to existing peer-activity in Schools. This was important to secure buy-in to a set of peer mentoring principles at discipline level. Opening provision to all students enabled more staff to be involved in the programme, since the scheme did not exclude international students for example.

A Full Student Life Cycle Approach

Student Peer Mentoring is an intervention which exemplifies adoption of a full student life cycle approach. Although the University's initial widening participation focus was upon outreach, the diversification of activity was afforded by a better understanding of students needs, and a more balanced approach to both access and student success, including student achievement, satisfaction, and employment outcomes. In response to the initial research, the Student Peer Mentoring Programme prioritised the first year student transition and second year placement preparation. Subsequently provision has diversified to include peer contact while students are on industrial placement, and graduate mentors supporting the transition of final year students into the world of work.

Cross-Institutional Developments

As the University started to work more strategically, it sought to identify links across existing projects and to develop cross-institution interventions to benefit a greater number of students. A prime example of this is the set up of the Learning and Development Centre in 2006, which built on and included the Maths Support Centre first set up in the School of Engineering and Applied Sciences. Relocating to the Library made the provision more transparent to students, and broadening the offerings to include study skills support and academic writing mentors, for example, meant that the service was used by many more students. The Learning and Development Centre is now well used by undergraduate and postgraduate students, by home and International students; mature students and Foundation Degree students.

Access to Institutional Data

In 2004 the University appointed a Widening Participation Data Officer (now 'Planning and Management Information Officer'), based in Registry and Planning, to support the data requirements of the University's Widening Participation Task Group and project staff engaged in widening participation programmes and research. This post was critical to the early institutional research for Widening Participation, and continues to perform a vital role in providing planning and management information to support equality and diversity. From a Widening Participation perspective it is possible to monitor student recruitment, progression and achievement and to identify any performance issues at institutional and local level.

Developing an Inclusive Culture

In 2008 the Postgraduate Certificate in Professional Practice (PGCPP) was launched, with a much greater focus on diversity and inclusion than its predecessor. The programme is mandatory for new lecturing staff. This new approach has been found to be effective in helping to raise awareness of cultural diversity and in challenging assumptions (Higson, 2009). Aston has also developed inter-cultural awareness programmes for students to help develop students' awareness of cultural difference and a way of managing this constructively in both their studies and in employment. Building on earlier work (Herzfeldt, 2007), the pilot has shown that the optimum time to engage students in this work is in their first year when they are fresh and eager to embrace new experiences (Higson, 2010).

Aston has also engaged with external partners through participation in two Higher Education Academy Summit programmes relating to inclusive practice. These were nine month programmes in which the University worked with a community of partners to enhance inclusion and student success. One Summit looked specifically at the attainment gap between white and BME (Black Minority Ethnic) students. Key outcomes of this engagement include the development of resources to enable staff to consider inclusive practice in design of the curriculum and learning and teaching practices; and in particular how to encourage student engagement and integration in the classroom.

EVIDENCE OF EFFECTIVENESS

In light of the developments described it is pertinent to consider what difference they have made, and to what degree the institution has been transformed. To some extent the steady and incremental nature of institutional change disguises the true level of transformation that the University has undergone. The student body has become increasingly diverse and the University is in a strong position to be responsive to those needs and to engage staff in a dialogue about the value of, and strategies for, inclusive practice. This approach has also enabled strategic connections to be made between widening participation and internationalisation agendas; two agendas which are rarely linked (Ippolito, 2007). This current position is in stark contrast to an institution 10 years earlier, when the University was preparing its first Widening Participation statement.

A key measure of success is the continued performance against Widening Participation benchmarks, but more importantly widening participation is now considered as part of a more inclusive approach in meeting the needs of a diverse student population. This represents a powerful change which immediately involved staff who had previously not been directly engaged in the widening participation agenda. New staff could see the founding principles of the work of the Widening Participation Hubs as well as bringing fresh and different perspectives. It has also been empowering for the Working Groups to focus on enhancement, rather than the earlier required focus on accountability in monitoring the effective usage of HEFCE widening participation grant.

Staff also have access to professional development programmes and cultural awareness programmes to enable them to reflect on the degree to which their own practices are inclusive.

CONCLUSIONS

This final section is a critical reflection of the process of mainstreaming widening participation, including the challenges, enabling factors and suggestions for practice.

Challenges

Widening Participation and Standards
Despite widening participation being achieved while maintaining entry standards, notions of a diminution of standards and the need for remediation are ongoing challenges. In a recent evaluation of the Learning and Development Centre there was evidence that such provision is still perceived by some as remedial, and the Centre is aiming to strengthen its relationship with Schools to work in partnership and to promote the Centre as part of positive student development practice for all.

Staff Engagement

Although the Widening Participation Hubs had cross-University represen-tation, staff engagement in this activity was typically with a community of already committed staff. An inclusive approach to learning and teaching is one which includes students at all levels and from all backgrounds, so cannot be considered to be the sole responsibility of widening participation-funded staff, for example. The inclusive approach adopted for widening participation interventions seeks to challenge notions of deficit and remedial provision, and to reinforce the notion that inclusive practice is for all students, and is the responsibility of all staff. This approach has helped the University to reach-out beyond staff involved in specific projects or remits relating to widening participation.

Access to Institutional Widening Participation Data

Another major challenge for widening participation was the difficulty of accessing widening participation data to inform policy, practice and research. This became such an issue for staff engaged in research that a case was made for the creation of a new role dedicated to data analysis to support widening participation.

A Widening Participation Data Officer was appointed in 2004 in the Registry and Planning Department. This post has proved invaluable and continues to provide a fundamental service across the University. Having access to institutional data that we had not had access to before, has enabled the University to go beyond anecdotes, challenge ill-informed assumptions, reduce the reliance on HESA data and facilitate prompt responses to performance issues.

Management of Change and Assisting Factors

A full student life cycle approach, rather than the more common focus on the earlier stages of the life cycle (Storan, Thomas, Wylie, & Berzins, 2009), has created opportunities for working jointly across the University. This would not have been the case if widening participation activity had been predominantly outward-facing. This approach recognises that there are multiple transition points in students' university careers.

A key assisting factor to changing practice was working across the institution, working jointly with other groups and focusing on strategic priorities collaboratively. This created opportunities to add value to existing areas of work and to other funding streams. The set up of the Learning Development Centre, for example, was enabled through task groups of widening participation and learning and teaching, working jointly and strategically.

Typically Aston's approach to change has been steady and incremental. It has begun with small case studies and evaluations to build an evidence base for impact. This has afforded the opportunity to engage staff and students in the process of change. This steady growth in response to need is illustrated by the first widening participation-funded post in Careers. This post was introduced in response to growing concern about the declining student uptake of the Placement Year and the possible impact of the changing student demographic; along with a desire to engage students who might be disadvantaged in the labour market. The appointment was initially made on a part-time basis. Through continued research and the success of provision in Careers this activity has now grown to a Placement and Employability Team of three, and is key to the Employability Strategy.

An early requirement for an evidence-based approach represents one of the most powerful assisting factors in the success of widening participation at Aston. This has meant that widening participation funding was well used in addressing real, rather than perceived, need. It has also been critical to the University to have access to institutional widening participation data so that both student access and success can be monitored. It is equally important for monitoring uptake of interventions by under-represented groups and enabling a quicker response to any identified performance issues.

The following lessons learned from this experience may be transferable to other Higher Education institutions:

1. Where possible, consider a full student life cycle approach.
2. Listen to your students and scrutinise your institutional data.
3. Although seeking to meet the needs of under-represented groups consider how interventions can support all students through inclusive practice.
4. When introducing new activity start small and grow steadily to give time to bring staff on board.
5. Build upon and add value to existing activity.
6. Focus interventions upon strategic priorities.
7. Work with others across the institution to focus jointly on strategic priorities, rather than working in isolation.
8. For each project, plan for embedding and sustainability from the start.
9. Add value through working in partnership both internally and externally.
10. Engage staff with the concepts of widening participation, diversity and inclusive practice; and integrate into the professional development of staff.

CHAPTER 3.2

ACHIEVING A 'FAIR GO' AT LA TROBE UNIVERSITY

Kerry Ferguson

ABSTRACT

Purpose – *This chapter highlights the general direction that Australian Universities are headed in Broadening Participation, including the impact of The Bradley Review of Higher Education (2008). More specifically, the chapter explains how La Trobe University has interpreted the review and set about a whole of university approach to delivering equality of opportunity.*

Approach – *Social justice and equity have always been core values of La Trobe University. The University aims to increase the diversity of the student cohort by engaging with communities through outreach and promoting collaboration which facilitates the increased participation of under-represented groups in higher education. The University also supports successful academic outcomes through the effective provision of services and a broad student experience.*

La Trobe University promotes and maintains a learning environment which provides opportunities for engagement, is inclusive, healthy, socially vibrant, accessible and free from discrimination.

Practical implications – *This chapter demonstrates how policy, training and small programmes and projects in various departments throughout the*

Institutional Transformation to Engage a Diverse Student Body
International Perspectives on Higher Education Research, Volume 6, 107–118
ISSN: 1479-3628/doi:10.1108/S1479-3628(2011)0000006011

University add to the emerging larger picture of success in creating an environment that embraces diversity and the successful participation of students from disadvantaged backgrounds.

Value of paper – *Australian universities are cognisant of the global issues faced by the higher education sector and believe that some of our experiences in addressing the issues may be of value to the wider international community of tertiary education.*

Keywords: Case study; Australian context; equity; partnerships

AN OVERVIEW OF BROADENING PARTICIPATION IN HIGHER EDUCATION IN AUSTRALIA

Managing equity and widening participation, balanced with competition for student numbers and funding, is a major challenge for all Australian universities.

The 'Fair Chance for All' agenda (Department of Employment, Education and Training; National Board of Employment, Education and Training, 1990) was introduced in all Australian states in 1990, and identified specific equity groups for action with regard to access, participation, retention and success in higher education. Following the election of a Labor Government in 2007, the higher education equity agenda had a major re-focus through a commissioned comprehensive review of higher education, referred to as the Bradley Review (Bradley, Noonan, Nugent, & Scales, 2008). A major outcome of the review was addressing social inclusion in higher education and policy for the sector. Recommendations from the Bradley Review were then presented in the Transforming Australia's Higher Education System Report (Department of Education, Employment and Workplace Relations, 2009a).

Higher education institutions are focusing on equity in creative and innovative ways. There is no one particular approach, with most institutions engaging in outreach activities, including communities and schools, building aspiration, addressing school curriculum choices and progress, financial aid through scholarships and other forms of assistance and specific academic support. Some institutions combine staff, student equity and diversity matters, with the equal opportunity legislation being the basis for both areas.

As part of the Government's response to the Bradley Review (Bradley et al., 2008), the focus on social inclusion and the drive to increase the number of low socio-economic students participating and succeeding in higher education, new funding initiatives, the Higher Education Participation and Partnerships Program, or HEPPP, (DEEWR, 2010) are being introduced to replace the current equity funding programme. The programme has two key elements: *Participation* and *Partnership*. Universities will undertake activities and implement strategies that assist in improving access and participation rates for Australian resident undergraduate students from low socio-economic from the current level 15% to 20% by 2020 (Department of Education, Employment and Workplace Relations, 2009b).

This programme represents a major increase in equity funding.

LA TROBE UNIVERSITY

La Trobe University is a multi-campus university in the state of Victoria with four regional campuses and a large campus in the outer suburbs of Melbourne. The University has a long history of social inclusion with a strong social justice agenda, being built on the principles of a 'fair go' (to give some one an equal opportunity or equitable treatment). The *La Trobe University Act 1964* was established to serve the community of Victoria by making knowledge available to the benefit of all. La Trobe was also committed to fostering the general welfare and development of all its students. The establishment of equity and access services within the University grew in the late 1980s arising from the need to offer additional support to students with disabilities. In a backdrop of reducing government funding and other market forces, the University has continued to provide education and support to a diverse student population including those students from the under-represented groups and disadvantaged backgrounds.

When the University enrolled its first cohort in 1967 there were approximately 500 students including undergraduate and postgraduate students. Of these, a significant number were women, the first in their family to attend a university, and students from migrant families. Student enrolments in 2008, some 40 years later, numbered 26,344 of which we have approximately 3,500 domestic students who were born overseas from 129 countries of origin. In a recent student survey approximately 40% of students surveyed indicated they were first in family to attend University. La Trobe has a major regional presence and a strong diversity profile and is able to offer opportunities and support services to low-SES, rural and isolated, migrant and refugee students, Indigenous students and students with a disability. The University's location and extensive entry policy allows students to attend who might otherwise not have met the entry requirements and be disadvantaged by their remote location.

The core values of the University include responsibility, for Social Justice, Equal Opportunity, Cultural Diversity and Environmental Sustainability and Relevance, ensuring education is a life long and interactive experience that produces responsible global citizens.

Institutional Policies, Processes and Practices to Mainstream Widening Participation

The University has extensive policies, procedures and guidelines covering all its functions. Equity-related policies include:

- Equal Opportunity
- Sexual Harassment, Harassment and Discrimination
- Policy for People with Disabilities, Mental Health Illness and/or Ongoing Medical Conditions
- Children on Campus (i.e. when parents or carers are unable to make alternative child care arrangements children can stay with them providing there is no safety issue or disruption to the work or learning environment)
- Equality and Diversity Awareness Program – staff attendance policy
- Work and Family

The ongoing review of policies and procedures is managed under the Quality Enhancement portfolio; each policy is mandated to address issues of inclusion and equity. Each area of governance that has responsibility for developing policies and procedures must review and amend in accordance with the quality framework for progressing through the University's senior committees.

Widening Participation

Within the OECD, Australia is currently 9th of the 30 in the proportion of 25–34 year olds with higher degree qualifications (29%), down from 7th a decade ago. The Bradley Review (Bradley et al., 2008) has set a target of 40% of this age group to attain a bachelor-level qualification by 2020. In widening participation, a further target is to ensure that those from disadvantaged backgrounds can aspire to higher education. The proportion of low socio-economic status students enrolled in higher education in Australia has remained static at approximately 15% over the past two decades, yet this group makes up 25% of the broader population, however, when compared with international trends, this figure may seem reasonable.

Defining Social-Economic Status (SES) has presented major problems in Australia as it is currently defined by the post code of the area where a person lives, leading to many disadvantaged Australians living outside these designated post codes not being counted. A further reform of government is to take other equity factors such as parents' level of education and occupation, immigrant status and disability into consideration when determining disadvantage. Australia has additional problems created by the vast distances and the fact that large urban areas are on the coast. The costs of travelling, accommodation and social isolation can create another layer of disadvantage for students who are from these areas that are also listed as low SES.

Table 1 indicates the progress of La Trobe University in attracting and retaining students from low SES backgrounds.

Evidence of Effectiveness

Trend data for low SES shows that La Trobe has been attracting these students at above sector average rates for many years. The low SES student participation data relates to both commencing and continuing students and shows a consistent and gradual upward trend at La Trobe over the five year period, 2004–2008. The retention and success data for these students were also at or above sector averages. It can be seen from the following table that the 2008 commencing rate for low SES students was above the previous four years, indicating a gradual improvement in low SES student enrolments. For all indicators, La Trobe remained above the sector averages (State and National) for the five year period. As shown in Table 1 the retention indicator is 1.0, which indicates that students in the equity group are persevering with their studies at the same rate as other students. A retention ratio of less than 1.0 indicates the equity group students are withdrawing at a greater rate than the general student population.

Table 1. State and National Access and Participation Rates for Low SES Students in Australia 2004–2008 (Undergraduate Data Only).

	2004	2005	2006	2007	2008
Low SES access					
La Trobe	16.53	17.69	17.15	16.98	18.07
State average	12.67	12.53	12.72	12.93	13.19
National average	15.40	15.46	15.69	15.92	15.82
Low SES participation					
La Trobe	15.95	16.32	16.65	16.88	17.39
State average	12.27	12.17	12.16	12.33	12.49
National average	14.80	14.68	14.78	15.02	14.95
Low SES retention					
La Trobe	1.00	1.00	1.01	1.01	1.00
State average	0.99	1.00	0.99	0.99	0.99
National average	0.98	0.98	0.98	0.98	0.97
Low SES success					
La Trobe	0.98	0.98	0.98	0.98	0.98
State average	0.96	0.97	0.97	0.97	0.97
National average	0.97	0.97	0.97	0.97	0.97

Source: Data from Department of Education, Science and Training Statistics

DESIGN FOR LEARNING: CURRICULUM REVIEW AND RENEWAL

In May 2009, the University's Academic Board approved a programme of curriculum review and renewal across the University in *Design for Learning: Curriculum Review and Renewal (*La Trobe University, 2009*)*. From 2009 to 2013 La Trobe University will review and renew every undergraduate course under the auspices of the *Design for Learning (DfL) Project* (La Trobe University, 2010). The overall project will consist of a number of inter-related initiatives across all faculties which will include addressing the first year experience, curriculum design guidelines, course mapping, and the evaluation of learning outcomes and standards. Entry requirements, alternative formats, alternative assessments and other equity practices are all part of this major reform. Early identification of students at risk is also a key focus of the DfL project.

Many new support roles have been created, including student engagement and transition officers. Student wellbeing and social support have been taken into account and a student hub has been designed which will provide a new and exciting workplace for Academic and Student Services staff and a more streamlined student resource area that will centralise a range of services and become a focal point for students.

Education Partnerships Team

The University has committed to increasing undergraduate domestic enrolment by 30% by 2025 and achieving this will include a significant increase in enrolment of students from low SES backgrounds. The University is establishing an Educational Partnerships team to facilitate the schools partnership agenda.

A Regional Strategic Plan addresses issues relating to increasing participation of disadvantaged young people who live in rural and isolated areas. Twenty five per cent of La Trobe students are enrolled at the regional campuses and additional Government funding to assist students from low SES families, will enable the University to contribute significantly to the Government's participation and attainment targets.

Broadening Participation

La Trobe University has embarked on the following collaborative projects and partnerships:

(a) La Trobe is a member of the Innovation Research Universities Australia (IRUA). The Network includes: La Trobe, University of Newcastle, Griffith University, Murdoch University, Charles Darwin University, Flinders University and James Cook University. These universities are located across the breadth of Australia.

Recently, representatives from equity-related areas at each of these universities met to establish the Broadening Participation Network. The group shared their successful outreach programmes and discussed how they could pool resources and develop collaborative programmes to improve the access, participation, retention and success from the low SES students.

(b) The Tertiary Aspirations Network (TAN) was formed in 2008, and is comprised of student equity officers from each university in Victoria. The network collaborates on outreach programmes to the under-represented in terms of transition to University and/or Low SES schools. The Network has divided the state of Victoria into sections, with each group managing one section. This is to ensure that all areas of the state are reached and there is no overlap or duplication of what is being undertaken.

(c) Development of the Learning Families Project: the focus of this project is support for families of current and prospective students where the family has little or no experience of university education.

Rationale for working with families include:

- To enhance support for students. Some families will be particularly unaware of how best they could support the student.
- To reduce family pressures which may impact on a student's studies so that families unfamiliar with university study can address concerns about changes in the students' attitudes and friendship groups, reduced contact with the student and failure to meet expectations for family involvement.
- To improve family support for school students as support and interest is important to students succeeding academically and setting goals for post-school education and training.

The Equality and Diversity Centre (EDC) also has responsibility for the following already existing projects that support the widening participation agenda.

Staff Training

The EDC undertakes University-mandated equity training for all new and continuing staff through the Equality and Diversity Awareness Program. The programme includes an online component and a half-day workshop. It is a promotion requirement that staff have completed equity training. Topics include equal opportunity, anti-discrimination, indigenous and cultural issues. A Culturally Diversity and Inclusive Practices Toolkit has been developed to ensure that all staff have a consistent approach to inclusive language and practice and can be accessed at www.latrobe.edu.au/cdip

The Curriculum, Teaching and Learning Centre (CTLC) supports and assists La Trobe University's academic staff and managers in designing, developing, and providing curricula, teaching, assessment, and feedback that are effective and efficient. Academic staffs are encouraged to undertake the Graduate Certificate in Higher Education Curriculum, Teaching and Learning.

Equity Grants

Over the past six years the EDC has provided competitive grants to Faculties, campuses and administrative areas which have contributed to the social inclusion agenda of the University. The Equality and Diversity Grants are available to improve access, participation, retention and success for the following disadvantaged groups as defined by the Department of Education, Employment and Workplace Relations (DEEWR):

- students with low socio-economic/low income backgrounds;
- students from regional or remote areas;
- students with a disability;
- students from non-English speaking backgrounds (domestic students less than 10 years in Australia) and
- gender.

Following a review of the Higher Education Equity Program (HEEP) undertaken by Department of Education, Science and Training (DEST), now known as DEEWR, in 2004, women in non-traditional areas of study was removed from the list and replaced by gender. This decision was in the large part due to the attainment of the targets set in 1991 in specified areas of non-traditional areas of study and to increase the number of male students in the disciplines of nursing and teaching despite protests from university practitioners across Australia.

Disability Support

La Trobe University is above the national average for students with a disability or long-term medical condition. In 2008, 710 students (2.4%) of the 29,273 enrolled students in 2008 were registered with the EDC and of these, 75 needed intensive support and a further 16 required additional specialist equipment to assist them to study successfully. Note-takers, study support and sign interpreters are part of the services provided. New developments in technology are adopted when suitable and the Centre has well established protocol and procedures for determining support. The partnership with the student is an integral aspect of the success of the support offered.

Refugee Programme

A programme offering additional support to refugee students has been operating at La Trobe University since 2008, and is administered by the EDC. In 2010, the University had 63 refugee students seeking support.
Results of the programme include:

• only two students have withdrawn from their studies (3% attrition compared with 18% across LTU) and
• six students have now graduated from their studies.

Support has included one year residential scholarships, provision of computers and bicycles.

The EDC sponsored three students studying International Development to attend the Millennium Development Goals conference in Melbourne, December 2009. The conference was organised by the Australian Council for International Development (ACFID) and Institute for Human Security, La Trobe University, with the key aim of bringing together development practitioners, academics, policy-makers and the business community to review progress of the Millennium Development Goals.

Scholarships and Financial Aid

The University has a significant number of institutional equity scholarships for undergraduate students. The scholarships on average are valued at AUS$3,000 per year and are for the normal duration of an undergraduate course.

Computers are given to students who are eligible for an equity scholarship but are unsuccessful because of the number of scholarships available.

The University also provides La Trobe Indigenous Support Scholarships to commencing full-time undergraduate students with a value of $5,000 per annum for the normal duration of their course.

Financial Aid Service

Students can obtain a non-interest bearing loan up to a total of $4,000 for a course-related purpose that is essential to continue their course of study at the University. Students are able to use it for course-prescribed texts, course materials/equipment, computer hardware/software and costs for study placements/travel.

Special Entry and Access Schemes

The Special Entry and Access Schemes are open to applicants whose education generally has been adversely affected by their life circumstances. The University has a number of special entry programmes to facilitate enrolments from students of low SES background, regional and remote students, Non-English Speaking Background (NESB) students, and students with disabilities. These include:

- The Rural and Regional Students Access Scheme which aims to encourage students who have completed Year 12 at a rural or regional school to study at one of La Trobe's regional campuses. The Scheme provides an automatic bonus of five aggregate points to eligible applicants.
- The Special Access at La Trobe scheme (SALT). The SALT scheme enables students from selected schools to apply for entry into a degree programme based on a written application supported by a school recommendation. This scheme is available to students in schools identified where the proportion of their Year 12 cohort enrolling at university has averaged 50% or less over the previous two year period and the school is located in a low socio-economic post code area.

La Trobe Golden Key Homework Club

This programme aims to develop a partnership approach to study support with local secondary high schools, which are located in low-SES areas in the university catchment region and also have a high NESB populations. Year 11 and 12 students from three local under-represented schools are invited to come on campus for 1.5 h per week and receive assistance with homework by University student tutors who are members of the Golden Key Honour Society. Membership to this society is restricted to the students in the top 15% of grades in their first year at university. The Home Work Club programme is offered for a six-week period during semester 1, and a seven-week period in semester 2. Two Homework Club sessions are offered each week, one during school hours, and another after school. The students are transported from the school to the University campus. The students receive a gift pack (La Trobe badged USB stick, pen and ruler) on completion of the programme evaluation.

Middle Years of School Project

The Equality and Diversity Centre has undertaken two research projects in one of the University's regional centres that has one of the highest drop out rates from the middle years of school in Australia. The region has a high proportion of indigenous, refugee and long-term unemployed people. Non-Government Organisations (NGOs) and Government agencies have been working to address many of the problems these young people encounter. Despite these efforts to establish cooperative partnerships and share the limited funding and resources over the past 10 years, the rate of school drop out appears unchanged. The project is seeking to find alternative ways for agencies, schools and the community to approach the problem.

Faculty Operational Plans

All faculties as part of their operational plans include objectives and strategies to address equity and indigenous participation and success. These plans are monitored by the Vice-Chancellor and University Council.

REFLECTION

All sections of the University have an important role in providing opportunity for students whose educational potential has been obscured by their social and economic circumstances. Today we look to a future with improved funding and objectives for 'social inclusion' in higher education.

There is much to do, however, with the current Government recognising and supporting universities in this critical area for our society, the future looks optimistic. Australian universities are on the threshold of dramatically changing the profile of participation and success for all Australians providing the financial commitment from Government does not decline.

ACKNOWLEDGMENTS

The author wishes to acknowledge the major contributions of Ms Beth Rankin and Mrs Stephanie Chard to the chapter.

CHAPTER 4

MAINSTREAMING WIDENING ACCESS TO ENGAGE STUDENTS IN HIGHER EDUCATION

Sue Hatt and James Tate

ABSTRACT

Purpose – *This chapter explores the reasons why higher education institutions (HEIs) have engaged with learners before entry into HE and examines the ways in which this transformed institutions.*

Methodology/approach – *The chapter draws on evidence collected in the South West of England about the ways in which HEIs worked with schools and colleges to reach out to learners with the potential to progress to HE but who come from backgrounds with little tradition of accessing HE. This evidence is set within a literature framework to contextualise the findings. The chapter considers outreach work as part of the whole student lifecycle beginning before university entry and continuing beyond graduation.*

Findings – *The chapter finds that outreach work is particularly valuable when it is undertaken by partnerships. Within a partnership framework, each institution can contribute their specialist expertise to provide a coherent, progressive programme of activities for young people to help them to consider progression to HE. Partnerships facilitated knowledge transfer so that all institutions benefitted from the lessons learnt particularly with*

Institutional Transformation to Engage a Diverse Student Body
International Perspectives on Higher Education Research, Volume 6, 119–128
Copyright © 2011 by Emerald Group Publishing Limited
All rights of reproduction in any form reserved
ISSN: 1479-3628/doi:10.1108/S1479-3628(2011)0000006012

respect to the training of student ambassadors and the use of data for targeting and evaluating the programme.

Implications – *Pre-entry engagement helped learners to acquire more information about HE so that they could make informed choices about mode of study, subject and institution. This, in turn, improved retention rates and helped HEIs to smooth the transition into HE, to diversify their entry profile and to enhance the educational experience.*

Keywords: Diversification; partnership; pre-entry engagement; summer schools

INTRODUCTION

The student experience is a brief but pivotal episode in a person's life. Engagement in higher education (HE) positively influences students, HE institutions (HEIs), the economy and society. For students, their opportunities and subsequent careers can be enhanced by their HE experience (DfES, 2003); HEIs are enriched by the quality and diversity of their students (Shaw 2009); the economy benefits from the development of workers with higher level skills while society is enriched by graduates who participate in their communities (DfES, 2003).

Successful engagement in HE is strongly affected by the availability and accuracy of the information students receive in school and college, which shapes their expectations and informs their choice of course, institution and mode of study (Ozga & Sukhnandan, 1998; Yorke & Longden, 2008). Hence, clear benefits ensue for young people and for HEIs from pre-entry outreach work, which promotes a greater awareness and understanding of HE, especially when the focus is on those groups with little tradition of accessing HE. By raising aspirations in sections of society where it may previously have been largely absent and by enhancing the preparedness of the individual student, pre-entry engagement offers an opportunity to transform the institution by extending the diversity of applicants, broadening the cultural base of the institution, increasing retention and improving student success.

Although some institutions in the United Kingdom have come to this agenda during the past decade, others have a long history of outreach work, as the case study for the University of Bedfordshire indicates. The Labour government elected in 1997 highlighted the role of education in upward social mobility and provided funding to HEIs and partnerships for targeted outreach work. An expansion of outreach work in England followed during the first decade of the twenty-first century and this has extended the professional knowledge base about what works, when and for whom.

In the South West of England (SW), the Aimhigher regional team has gathered a considerable body of evidence about the development of its outreach programme, its challenges and the extent to which it has realised its objectives. The Aimhigher SW team has collated evidence from managers, practitioners and participants in schools, colleges and HEIs to establish the impact of the collaborative outreach programme. Qualitative and quantitative data has been collected to evaluate the ways in which the programme has influenced partner institutions, the extent to which it has met its objectives and the factors that have contributed to its effectiveness. This evidence has been supplemented by the analysis of secondary data from the Higher Education Statistics Agency (HESA) and the Universities and Colleges Admissions Service (UCAS) to assess changes in applications and accepted applications to HE by entrants from lower socio-economic groups. The primary data has thus been located within the context of the secondary data to provide a series of rich and detailed reports and articles (see, e.g., Austin & Hatt, 2005; Tate, Hatt, & Baxter, 2006; Hatt, Baxter, & Tate, 2007, 2009) about widening participation outreach work in the SW. This chapter draws on that evidence base to explore the reasons why, and the success with which, HEIs have engaged with learners before their entry into HE and will examine the ways in which this engagement has transformed the institutions.

THE STUDENT LIFECYCLE AND PRE-ENTRY ENGAGEMENT

Although HE study begins on entry, the extent to which a person benefits from this experience and successfully attains their educational objectives depends on a series of factors before and after this point. It is therefore useful to adopt a student lifecycle (HEFCE, 2001b) approach to widening participation in which HE is seen as part of a progression along a continuum of learning experiences, beginning before HE entry and continuing after graduation. This locates the student experience within a wider context and explores the reasons why students enter HE, the factors that facilitate their adjustment to the new environment and contribute to their success.

The lifecycle approach begins when the student becomes aware of HE as a possible option for their own future. During this 'aspiration raising' stage

(HEFCE, 2001b), a series of steps on the 'aspiration stairway' (Hatt et al., 2009) need to be negotiated to help the potential entrant discover and understand what HE entails, whether it can help them to attain their aims in life and how they might access HE by choosing the programme, institution and mode of study best suited to their circumstances and preferences. Raising aspirations is more than simply the creation of an aspiration; it also involves nurturing, sustaining and developing that aspiration so that the learner becomes sufficiently confident to take the steps necessary for its realisation.

In this model, raising aspirations is an extensive process and pre-entry engagement can be spread over several years, starting perhaps in primary school. An example of engagement in secondary school might include a drama workshop to introduce 12- or 13-year-olds to HE, a taster day on an HE campus in the following year, a mentoring programme with HE students when they are 15 and 16 years of age and, in their first year of post-compulsory education, a subject-specific summer school, which extends their learning and prepares them for the UCAS application process.

Integrated programmes that combine contributions from different institutions and progress young people from considering HE to making an application for a course at a particular institution have been found to be more effective than isolated events (HEFCE, 2006b). HEIs also share in the immediate benefits of pre-entry programmes because these activities provide opportunities for HE staff to appreciate the different educational pathways through which pre-HE learners have accessed HE and to smooth the transition from pre-18 learning to HE (Thomas et al., 2010a, 2010b). Learners entering HE from vocational programmes, for example, have experienced different approaches to teaching, learning and assessment compared with those who have taken the traditional academic route into HE as the case study from the Netherlands shows. Coming into contact with learners from different entry routes offers HE staff an opportunity to inform curriculum development and facilitate cross-sector progression. Pre-entry programmes form part of an extended orientation to HE, while strengthening the relationship between the entrant and the institution at the same time.

The Higher Education Progression Framework (HEPF) provides a set of principles to guide partnerships and institutions as they move beyond one-off widening participation interventions to a sequence of experiences for learners (Action on Access, 2008). It identifies three stages for outreach work – the introductory, the developmental and the consolidation phase. Taken together, these provide a coherent framework within which widening participation outreach work from different partners can be located.

An alternative model of pre-entry engagement has been evidenced by the Plymouth and Peninsula Tri-level model (Reynolds et al., 2010), which is based on a 'genuine partnership with parity of esteem between HEIs, schools and local authorities' (Reynolds et al., 2010, p. iii). This approach seeks to build HE school liaison and facilitate institutional change in schools and universities through professional development.

This model, like many other programmes, makes extensive use of HE students to 'act as long-term role models, coaches, mentors and "buddies"' (Reynolds et al., 2010, p. v) to support school students over the course of a school year to realise their potential. The training and employment of HE students to work on pre-entry programmes brings extensive benefits to HE students and their institutions. It provides opportunities for students to earn money, confirms that the institution values applicants from their backgrounds, increases their self-confidence, extends their curriculum vitae and strengthens their bond with their institution (Austin & Hatt, 2005). As a result, the HEI can benefit from improved retention, a diverse student body and better opportunities for its alumni in the graduate labour market.

WORKING WITHIN A SHARED FRAMEWORK

In the early years of the twenty-first century, the policy focus in England has been on partnerships to promote HE progression. These partnerships have been both horizontal and vertical. From 2000–2002, the HEFCE Special Initiative projects (HEFCE, 1999a, 1999b) provided an example of horizontal partnerships by encouraging HEIs to work together to raise awareness of the opportunities HE offered. Vertical partnerships between providers at different stages in the education sector have been exemplified by Aimhigher (HEFCE, 2008a) and by Lifelong Learning Networks (HEFCE, 2004), which brought HEIs, colleges and training providers together to build and promote vocational pathways to HE.

Partnerships focused on working with groups with little tradition of entering HE and which are under-represented in HE. They have been well placed to establish a collaborative framework for outreach work within which the contributions of different partner institutions can be located and they offer opportunities for knowledge exchange between institutions.

In the SW, the 13 HEIs, 31 colleges, 15 local authorities and over 160 targeted secondary schools have collaborated in Aimhigher partnerships to work with pre-HE learners. As the institutions have undertaken independent activity on their own behalf as well, a complex cross-sector collaborative framework has been constructed to raise HE awareness, improve the motivation to study and promote progression to HE. As one senior practitioner reflected,

> 'what I think Aimhigher has done ... is foster the culture of collaboration and partnerships. And the fact that partnerships can do things and work ... the notion that institutions within sectors and between sectors should collaborate, I think, has been a major contribution of Aimhigher. (Chair of Aimhigher partnership).

Aimhigher funding has been closely monitored by HEFCE to ensure that it was targeted on identified groups of beneficiaries (HEFCE, 2007a) and met the programme's objectives. As a consequence, Aimhigher has been encouraged to develop techniques for using data to target schools and beneficiaries and for evaluating programmes. Interviews with the widening participation managers in SW HEIs found that they were aware of and wanted to share Aimhigher's expertise,

> I think in terms of Aimhigher influencing the institution, the things like thinking about targeting and being explicit about your criteria and things like that. Evaluation approaches are another thing that has kind of fed in. (HEI widening participation manager)

Knowledge exchange has moved institutions to become more rigorous and has brought practitioners, managers, researchers and policy-makers together to discuss widening participation issues and learn from each other. Consequently, widening participation has become 'serious business' and, in the words of one Aimhigher senior manager,

> Aimhigher has helped to professionalise (widening participation). It's produced a sort of professional cadre of groups of people who've been enabled to talk to each other ... So in a sense Aimhigher has acted as a sort of *academy for widening participation.* (Aimhigher senior manager; emphasis added).

Partnerships have been influential in pioneering approaches to widening participation, which have then been imported into institutional outreach work. The training of student mentors and ambassadors provided another example of this knowledge transfer process as the following quote illustrates:

> We've probably benefitted through our experiences of working with the student ambassadors strand ... Certainly that's given us a lot of ideas around that and her team are a great resource to go to around anything like this. You know, they are so happy to share. (HEI widening participation co-ordinator)

Partnerships have thus professionalised the ways in which widening participation has been undertaken, and the HEIs have benefitted from sharing that learning to transform the ways in which their own institutional outreach programmes are organised, delivered and evaluated.

OUTREACH, RECRUITMENT AND RETENTION

HEIs have focused the majority of their activities near to the point of HE entry, providing opportunities for incidental institutional recruitment even when the content of the activity has been largely generic. In the SW, the broad pattern was for HEIs to focus their outreach activities on post-16 learners, whereas Aimhigher worked with schools and colleges to cater for the pre-16 age groups. One HE co-ordinator noted that

> one of the things that was decided by the [Aimhigher] programme quite early on, was that the standard post-sixteen work would be left to the institution, so quite a lot of our institutional WP strategy dovetails with Aimhigher, because Aimhigher stops [at sixteen]. (HEI WP co-ordinator, Aimhigher Peninsula area)

This division of labour enabled the HEIs to use outreach work to smooth the transition between school or college and HE. They can use outreach activities to address issues such as independent study, budgeting and time management so that students are well prepared, ready to adjust to HE study, be retained and succeed in realising their educational objectives (Yorke & Longden, 2008). Similarly, outreach activities provide opportunities for HE staff to improve their understanding of the pre-HE curriculum. The reform of the 14–19 curriculum involving changes to A levels, and the introduction of the diploma lines has had implications for HEIs and their entrants. Working in partnership with schools and colleges through the Aimhigher programme has enabled them to keep in touch with these developments as the following quote indicates:

> The 14–19 (agenda) has taken off in the last 2 years ... We were the host of the joint conference last year, with Aimhigher ... So there's been some core policy areas on which we did really see them as experts. (HEI widening participation manager)

The widening participation activities in which HEIs have engaged have furthered institutional goals and provided opportunities for institutional change. In 1997, the Dearing Report (NICHE, 1997b) showed that the expansion of HE in the early 1990s had not extended participation to those from lower socio-economic groups. These 'under-represented groups' became the target for widening participation activities as HEIs sought to diversify their profile by encouraging applications from these social groups.

The contention that a diverse student body contributes positively to excellence in education and enhances the quality of the student experience (Shaw, 2009) is supported by evidence that curriculum changes to accommodate diversity can be beneficial to all students (Powney, 2002). It has been reflected in the Widening Participation Strategic Assessments (HEFCE, 2009) of several HEIs in the SW. One HEI, for example, noted its commitment to attract and retain:

> students from a wide range of backgrounds, creating a diverse and international University community. (University of Bristol, 2009)

Residential summer schools, which enable young people to spend several days at a university campus, fit into this framework. They are like the Foundation Studies programme detailed in the case study from the University of South Australia in that they offer participants an immersive university experience and support informed choice so that young people apply to institutions where they can succeed. In the SW, the objective of residential summer schools is to build confidence and develop participants' plans for entering HE (Hatt et al., 2009). They replicate the HE experience sufficiently well for participants to feel confident in moving towards an HE application.

A longitudinal tracking study in the SW suggested that summer schools were more successful than other outreach activities in encouraging HE applications. This study (Aimhigher South West, 2007) compared summer school participants with those who had taken part in less intensive widening participation activities and found that summer school participants were more likely to submit a UCAS application at their first opportunity than those who had taken part in other activities. For summer schools, 32% of past participants applied to UCAS at their first opportunity compared with only 25% of those who had taken part in less-intensive Aimhigher activities (Hatt et al., 2009). Summer schools are thus contributing to HE recruitment and to diversifying the profile of HE applicants. An analysis of HESA data on HEIs in the SW showed that, between 2002 and 2007, the number of accepted young applicants to HEIs in SW from lower socio-economic groups rose by 1,255 entrants representing a 34% increase (Harrison, 2009).

Although diversity in the student population enhances the quality of the student experience, HEIs have also been mindful of the perceived 'risk' that admitting learners from under-represented groups might lead to higher rates of non-completion. Despite some evidence to the contrary (Harrison, Baxter, & Hatt, 2007; West, Emmerson, Frayne, & Hind, 2009), the perception is that such learners will be less gifted academically, less well-prepared and more vulnerable to early withdrawal than students from higher social groups. The case study from the University of Australia illustrates that similar issues arise in Australia. Although learners from under-represented groups may start with additional barriers to overcome, pre-entry engagement provides institutions with an opportunity to minimise the risk. Summer schools, for example, have enabled participants to explore courses, institutions and locations. Several participants in the SW noted that they had changed their plans for where or what they wanted to study as a result of the summer school (Hatt et al., 2009). For example, one summer school participant said,

> I was thinking about staying at home and now I definitely want to go away to uni. (summer school participant)

If learners find out about courses and institutions before entry, then they are better positioned to enter a programme of study that meets their expectations, to which they can feel committed and on which they will be retained (Ozga & Sukhnandan, 1998; Yorke & Thomas, 2003; Yorke & Longden, 2008).

Using current HE students to reach out to potential HE entrants provides another example of work, which benefits school students, HE students and the institutions at which they study. During the past decade, HE students have been used extensively to work with young people before HE entry. The great advantage of HE students is that they can act as role models who

> play an important part in an individual's expectations and aspirations. (HEFCE, 2003, para 44)

HE students are close in age to school students; yet, in their journey from school to HE, they have passed through a series of important transitions that they can help the school students to negotiate successfully.

Furthermore, the process of training and working as an ambassador increases the HE students' skills, self-confidence and relationship with the institution so that they are more likely to persist with their own studies and be successful in realising their own educational objectives (Austin & Hatt, 2005). The employment of students as outreach ambassadors sends out a powerful implicit message that the institution welcomes diversity. One study (Austin & Hatt, 2005) found that HE students were able to draw on their outreach employment to complete their academic assignments and that 18% of students considered that working as an ambassador had helped them a great deal in their studies. A further 42% considered that it had helped to some extent and, interestingly, no one reported that working as an ambassador had interfered with their studies. This evidence indicates that training students to work as outreach ambassadors increases their skills and offers new ways for institutions to enhance the quality of their graduates.

CONCLUSION

As the name implies, outreach programmes are essentially outward facing. They develop mutually beneficial links between HEIs, schools and colleges and other HE providers that over time can develop into mature relationships. These links provide opportunities for knowledge exchange, which, in turn, enables institutions to establish a positive cycle of change. Through pre-entry engagement with learners from under-represented groups, HEIs help to promote progression to post-compulsory education and to HE, diversifying their student intake.

Pre-entry engagement also provides opportunities for HE staff to increase their understanding of the pre-HE curriculum so that they can ease the transition into HE and reduce withdrawal rates. As students from under-represented groups are recruited and retained by the HEI, a diverse student community is created. A socially inclusive student body requires adjustment to the curriculum, and developing the teaching and learning provision enhances the quality of the educational experience for all students. Finally, the training and use of HE students as outreach ambassadors and mentors improves their capacity for study and develops their employability skills. The student experience can be enhanced at all stages of the student lifecycle. Widening participation outreach programmes can thus transform the ways in which HEIs recruit, orientate and educate their students to prepare them better for progression beyond HE.

CHAPTER 4.1

THE ACCESS TRADITION: WIDENING PARTICIPATION AND THE UNIVERSITY OF BEDFORDSHIRE

Steve Kendall

ABSTRACT

Purpose – *To offer an account of widening participation practice at the University of Bedfordshire as a case study of how higher education can approach 'access' and embed practice across the institution. The paper explores the contribution of widening participation policy and practice to the development of the University.*

Approach – *The paper considers the part played by widening participation policy and practice in the development of the University from the organisations out of which it has grown; it provides a brief overview of some of the ways in which the University pursues and fulfils its widening participation objectives; and it offers some reflection on the prospects for widening participation in the context of new arrangements for funding students and higher education institutions.*

Findings – *The paper provides some outline evidence for the success of its practice and for its mainstreaming across the organisation and offers some reflection on areas where further work is required to develop the University's strategies and processes.*

Institutional Transformation to Engage a Diverse Student Body
International Perspectives on Higher Education Research, Volume 6, 129–135
Copyright © 2011 by Emerald Group Publishing Limited
All rights of reproduction in any form reserved
ISSN: 1479-3628/doi:10.1108/S1479-3628(2011)0000006013

Originality/value of the chapter – *The paper provides an account of a UK university with a particularly strong commitment to widening participation, which it has sustained throughout a period of growing reputation and increasing pressure to adopt a more 'traditionally' selective approach to recruitment and participation. Widening participation remains a core value within the university and continues to be one of its defining characteristics.*

Keywords: Access; progression; widening participation; transformation; Aimhigher

INTRODUCTION

Universities and other higher education providers seek to widen participation for various reasons (and with varying degrees of enthusiasm). They do so perhaps to reach new sources of students or because government policies press them to, providing them with financial incentives or subjecting them to external scrutiny. Where they are most successful in widening access, however, is where the impulse to do so flows from the essential character of the institution and is fully embedded in its core values. In our case, 'access' is the first of our values.[1]

Universities are, in our view, agents of social transformation, although it should be acknowledged that this is not necessarily a generally held view. Excellence in the generation of opportunity is, or should be, of equal importance with excellence in innovation and research, excellence in teaching and learning, excellence in employer engagement or excellence in international reputation. This view is encapsulated in the University 'vision' of 'a world where all are able to benefit from transformational educational experiences'[2] and in its strategic plan whose first objective is 'to enhance the opportunities to access higher education for all those able to benefit'.[3]

WIDENING PARTICIPATION AND INSTITUTIONAL TRANSFORMATION

The University of Bedfordshire exists as the result of a series of major transformations – from a technical school into a technical college and then from a college of higher education to a university (initially, the University of

Luton and now the University of Bedfordshire.) Twenty-five years ago, the then Luton College of Higher Education launched its first Access Course for adults and was for many years the main provider of Access Courses in Bedfordshire.

'Access' predates the University but persists into and continues to permeate the present institution. The access mission of the University thus provides continuity, helping to keep it on track throughout the various changes it has undergone. This was particularly evident just before the formation of the new University of Bedfordshire at a time when the University was experiencing financial difficulty and struggling to recruit. There was considerable internal debate about the future direction of the University, with one strand arguing for a repositioning of the organisation towards a more 'traditional' student market and an increased emphasis on postgraduate recruitment. Following the appointment of a new vice chancellor, the debate was resolved in favour of a resounding reiteration of our commitment to widening participation – a commitment firmly embedded in the University's mission and strategic plan, which in turn helped to steer the institution into and through the merger, which resulted in the formation of the new University in 2006. This reassertion of the 'access tradition' can be understood as the convergence of pragmatism and principle, involving both a realistic recognition of the University's niche in the student recruitment market and consistency in the application of its core values.

Widening participation activity did not drive, nor was it a response to, these changes. It would be more accurate to say that the long-established history of widening participation practice helped to frame successive transformations. The access mission had woven itself sufficiently into the character of the University (although not without challenge and debate) that it formed part of the prevailing conditions within which change took place. Access had come to form a 'tradition' within the culture of the organisation, which helped crucially to shape its identity.

At the time of writing, four years after the formation of the new University, it is fair to claim that the widening participation mission permeates the whole institution. It is at the heart of the strategic plan. It is firmly and consistently upheld by the senior management team. It is enshrined in a range of strategies and policies that deal with the curriculum, partnership working, schools liaison, marketing and communications and equal opportunities. It is woven into the University's financial planning and reflected in the proceedings of the corporate management team, the Academic Board and the Board of Governors. Although it is true that certain central functions (the Partnership

Office, the Teaching and Learning Directorate, the Marketing, Admissions, Recruitment and Communications Department would be key examples) take a particularly keen interest, the mission of the University to widen participation would be universally acknowledged and generally supported across the institution.

WIDENING PARTICIPATION PRACTICE

This commitment manifests itself in a range of ways. These include the systematic provision of opportunities for potential students from under-represented groups to be in contact with the University and encouraged to progress to higher education. We have a lively and well-received programme of liaison with schools and colleges, providing, for example, campus visits, which 'showcase' higher education and subject-specific 'taster' days, which set out the particular opportunities, associated with specific disciplines. Each academic department has its own 'education champion' whose role is to form links with student groups and staff in local schools and colleges where there is the greatest scope to increase progression (especially from among students from groups under-represented in higher education, such as those from the lower socio-economic groups and some minority ethnic groups).

The University takes a leading role, locally and regionally, in the Aimhigher project (a national initiative enabling partnerships of higher education institutions, further education colleges and schools to work together to improve aspiration, attainment and progression from among those who are under-represented in higher education). Aimhigher's target groups (which, locally, are learners from backgrounds that are income-deprived, educationally deprived and from neighbourhoods that have low participation in higher education) are well aligned with the University's own recruitment strategy. Aimhigher funding has been used to appoint Higher Education Progression Officers who work with local schools and colleges to promote and facilitate progression to higher education.

The University's work with Aimhigher involves a number of specific projects, which target vulnerable groups of learners, specifically young people in care, young people being educated outside the classroom (e.g. in Pupil Referral Units) and boys from black Caribbean backgrounds at risk of disengagement. There is also work in partnership with Aimhigher, local and regional government agencies, and young people themselves to exploit the opportunities afforded by the London Olympic Games, to promote educational aspiration and achievement. One example of the success of these initiatives is the increase in progression to higher education among young people in care in Luton from 2 in 2007 to 13 in 2010: modest numbers, admittedly, but still a significant improvement.

The University's partnerships with further education colleges also make a significant contribution to widening participation bringing around 1,000 students into higher education, through foundation degrees (two-year degree-level courses with a strong vocational focus), from which three-quarters of those who pass, progress to an honours degree. We are also a sponsor for a new Academy (a school which is independent of local government control and directly funded by central government) and a partner in another. Both schools have very high concentrations of learners in the Aimhigher target groups.

The University's admissions policy is similarly directed and includes explicit progression agreements for learners from non-standard routes such as Access Courses, learners on vocational programmes in further education colleges and learners in the target groups described earlier. These practices have recently been re-examined (and reaffirmed) in the context of the government cap on the recruitment of students to full-time undergraduate programmes. The cap, in combination with a huge increase in applications (more than 50% in 2010), clearly exerts pressure on admissions staff. However, because admissions are conducted centrally, we have found it possible to maintain a clear direction and sustain our emphasis on widening participation. Evidence for the success of this approach includes the increase in acceptances this year in students from Access Courses and the maintenance of student numbers on foundation degrees in partner colleges at the same level as before the imposition of the cap.

Much of this work is supported through the widening participation premium received from the Higher Education Funding Council for England (HEFCE). It supports marketing, information, advice and guidance for learners in the key target groups; the management and delivery of the college partnerships; the additional administrative infrastructure required to support this and a specific bursary paid to students progressing from partner colleges. The use of the funding is transparent and can be distinguished within the key cost centres involved. We calculate, however, that our expenditure on widening participation is significantly greater than the premium we receive, which accounts for less than two-thirds of the total relevant expenditure. If further allowance were made for the general bursary payments, the HEFCE widening participation premium would account for less than 50% of our total widening participation expenditure, the balance of which comes from our mainstream funding.

REFLECTION – THE PROSPECTS FOR
WIDENING PARTICIPATION

It remains to be seen how changes to the funding regime for higher education students and higher education teaching will impact on the emphasis given to widening participation at the University of Bedfordshire. The proposed further shift of the responsibility for funding higher education from state to citizen will certainly exert increasing pressure on institutions such as ours, and our commitment to widening participation will be challenged and tested.

Even so, the clarity of institutional purpose described earlier is, we think, a considerable advantage. The strong leadership of the vice chancellor is a particular and signal instance of this clarity. Prof. Les Ebdon is indefatigable in his consistent insistence that the University of Bedfordshire is a university for those who would otherwise find it difficult (if not impossible) to go to university.

Although we are crucially shaped by the funding regime in which we find ourselves, of course, we are not driven to seek to widen participation primarily by any legislative, regulatory or financial imperatives. In fact, we would probably argue that national policy, especially at the moment, tends to lag behind our ambitions.

The main challenge we have so far encountered is the cap on full-time undergraduate recruitment – not just for the limit it places on expansion but also for the challenge it introduces, by implication at least, to an access mission. It is all too possible for such a shift to be misunderstood as necessitating a concomitant shift to a more 'traditionally' selective approach to student recruitment. The University has set its face against this and continues to explore ways in which it can continue to meet its obligations to the 'under-represented' by expanding its part-time and work-based provision and by beginning to explore the introduction of 'contextual data', which can be sensitive to the educational background and experience of applicants.

The limits to the recruitment of full-time students and the proposed changes to student funding notwithstanding, there is much that we can do to sustain and extend the 'tradition of access.' Even though in a university such as this where widening participation (WP) is embedded in the institutional ethos, we would expect WP policies and above all action to be strongly reflected in all key documents; there are nonetheless some evident gaps, requiring some further work to balance our WP activity across a wider range of beneficiary groups. Our success to date mainly involves our work with the full-time undergraduate population. Attention needs to be paid to part-time and mature students also, and these will require a different approach that will nevertheless be strongly rooted in the University's links with local further education colleges.

On disability, there is scope to widen our focus to include learners whose 'learning difficulties' may not trigger applications for Disabled Students Allowance but who nonetheless may require our intervention, especially as part of our teaching and learning strategies. It would be helpful if there were more explicit linkages between employer engagement work and WP, particularly around progression from advanced apprenticeships to higher education. This is one area where we would like to broaden the scope of our work with Aimhigher (if political and funding changes continue to permit us to do so).

Our future plans involve the expansion of our network of collaborative partners, addressing the need for a growing number of graduates with higher skills and continuing to develop the access tradition. By so doing, we aspire to become a university that combines the pursuit of social justice with an effective response to economic necessity.

NOTES

1. http://www.beds.ac.uk/aboutus/mission-statement
2. http://www.beds.ac.uk/aboutus/mission-statement
3. http://www.beds.ac.uk/aboutus/strategic/strategicplan0712.pdf

CHAPTER 4.2

ACCESS, ASPIRATION AND ATTAINMENT: FOUNDATION STUDIES AT THE UNIVERSITY OF SOUTH AUSTRALIA

Christopher M. Klinger and Neil L. Murray

ABSTRACT

Purpose – *The case study described here showcases the way in which the University of South Australia (UniSA), an institution with a long history of being at the forefront of educational opportunity for all and with equity principles embedded in its founding legislation, has responded to the mainstreaming of widening participation and engagement. It does so by focussing particularly on the Foundation Studies access education programme, the cornerstone of the University's widening participation strategy for adults (although in Australia the vast majority of university entrants are aged 18 years and above and, therefore, by definition, categorised as adults).*

Approach – *We provide an overview of the development and structure of the Foundation Studies programme, the national and institutional contexts in which it operates, and key characteristic of students who undertake the programme. We also report on participation and success*

Institutional Transformation to Engage a Diverse Student Body
International Perspectives on Higher Education Research, Volume 6, 137–146
Copyright © 2011 by Emerald Group Publishing Limited
ISSN: 1479-3628/doi:10.1108/S1479-3628(2011)0000006014

rates and briefly describe how successful access education students gain admission to undergraduate study.

Social implications – *UniSA's approach to equity and widening participation provides an effective means of redress for people who have experienced educational disadvantage. It does so not merely by providing access but by also actively preparing them for future academic success. That success in turn builds social capital – serving a wider and increasingly pertinent imperative in today's global market economy.*

Value of chapter – *The case study described presents what has proven to be a viable and effective model, one which suggests strongly that socio-economic and educational disadvantage can be overcome and that 'second chance' does not imply 'second rate'.*

Keywords: Access education; widening participation; foundation studies; equity; opportunity; non-traditional students

INTRODUCTION

In 2008, the government-commissioned Bradley Review (Bradley, 2008) drew attention to Australia's need to increase the representation within higher education (HE) of those in society who have been variously disadvantaged. This led to the Australian Government's current HE participation target that by 2020 students from low socio-economic backgrounds should account for 20% of all undergraduate enrolments. To put this in perspective, 25% of the Australian population is categorised as low socio-economic status (SES) (Phillimore & Koshy, 2010). The Review and the Government's response have given unprecedented prominence to widening participation, encouraging universities to reflect on their role as educational institutions and agents of social change. The University of South Australia (UniSA), however, has a long history of being at the forefront of educational opportunity for all and, in many respects, has extant policies and strategies that might be viewed as having anticipated the thrust of the Bradley Review. This is perhaps unsurprising, given that the lead author of the Review, Denise Bradley, was the University's vice chancellor from 1997 to 2007. UniSA takes particular pride in its history, which is centred on community engagement, maintaining cultural diversity among staff and students and providing equitable access to HE. Here, we outline the university's background in relation to equity principles and, in particular, relate aspects of its *Foundation Studies* access programme and the role it plays in providing opportunities for those whose talents and potential might otherwise have gone unrecognised and unrealised.

INSTITUTIONAL CONTEXT

Established in 1991 with a strong equity mission in its founding legislation (Government of South Australia, 1990), UniSA is the youngest of the state's three HE institutions, having evolved through the amalgamation of South Australia's Institute of Technology and College of Advanced Education, thereby drawing on more than a century's experience of educational leadership. UniSA is part of the Australian Technology Network (ATN), an alliance of five prominent universities from each mainland Australian state. It offers over 600 undergraduate and postgraduate degree programmes in education, arts and social sciences; health sciences; business; and information technology, engineering and the environment. Of approximately 38,000 students (growing on average by 3.2% annually), some 27,000 are undergraduates and almost a quarter are from one or more of six government-defined equity groups, with about 5,000 of these having low SES. Around 50% of all students are aged 25 or older and 57% are female. The institutional retention rate is typically around 85%.

FOUNDATION STUDIES AT THE UNIVERSITY OF SOUTH AUSTRALIA

UniSA has numerous policies and strategies that serve to mainstream widening participation and engagement. Most prominent among these is its Foundation Studies programme, established in 2006 as a *university-wide* initiative funded through the Commonwealth Government under provisions for 'enabling education' – a term that can, and does, mean many things to many people: it comes in numerous flavours and, given that no standard model exists, it can be difficult to generalise from one setting to another. For the present purposes, however, we use the term synonymously with 'access' in the sense of bridging or foundational programmes that provide opportunities to undertake HE for those adults (including immediate school leavers) who, exclusively, lack the usual (traditional) pre-tertiary qualifications for university entry. As such, the Foundation Studies programme is a pathway to *any* of the University's undergraduate degrees, including high-demand programmes such as law, medical radiation and midwifery.

Foundation Studies superseded several distinct preparatory programmes within the university. It is designed to encompass all facets of its antecedents and goes further by virtue of its university-wide focus, which integrates this key participation initiative into the core work of the institution, while also allowing the programme to appeal to a broader segment of the population.

Foundation Studies has made a significant contribution to the University's equity mission to provide HE opportunities for people who have experienced educational disadvantage, either through being numbered within margin-alised, social groups that are notable for low educational achievement and aspirations or due to life events that negatively impacted their pre-tertiary educational attainment. A key performance indicator for equity at UniSA is the percentage of Australian students enrolled with one or more equity characteristics – that is, being counted among one or more designated equity groups defined by the Australian Commonwealth Department of Education, Employment and Workplace Relations – DEEWR): 'ATSI' (Aboriginal and Torrens Strait Islanders), 'Disability', 'Isolated', Low-socio-economic status' (Low-SES)', 'Non-English-Speaking Background' (NESB) and 'Rural' (NBEET, 1990).

Over 2006–2008, some 55% of Foundation Studies students came from at least one of these targeted equity groups, compared to the 42.5% institutional average, as illustrated by Table 1, where the terms 'access' (a ratio of *commencing* students in an equity group as a proportion of all commencing students) and 'participation' (a corresponding ratio but with respect to total student numbers) are adopted nationally for use across the HE sector (UniSA,

Table 1. Access and Participation rates – 4-Year Averages (2006–2009).

| | Access | | Participation | |
	Foundation studies (%)	University-wide (%)	Foundation studies (%)	University-wide (%)
ATSI	3.6	1.4	3.1	1.4
Disability	10.9	5.6	11.7	7.1
Isolated	0.9	1.0	0.8	1.0
Low-SES	39.5	25.1	38.5	24.7
NESB	7.7	3.5	9.0	3.3
Rural	21.5	13.6	20.9	12.8

2010). Notably, the access and participation rates for Foundation Studies are substantially stronger for students from low-SES, rural and non-English-speaking backgrounds. Although the antecedent programmes had strong equity profiles, representation of most equity groups is generally higher in Foundation Studies, indicating that the programme is effective in providing second-chance opportunities to access HE for people who have experienced educational disadvantage.

Foundation Studies *enables* students not just by providing a means of access to university but, in particular, by actively preparing them for success in their future undergraduate studies – an approach emphasised in Tinto's (2008) admonition that 'access without support is not opportunity' in a paper with that title. To that end, rather than adopting a 'one size fits all' approach, the programme is offered in six strands: five corresponding to major discipline areas across the university, whereas the sixth caters to students attending two regional campuses. All students undertake core courses for the programme as a whole, including 'Introduction to Tertiary Learning', 'Critical Literacy' and 'Introductory Computing', which reflect a deliberate focus on developing a range of generic academic and study skills that also anticipate the University's specified graduate qualities. Students also undertake strand-specific, discipline-related core courses and elective (non-core) courses that align with their intended degree-level pursuits. UniSA, like all Australian public universities, admits students to undergraduate degrees on a competitive basis, for which quotas are an integral factor. Most undergraduate programmes also have, within mainstream quotas, sub-quota allocations for 'special entry' applicants who do not meet traditional, school-based entry criteria – for instance, mature students who sit a special entry admissions test and others who undertake bridging or foundational/access programmes. On completion of Foundation Studies, students are not guaranteed admission to undergraduate programmes but compete with each other on merit (using their Foundation Studies grade point average) for these special-entry sub-quota places; however, they do not compete with traditional applicants.

Flexible study options are an integral part of UniSA's Teaching and Learning Framework, and this extends to the Foundation Studies programme, which may be undertaken full time over one academic year or part-time equivalent and in internal (on-campus) or external (off-campus) study modes (or any combination), supported by a suite of online learning facilities. Significantly, Foundation Studies students are full students of the University in every respect and have the opportunity to gain an immersive university experience; that is, one that acclimatises them to the University culture – academically, socially and geographically. Indeed, the proportions of those who choose to study internally and full time (typically 70–75% on both counts) are similar to those of the overall undergraduate population.

As an accredited programme, Foundation Studies courses must comply with UniSA's Teaching and Learning Framework, and its students are inducted into the University's teaching and learning culture, with its emphasis on producing work-ready graduates. The Framework is founded on principles of *experiential learning*, which encompasses 'practice-based learning' (incorporating workplace learning, embedded industry input and professional development); 'service learning' (developing professional knowledge in practical settings directed to the support of others, i.e. with a 'public good' dimension) and the 'teaching/research nexus' (emphasising enquiry-based learning experiences that develop research skills and critical dispositions). However, whereas the Teaching and Learning Framework is expressed in terms of *graduate* destinations (work-ready professionals), clearly the immediate destination for Foundation Studies students is different – their objective is to become effective undergraduates, requiring that the language of the Framework be re-interpreted so as to make it relevant and meaningful to this context. For example, the usual interpretation of 'workplace learning' (to give students an in-depth understanding of the workplace and opportunities to practice their emerging professional skills) shifts to giving Foundation Studies students a sound appreciation of, and capacity to function in, an undergraduate learning environment. Similarly, 'embedded industry input' translates to providing Foundation Studies students with authentic discipline content within which to develop a broad academic skills set. One might ask how this re-interpretation might be relevant for those who do not transition to undergraduate study; however, this is a highly unusual scenario as the overwhelming majority of students who complete the programme *do* go on to degree-level work. The rare instances when this is not the case have tended to be the result of changing circumstances and life priorities. Nonetheless, while no formal study has been conducted at UniSA (in part due to the very small incidence rate), anecdotal evidence suggests that these individuals leave the institution having acquired an enhanced skill set, which, one might speculate, could benefit them in terms of job prospects and workplace performance.

EVIDENCE OF EFFECTIVENESS

The performance of students in Foundation Studies reflects the role of the programme as both preparatory and exploratory. Across Australia (and elsewhere), success, retention and completion rates for access programmes have always been well below the sector average (DETYA, 2001; Ramsay, 2004). An early report on the attrition of students in the (now superseded) diploma in university studies found that 80% of those who withdrew did so not because of difficulties with their studies per se but because of the pressures of combining study with life responsibilities (Ramsay, Tranter, Sumner, & Barrett, 1996). Whereas that report is dated, recent evidence suggests that its findings remain germane: in an ongoing study involving focus groups and one-on-one interviews with Foundation Studies students, two of the three dominant emergent thematic constructs related explicitly to family and work responsibilities and their impact on students' aspirations and capacity to study (Murray & Klinger, 2011). Moreover, anecdotal evidence consistently reinforces the currency of Ramsay et al.'s findings – unsurprising, perhaps, given that, on average, in any year, some 50% of students in the Foundation Studies programme are aged 25 years or older, compared to some 31.5% of those undertaking bachelor-level degree studies, suggesting that family and employment commitments are likely to impact on enabling students more than on undergraduate students generally.

The definition of academic success used at UniSA is that employed by DEEWR, namely, the proportion of enrolled load for which students achieve passing grades. For undergraduate students, the success rate is typically a little under 90%, while for Foundation Studies students, it is 52–53%, on average. The latter, however, needs to be viewed with some caution. Firstly, it is not possible to make direct comparisons with the success rates for undergraduate programmes because the nature and purpose of enabling education is to enable people with no entry qualifications to prepare for university study. Some will find that university study is not for them; others will need additional time to be fully prepared, and still others will find their studies impeded by life factors. Secondly, success rates can be skewed by factors applicable only to Foundation Studies – for instance, we have found that the obligation for recipients of certain welfare payments to be 'learning or earning' has meant that a proportion of access students enrol merely to satisfy those requirements, sometimes never attending classes at all. Furthermore, being fee-free, means that there is no incentive for access students to withdraw formally. Finally, the DEEWR definition of 'success' might be considered too narrow for access education – where withdrawal signals an informed, *adult* decision that university is not for them, this should be viewed as a form of success because the equity objective has been served, in that people who otherwise may have been denied the opportunity to attempt university study have now had that chance. One might also speculate that even in their withdrawal, many of these students leave richer for their experience and will have developed skills that can benefit them in other life contexts.

Given this context, due recognition must be given to the proportion of enabling students who *do* successfully complete their programmes and transition to undergraduate studies. These represent a substantial number (around 100 each year) of new undergraduate students who would not otherwise have gained access to HE nor have been well prepared to succeed once there. Moreover, some of the students who withdraw subsequently return to make a successful attempt (according to the DEEWR definition of success). Thus, we estimate that of the 45–50% who 'fail to succeed', only around 10% do so after persisting in their efforts to finish the programme. This suggests that the 'actual' failure rate (i.e. computed for those who persist to completion) may not be too dissimilar from undergraduate rates.

Further evidence to support the above interpretation is provided by considering how successful Foundation Studies students perform following their transition to undergraduate degree studies. Fig. 1 shows distributions of students' undergraduate grade point averages (GPAs) for those who enter through Foundation Studies as well as for those admitted by all other entry pathways (GPAs of 1.5 and below were discarded as these outliers are due to students who did not persist in their programmes, and this analysis is concerned with comparing the performance of continuing/active students). Comparing these distributions, on average, those admitted through our access programme have a higher mean GPA (4.90) than those admitted by other methods of entry (4.74).

Statistical analysis of the data in Fig. 1 reveals that the higher average GPA for former Foundation Studies students in undergraduate programmes is statistically significant at a level above the 95% confidence level. This provides very strong evidence that the observed difference in the means is a real effect – that is, transitioned Foundation Studies students are significantly more likely to have a higher undergraduate GPA than students who enter university by other means. This stronger performance is also reflected in the retention rates: the university-wide retention rate for undergraduates is typically around 85%, whereas that of former access students is some 90% – attesting to the generally greater motivation often attributed to mature, non-traditional university students and offering some further indication that the access education provided by the Foundation Studies programme prepares them effectively for future success at university, going beyond merely providing an alternate pathway.

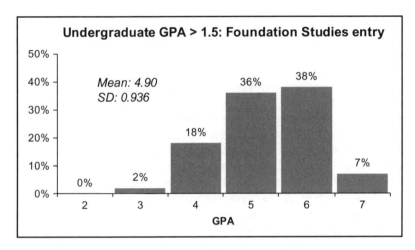

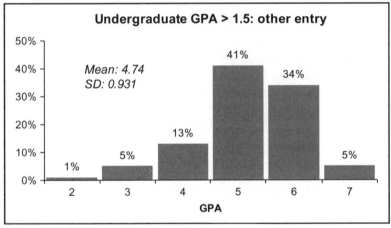

Fig. 1. Comparison of Undergraduate GPAs by Method of Entry.

REFLECTION

Although we have focussed on the Foundation Studies programme, in the present rapidly changing educational, social and political environment, UniSA continues to demonstrate its commitment to equity principles and the capacity to respond dynamically and flexibly. Indeed, UniSA has numerous allied policies and strategies directed at the widening participation agenda, and we have alluded to these in framing our discussion.

A significant development is the establishment in 2011 of the UniSA College, bringing together community engagement, pathway development and delivery of preparatory programs, including the Foundation Studies programme, which, as a result, is undergoing a process of renewal and transformation. New arrangements include the introduction of a stream to cater specifically to the distinct needs of the growing cohort of 18- to 20-year-old students accessing the programme and revised delivery arrangements to provide a teaching-intensive focus. This case study necessarily reflects the first five years of Foundation Studies at UniSA and provides a base against which in, say, a further five years, one might return to consider how, and in what ways, the new model has been successful (or otherwise).

In the meantime, Foundation Studies remains the mainstay of the University's equity mission. More than that, the programme demonstrates clearly that socio-economic and educational disadvantage can be overcome and that 'second chance' does not in any way imply 'second rate' – quite the reverse: many of those who enter HE by a non-traditional pathway such as ours will go on to become some of their institution's highest achieving students and graduates. Their success builds social capital, in the sense of 'the economic and social opportunities which a higher education provides' (Bradley, 2008, p. 10) – a vital commodity in today's global market economy where the need for a more skilled, better educated workforce is increasingly critical.

CHAPTER 4.3

TRANSFERRING FROM SENIOR TO HIGHER VOCATIONAL EDUCATION IN THE NETHERLANDS

Sabine Severiens, Rick Wolff and Wâtte Zijlstra

ABSTRACT

In the Netherlands, the route to higher education is not equally accessible for all (ethnic) groups. In this chapter, we focus on the transition from senior vocational education (MBO) to higher vocational education (HBO). Four focus group sessions of professional representatives from both MBO and HBO in Amsterdam, Rotterdam and The Hague (a total of 53 people) were held to examine the transfer policy measures and possibilities for improvements. The focus groups showed that most transfer projects are related to students themselves (the academic/utilitarian approach). More projects need to focus on the education itself (the transformative approach). It also is recommended to establish a transfer-infrastructure in each region, both to improve the quality of transfer and to promote study success of all (ethnic) groups.

Keywords: Transfer; transfer students; institutional reform; vocational education; ethnic minority students; collaborative models; diversity in education

Institutional Transformation to Engage a Diverse Student Body
International Perspectives on Higher Education Research, Volume 6, 147–154
Copyright © 2011 by Emerald Group Publishing Limited
All rights of reproduction in any form reserved
ISSN: 1479-3628/doi:10.1108/S1479-3628(2011)0000006015

INTRODUCTION

Research conducted by the TIES network has shown that the route to higher education is not equally accessible for all groups. The TIES project is undertaking comparative research on the integration of second-generation youth from Turkish, Moroccan and former Yugoslavian descent in 15 cities in 8 European countries (for detailed information, see http://www.tiesproject.eu/). 'Early tracking' shows that there are major differences in the progress made by students after primary education. Young people with a non-Western background are more likely to transfer to vocational education rather than general secondary education. They have to take an indirect route to higher vocational education (HBO) through secondary vocational education (VMBO) and senior secondary vocational education (MBO), which – on average – takes three years longer than the general track. Half of the second-generation Turkish young people in higher education have taken this indirect route, compared to 25% of the young people in the control group, which comprises young people living in similar neighbourhoods or communities (Crul, Pasztor, Lelie, Mijs, & Schnell, 2009). Both the OECD and the TIES network point out that improvements can be achieved in study success in higher education by providing better preparation to young people for their transfer to higher education. What improvements can be made to facilitate this transition? This chapter describes the results of a study among professionals: what solutions do they identify and what interventions are being deployed to promote transfers?

Two studies in particular form the framework for our research. The first is the research carried out by Jones and Thomas in 2005. They conducted an analysis of policy measures relating to diversity in British institutions of higher education and identified three distinctive approaches. Their study primarily concerns diversity in terms of socio-economic and ethnic cultural backgrounds. Our study concerns diversity in terms of previous education: The percentage of non-Western ethnic minority students in higher vocational education whose previous education involves an MBO is much greater than the percentage of students with a HAVO or VWO qualification. As such, this diversity in previous education is to some extent an indicator of diversity in ethnic cultural background. Despite this, the framework remains useful for our analysis.

The first approach identified is the academic approach. According to this, differences in study success are attributed to the students' attitude and motivation (or lack thereof). There is a focus on talent and efforts are made to recruit motivated students who have high aspirations. Projects that typify this vision include talent scouting, information campaigns at schools in deprived areas and so on. This constitutes an acknowledgement of the fact that higher education is less accessible for certain groups than it is for others. Efforts are made to improve accessibility by means of projects on the periphery of the institution.

The second approach is the utilitarian approach. Here, the focus is on maximising returns from an economic and financial perspective. Institutions apply diversity policy to enable as many students as possible to successfully graduate. Ultimately, the greater the number of successful graduates, the more financial resources the institution will receive. In this case, differences in study success are attributed to students' deficiencies in knowledge and skills. Typical projects applied in this approach include language courses, courses in study skills, job application courses and additional mentoring, and the third approach is the transformative approach. According to this, differences in study success are always partly attributable to the quality of the education provided. This is what distinguishes this approach from the other two. The first approach does not question the system of education itself. In the utilitarian approach, it is also up to the student to adapt to the institution. The basic concept of the third approach is that the institution changes *to* ensure that students are successful. Put another way, the structure of the institution is placed in question.

Policy measures applied from the perspective of this third approach are different in nature – there is a programmatic strategy, and policy is safeguarded within the structure of the institution. Jones and Thomas do however stress that the projects inspired by the first and second approaches remain important and certainly need to be implemented, but that their effect will be minimal unless the structure of the institution also changes.

The second study we are using is the research conducted by Floyd and Arnauld (2007) who describe a series of collaborative models between educational institutes at consecutive levels (in this case, *community colleges* and *four-year institutes*). The first model involves a type of covenant known as an articulation agreement. Institutes enter into agreements about the acceptance of each other's credits, which ultimately comes down to agreeing which students will be granted exemptions. The second model is the higher education centre model. This model often involves consortia of institutions that share faculties and offer joint programmes that prepare students for higher education. The third model is the higher education extension model. In this model, institutes of higher education provide a separate programme for transfer students. Finally, in the fourth model, the community college baccalaureate model, the supplying institution itself offers an additional programme that prepares students for the subsequent level. On the basis of this framework, Lang (2009) conducted a study into the effects of covenants. The study showed that students were no more likely to opt for institutions that had agreed a covenant with their previous course. However, the type of collaboration was shown to be important: students are more likely to choose a course structured along the lines of the higher education centre model, especially if both institutions share the same campus. Transfer students also showed a preference for agreements at programme level (rather than at institution level).

In our search for strategies to promote the transfer of students between MBO and HBO, we are using the approaches described by Jones and Thomas and the collaborative models of Floyd and Arnaud.

In line with Jones and Thomas, we begin by questioning the assumptions relating to differences in study success. We will then ask what efforts are currently being made to promote transfer and the extent to which this policy or the interventions are proving to be effective.

We have formulated the following research questions:

1. What explanations are given for successful transfer?
2. What interventions are deployed by educational institutions to promote successful transfer and to what extent are these effective?
3. What solutions do participants envisage for the short-term future?

METHOD

Four focus group sessions were held to answer the question of how transfer can be promoted. The above-mentioned questions formed the framework for these sessions. The sessions took the form of interactive brainstorm sessions.

The groups included representatives from both MBO and HBO who are directly associated with the transfer between these two types of education and came from each of the three major cities in the Netherlands (Amsterdam, Rotterdam and The Hague). A total of 53 people took part in the workshops.

RESULTS

The results of these sessions were then analysed on the basis of the three approaches to diversity and the set of collaborative models. The analysis of the workshop results shows that it is possible to distinguish between the following different perspectives: students, education and collaboration. In Table 1, this is shown in terms of *factors* and *types of approach:* what factors

Table 1. Factors and Types of Approach.

Perspectives of Intervention to Achieve Successful Transfer	Factors on which Intervention is Focused	Intervention Approach
Student	• Expectations • Choice of study programme • Motivation • Competencies and skills • Knowledge • Background	• Deficit • Aspiration
Education	• Teaching staff • Curriculum • Quality of education	Transformative
Collaboration		• HBO extension model • MBO extension model • Centre model • Covenants model • No collaboration

do the interventions focus on to achieve a successful transfer and what approach has been adopted? Is the approach based on deficiency (deficits) or on aspiration (potential)? Or in other words, is it a utilitarian or an academic approach? In addition, there may also be interventions that lead to structural changes in the education provided (transformative approach).

Below, we deal with each of the research questions.

EXPLANATIONS OF SUCCESSFUL TRANSFERS

The professionals have the impression that many teachers consider MBO students to be a problem group and especially those who use their entitlement to transfer even though they have not actually chosen to move on to HBO level. There is a general feeling that this group is growing. According to the professionals, the primary precondition for a successful transfer is that the student is motivated and effectively prepares for study at HBO level. To achieve this, the student must begin to focus on the HBO during the MBO phase, in terms of both their choice of programme and the learning environment. Currently, very little is done at MBO institution level to facilitate this focus and the responsibility remains that of the individual student. The student's ethnic or socio-economic background also plays an important role in this transfer, although the professionals highlight the fact that there is very little actual knowledge to corroborate this. It is largely based on assumptions.

Knowledge and skills are another important area of focus. The professionals indicate that a successful transfer is partly dependent on the skills of 'reflection' and 'abstract thought'. An HBO student must be capable of effectively relating theory and practice. A successful transfer in the first year of the HBO is no guarantee of a diploma, as the later years place increasing demands on the skill of reflection. Students' language skills are also cited in this context. According to the participants, proficiency in the Dutch language and reading comprehension are absolutely essential for a successful transfer.

WHAT INTERVENTIONS HAVE BEEN DEPLOYED AND HOW EFFECTIVE ARE THEY?

The explanations of successful transfers are generally in line with the assumptions reflected in the academic and utilitarian approaches highlighted by Jones and Thomas. Most projects instigated to improve transfers have so far related to students' deficits or promoted a sense of connection or aspiration among students. Most interventions that focus on rectifying deficits are at pre-entry level: transfer courses, preliminary programmes, pre-entry crash courses and summer courses. In addition, language interventions and tutoring are offered at post-entry level. Interventions focusing on aspiration take place at both pre-and post-entry levels (intake and welcome interviews, excellence tracks). Talent development and the promotion of a sense of connection are the most important objectives in this.

There are also interventions that relate to the education itself, but these are isolated. They focus primarily on the curriculum and to a lesser extent on the teaching staff or the quality of the education provided. Examples of interventions relating to education concern the attitudes of teachers (diversity training) and improvements to the way in which curricula are linked to associated MBO and HBO programmes.

According to the professionals, rigorous collaboration between MBO and HBO is an important precondition for successful transfers. In addition to the types of collaboration required to ensure that the interventions highlighted earlier are successful, other types of collaboration were also mentioned during the sessions, including a project agency that offers projects/internships in which MBO and HBO students can work together, a joint location where MBO and HBO students can study together under the same roof, a regional network and the joint development of a self-assessment tool for MBO students enabling them to evaluate the extent to which the seven competencies required at HBO level had been included in their programmes.

Despite all the interventions referred to, very little can be said about their impact. Few attempts have been made to measure the effects. Although there is monitoring of students' satisfaction with regard to the interventions, no assessment is made as to whether they are also likely to be more successful in transferring.

SOLUTIONS FOR THE SHORT-TERM FUTURE

The professionals indicate that additional transformative projects will be required, which relate to the education itself (the teaching staff, the curriculum and the quality and coordination of learning environments). One of the key aims of these projects should be to teach HBO and other teachers to adopt a more positive attitude to their MBO students and better equip them to deal with student diversity. There is an assumption that teacher's perceptions of MBO students and particularly those with non-Western background as a problem group are having a negative impact on study success. Preparations within MBO programmes for HBO education will also require improvement through the development of ongoing career support lines from MBO to HBO and better coordination of skills profiles between the two levels. An alternative solution is to use the elective components or the internship in the MBO curriculum to prepare MBO students who wish to transfer to HBO. All of this would need to be formally included in the MBO-HBO policy of the various institutions by incorporating specific sections on the transfer process in the policy framework.

In addition, the participants indicate that policy needs to be conducted at a macro level. For example, there is a clear need for a regional policy framework, and the skills profiles at MBO and HBO levels need to be more effectively coordinated with each other.

CONCLUSIONS AND RECOMMENDATIONS

The focus groups showed that most projects implemented to improve transfer are related to the students themselves and generally involve rectifying deficits or focus on the promotion of a sense of connection or student aspiration. Most of these projects are based on the academic or utilitarian approaches. Although there is generally no measurement of the effects of the interventions, most of the professionals indicate that these projects are not sufficient. They highlight the following points.

Greater numbers of projects need to focus directly on the education itself (the teaching staff, the curriculum and quality and coordination of learning environments). It is also necessary to ensure that the MBO-HBO policy is effectively embedded by including specific transfer sections in the policy frameworks and where possible also developing regional policy frameworks. HBO institutions need to make concrete agreements at regional level with the MBO institutions to optimise linkage for MBO students and especially those from a non-Western background. It is therefore recommended that an infrastructure be established in each region, both to prepare for successful transfer to HBO and to promote retention and study success while taking account of the diversity of the student population. From our literature review, we can also add that although the agreement of covenants is essential, it is not sufficient to effectively improve linkage. The application of the higher education centre model, in which related institutions share facilities and offer joint programmes, increases the likelihood of successful transitions.

CHAPTER 5

WORKING TOGETHER ON WIDENING ACCESS, ADMISSIONS AND TRANSITION INTO HIGHER EDUCATION

Janet Graham and Dan Shaffer

ABSTRACT

Purpose – *To raise awareness of Supporting Professionalism in Admissions Programme's (SPA's) development of the concept of the applicant experience strategy and the use of contextual data to support good practice in widening access and fair admissions.*

Design/methodology/approach – *SPA worked with Higher Education Institutions (HEIs), HEI groups and funding agencies through visits, discussions, desk-based research and literature reviews to develop an evidence base. Definitions and preliminary findings from SPA's review and analysis were released to HEIs in stages throughout 2009 and 2010 for the formative production of good practice.*

Findings – *The research and analysis of the information gained from the institutions and other stakeholders enabled SPA to develop the applicant experience strategy for the benefit of institutions and potential students and has enabled SPA to develop principles for the use of contextual data.*

Institutional Transformation to Engage a Diverse Student Body
International Perspectives on Higher Education Research, Volume 6, 155–168
Copyright © 2011 by Emerald Group Publishing Limited
ISSN: 1479-3628/doi:10.1108/S1479-3628(2011)0000006016

This was shared with HEIs enabling them to develop and enhance what they do in these areas.

Originality/value – *The applicant experience strategy is an original concept developed by SPA as there was no comprehensive research on this in the United Kingdom. It is the precursor to the student experience, which has had much more coverage. The use of contextual data while not new has been taken to a new level United Kingdom wide through the work of SPA. Both these areas of SPA's work support institutions working on widening access, admissions and transition into higher education to enhance professionalism and good practice and to aid retention.*

Keywords: Widening access; admissions; transition; applicant experience; contextual data

INTRODUCTION

Students contribute financially, academically and culturally to the value of their higher education institution. 96% of respondents to the first Schwartz consultation on fair admissions in 2004 (Admissions to Higher Education Steering Group, 2004), and 98% to the review in 2008 (Supporting Professionalism in Admissions/DIUS, 2008) felt it was important for higher education institutions to have students from a wide range of backgrounds. However, according to a House of Commons Public Accounts Committee report (2008-2009), despite government grants of £392 million over five years up to 2008 to universities to widen access, participation of working-class young people has only increased 2%. Clearly, the desire for diversity from within the community itself has not yet realised the dramatic change envisaged, despite great efforts to raise aspirations to enter higher education and to support and retain students through the transition to higher education. There is, however, a gap between raising aspirations and transition, which is commonly referred to as 'admissions'.

Most student experience strategies recognise the influential role pre-entry engagement can have. The 1994 Group's (2007) report *Enhancing the Student Experience*, noted that,

> A student's experience of university does not begin at the moment they step onto campus at the beginning of October, and it does not end when they are shaking the hand of the Vice-Chancellor at graduation. The early relationship between student and university is important during the applications and admissions process, in preparing students for university life, and to initiate their engagement with and attitudes towards their

university in the best way possible. A student's experience of university can stretch back even further through effective HE engagement with schools and colleges. (p. 16)

Such a holistic view of an individual's engagement with and contribution to an institution links the experience from pre-higher education through to post-graduation, meaning that there is a mutually beneficial and enduring relationship between institution and student. However, if admissions processes are not fully integrated into that engagement, then there is a real risk of a broken link between all the early aspiration–raising interaction and transition to higher education.

THE APPLICANT EXPERIENCE

The applicant experience should be considered as far more than just a one-way or passive journey taken by an individual. Experience is gained through participation, so there should be an interactive path of engagement in which all potential students have the opportunity, knowledge and understanding to gain admission to a course suited to their ability and aspirations and in which higher education providers can inform, inspire and attract students who can add to that institution's character and succeed in their studies. Both applicant and institution benefit from the kind of experience where ability and aspirations are accurately matched with an appropriate place. The Schwartz Report's five principles of fair admissions form the bedrock to such an applicant experience, but as the experience is valued in terms of the outcomes as a student, it is a vital foundation to the whole student experience.

Schwartz's belief in, 'Equal opportunity for all individuals, regardless of background, to gain admission to a course suited to their ability and aspirations' (Admissions to Higher Education Steering Group, 2004) is a key statement in defining the applicant experience, because fair admissions is mutually beneficial to both applicant and institution. It opens up access to an increased number and wider range of potential students and, thorough transparent and professionally applied practices, raises awareness and understanding of appropriate choices, thus facilitating transition into and retention within suitable higher education studies. Any strategy that aims to nurture potential within the educationally disadvantaged pre-higher education and then support such potential through transition into higher education must also consider how it recognises and guides those with potential through a fair admissions process. Without this vital link in the provision of widening access, admissions may perpetuate the barriers to entry that aspiration-raising beforehand and transition support afterwards work to remove, resulting in wasted effort for institution and learner alike. Institutions should therefore consider the points in Table 1 (What makes a good or bad applicant experience?)

Admissions must therefore be seen as part of the mainstream recruitment and retention practice, rather than a separate process. According to Black (2001), Jack Maguire, generally cited as the principal developer of enrolment management in the United States, described it as, 'A process that brings together often disparate functions having to do with recruiting, funding, tracking, retaining and replacing students as they move toward, within and away from the University'. It constitutes a co-ordinated approach to manage both the quantity and the quality of students and recognises that interaction with potential students before they apply represents the enactment of any institution's mission to preserve its vitality through enrolling and retaining students. It involves the overarching stages of the applicant experience (pre-application, application, post-application, transition) and continues through the student experience including retention, completion and progression beyond the first degree.

FINDING THE BEST MATCH

An integrated approach to 'admissions' in its broadest sense should be part of an institution's mission, its teaching and learning strategy and its drive for quality and standards. Even before the student registers, how the institution conducts itself with regard to potential students, their families and advisors plays a crucial part in supporting applicants and in the development of the

Table 1.   What Makes a Good or Bad Applicant Experience?

A Good Applicant Experience	A Poor Applicant Experience
• Is mutually beneficial to both the applicant and the higher education provider • Prepares, informs and provides equality of opportunity to enter higher education • Should accurately match the student's aims, abilities and aspirations with the character of the institution • Therefore improves student retention and enhances the strategic mission of the institution	• Is inherently detrimental to both the applicant and the higher education provider – *both lose out* • Perpetuates barriers to entry • Disengages potential applicants and their advisors • Risks incongruence between student expectations and institutional character • Therefore embeds an enrolment strategy leading to unfulfilled potential and increased drop-out

institutions reputation, and even its competitive advantage. Saying that you work in widening participation but not in admissions, that you make offers to applicants but you're not responsible for any retention strategy or that you teach students but you don't know how they're recruited is like saying you're a chef but you're not interested in where your ingredients have come from or how good the food tastes. A good chef knows the difference provenance can make to the quality of a dish: the chickens from down the road may not be as plentiful and may have to be collected rather than delivered. They may not be as consistent a standard, and they may not be as cheap. However, a good chef knows that the time, effort and money to select the best is worth the investment and will build a relationships with the farmers, with the rest of the staff (front and back of house) and with the patrons. All involved benefit from such relationships and the end result is far greater than just one good dish. If your admissions doesn't function like this, if it is disassociated from investing in the quality of potential applicants and of potential graduates, then how does it define its purpose?

Building knowledge of the potential student can be developed by using additional data and contextual factors in targeting outreach, widening participation and student recruitment activities to the admissions process and transition into the institution. One of the characteristics of fair admissions indentified in a JISC scoping study is that 'Fairness does not necessarily mean the same treatment of all applicants, but all applicants should have the same equality of opportunity' (JISC Report *Scoping Study 2:* 2008). In the current climate in admissions

- there is an increasing number of applicants applying for the same number or even reduced places (2011 entry) for full-time undergraduate study and
- courses that in the past that have been recruiting courses, making offers to most applicants, are now moving, often for the first time, to selecting students.

Such increasing demand from well qualified applicants in a higher education environment that is no longer looking at increasing participation means that institutions seeking fair measures of potential are turning to the use of contextual data.

Supporting Professionalism in Admissions Programme (SPA) has highlighted the many ways in which contextual information may be used by institutions within the applicant experience strategy including:

- For widening participation – to target aspiration raising and fair access activities
- To inform the decision as to who to interview

- To inform admissions decision making
- To identify applicants who may need additional learner support or practical advice during their application process, transition or when registered as a student
- To help assess applicants eligibility for bursaries or other financial support
- For statistical and qualitative monitoring and reporting purposes.

In line with the huge interest in the use of contextual data by the public, media, schools and colleges, government and the institutions themselves in 2010 SPA developed a set of principles for the use of contextual data in admissions:

1. The use of contextual data within a course's entry criteria/decision making must be
   - research based and justifiable to ensure the use of data adds value to the process and that HE providers adhere to good practice
   - relevant to the purpose for which it is being used, for example to add context to the admissions decision making process
   - valid and reliable (noting that some data, for example through the universities and colleges admissions service (UCAS), is self declared)
   - used to improve inclusivity, by recognising potential assessed using evidence based judgement (i.e. applicants may not be treated in exactly the same way as different factors may be considered; all applicants are individuals with different backgrounds)
   - transparent to applicants and their advisors in terms of what contextual data is used, if any, how it will be used, when it is used and how it was used in the previous cycle. This must be communicated to applicants in a transparent, clear and timely manner through websites, publications, events, in feedback to unsuccessful applicants etc.
2. Regular monitoring of the use of the data and related audit trails should be an integral part of the admissions process.
3. Admissions staff using contextual data in decision making should be aware of the issues surrounding contextual data. Professional development and training may be appropriate to ensure staff understand and can interpret and use the data. Contextual data should be used as part of the overall consideration of an individual applicant and not in isolation; a combination of various items of contextual data should be used to arrive at a holistic assessment of the applicant's potential for the course/ programme. Contextual data informs the process of professional judgement that ultimately decides whether an offer is made.

4. Applicants needing additional learner support or practical advice during their application, transition or when registered as a student, should receive appropriate transition and in-session learner support to ensure their potential continues to be developed.
5. Whilst there may be shared principles in the use of contextual data, it is recognised that individual institutions are autonomous in the contextual data they use and how it is used within their admissions decision-making process.

One of the issues in the United Kingdom has been access by universities and colleges to verified and reliable data relating to potential students and their backgrounds. Various forms of data are available publicly, but it is held in different ways and in different places. Working with the different UK administrations, a number of universities, Higher Education funding councils and the UCAS, it was possible for SPA to gain the agreement that datasets of use to institutions can be provided to them, through UCAS, as both generic data sets and, where possible, data such as progression rates to higher education (percentage determined by cohort size) matched to applicants. An initial basket of data comprised items of educational data such as school General Certificate of Secondary Education (GCSE) performance for 5A*-C GCSE (including English/Welsh and mathematics) and average (mean) school 'Best Eight' GCSE performance as well as socioeconomic data such as 'lives in a low progression to higher education neighbourhood' and socioeconomic class 3–7 (intermediate to routine occupations). UCAS aims to provide much of the basket of data, cost free, to institutions for 2012 entry.

Data for widening inclusion and admissions strategic and tactical planning has not until recently featured heavily in most institutional planning, but is more likely to do so in future with increasing competition between institutions to recruit the 'best' students for them. In England, a changed tuition fee environment from 2012 will be required for institutions that charge fees over £6,000 per year to demonstrate they have fair access and participation for disadvantaged students, through their Access Agreement with the Office for Fair Access (OFFA). In the United States, data are available for universities and colleges to purchase about the students who have taken the SAT or ACT tests in high school who are planning to go to higher education. Over a million students take each test and provide around 120 data items about themselves and their families as part of the process, something not available in the United Kingdom. In Australia a wide range of data is available to the state admissions centres and institutions from public data sets. The systems in those countries may not feature holistic assessment of individuals as in the United Kingdom, but they have a huge amount of data for planning, management and decision making. In a global higher education market, the UK higher education institutions are now in a position to start a more integrated and strategic approach to the management of applicant and student numbers.

AN INTEGRATED STRATEGY

To help institutions identify and plan ways of integrating strategies, data and staff practice, SPA has developed an Applicant Experience Strategy Map (Diagram 1), incorporating student experience elements from existing strategies within the United Kingdom (notably specific influence from Glasgow Caledonian University's 'Moving Forward' project and Newcastle University's Widening Participation Strategy map). An institution with an existing comprehensive student experience strategy map may decide these applicant experience elements would be best absorbed as a key component

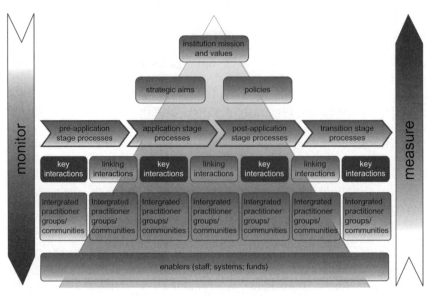

Diagram 1. The Applicant Experience Strategy Map.

of that student strategy. Alternatively, there may well be operational or tactical advantages to develop the applicant experience as a distinct strategy, at least in its formative years. It is worth remembering that applicants and students have a different legal status with an institution, that restrictions on student numbers may mean that not all suitable applicants will be entitled to progress and that funding streams may vary. In addition, a distinct strategy may be more readily highlighted and championed. Distinct should not be confused with separate, though: attention should always be given to ensure synergy between the applicant and student experience strategies and that benchmarks link between the two.

The strategy map is composed of 'blocks of productivity'. Each one would need to be filled with the actual input and output detail of activities, and it would be for the institution to decide, based on its own mission and values, what content is relevant to the strategy and what weighting to apply to different blocks. Additional links may become apparent as the mapping process develops, so it is best to approach development of such a strategy map by considering how the blocks are pieced together.

The strategy map is built up in seven steps, with each step piecing together the building blocks into a coherent framework:

1. *Define boundaries*

   All good project management is based on firstly defining the boundaries of the project: objective; time; budget. This ensures that anything falling within that scope is achievable and anything that cannot be met is either excluded or early approval is given to shift the boundaries and permit more to be achieved. Each block that is added to the strategy map should be checked against these requirements to ensure it fits and can be achieved. Most institutions will already have a well-defined project management structure to follow.

2. *Identify 'what'*

   The application cycle may be broken down into four broad stages of the applicant experience: pre-application, application, post-application, transition. These stages set out the route taken in gaining entry to higher education and so define the opportunities for engagement. Understanding the processes within those stages will:

   a. help identify which specific points to target engagement;

   b. aid identification of any potential impact on points in later stages;

   c. highlight any barriers along the route that may disproportionately affect specific groups;

    d.   indicate any gaps along the route where individuals are at risk of
       disengaging.

3. *Identify 'why'*

The strategy should always stem from the institution mission and intrinsic character of the institutional community. This drives the strategic aims and policies and sets the purpose behind the strategy. Without these as objectives, there would be no direction to any approach, no benchmark for success and no justification for performing any action.

The admissions policy is crucial, but by no means the only policy to influence the applicant experience. Careful consideration should be given to which other institutional aims and policies should be included. Equality, widening participation, marketing, accommodation, enrolment, student experience and teaching and learning are some but not necessarily all the areas whose aims and policies would need to be included.

4. *Identify 'how'*

The key interactions, or activities, will determine the nature of the experience, as they will be the points at which the institution and applicant engage. Such engagement can target barriers and gaps in the process, adding greater institutional control over applicant direction.

Key interactions may comprise direct engagement such as open days, interviews or summer schools, or indirect ones such as prospectuses, web-publicity or talking to advisors. Plotting existing activities against each stage will help structure those interactions, put them into the context of the wider purpose, facilitate targeting and tracking and highlight where weaknesses in support exist, where aims and policies are not being supported by activities and where new avenues for engagement may be opportune.

However, consideration should also be given to linking interactions. These may be similar to key interactions, but are ones specifically designed to bridge the gap between stages and facilitate the smooth transition of applicants from one stage to the next. For example, an institution may decide to bridge the gap between receipt of application and a decision by sending the applicant an acknowledgement that outlines the next stage of the process, including how long the decision-making process is expected to take. This is particularly helpful if the applicant receives offers from other institutions during that period as there might otherwise be ambiguity over whether or not to continue waiting. Alternatively, they may be more internalised activities to ensure applicants who engaged with a key interaction in one stage are tracked through the process into the next and that staff involved in those stages share knowledge and intelligence.

5. *Identify 'who'*

All identified interactions will require the best people to perform them. Integrated practitioner groups (IPGs) constitute communities of experts to oversee, guide and shape activities in the strategy and to identify where improvements need to be made, where new interactions can be delivered and when existing ones have run their course or are no longer fit for purpose. These communities may be formally structured and longstanding, as with committees or could be ad-hoc teams drawn together to deliver a specific task. The structures themselves should be determined by what best fits the operational style of the institution and the requirements of the task itself and can be called whatever best suits existing conventions.

They should not be limited to or confined by segregated departmental roles, but should be wholly inclusive, making best use of the most relevant practitioners needed to deliver the tasks. Each IPG should have a remit to consider who the relevant stakeholders are and identity communication routes to ensure they remain informed and involved. Some IPGs may cover a portfolio of activities that spans more than one stage, or be oversight groups that coordinate, review or approve the work of several IPGs. Therefore, lines of reporting should also be included in IPG remits.

6. *Identify enablers*

Enablers underpin the whole strategy. These should be viewed as far more than just resources: they will directly affect the effectiveness of the strategy and no part of it can be implemented without knowing what enablers are immediately available, how long they will be available for, what scope there is for change and how accessible new or additional enablers will be.

The same resources that constitute enablers can readily become limiters if not embedded as part of the whole strategy from the start. For example, if it is decided to develop a customer relationship approach that tracks learners through all stages of the experience and delivers pertinent information and advice at distinct points of the process, then consideration of how that will be enabled is vital. If the institution does not already have dedicated customer relationship management (CRM) software and does not have allocated budget to develop one, then such an approach will be staff and time intensive and would impact on the effective delivery of other interactions, potentially having an adverse effect on the strategy as a whole.

7. *Plan for change*

No strategy should be static. The character and values of an institution will evolve over time. Interactions will need to change as applicant demographic, institution targets and market requirements change. IPGs will need to change to accommodate the best practitioners and best practice for delivery. Enablers will need to change to meet new technological demands and to incorporate practical financial considerations. The only way to inform and to pre-empt such changes is through rigorous monitoring and measuring throughout the strategy.

- Top-down monitoring
  - ensures that the vital purpose of the strategy is reflected throughout
  - retains direction and checks that practice is efficient to that end
  - will inform the strategy and allow scrutiny of activity
  - allows planners to prepare enablers in response to demands.
- Bottom-up measuring
  - ensures that performance is meeting the needs of the strategy
  - provides a quantitative value on activity as indicators of success
  - identifies where the strategy is working, where further development is needed or where activities are redundant
  - allows managers to assess the use of enablers and justify redistribution or reallocation.

Without proper monitoring and measuring, there can be no realistic evaluation of the strategy, and its success is reduced to the anecdotal.

Following these seven steps should highlight opportunities for disparate staff to work together, using and sharing greater detail of information on potential applicants, to ensure all aspects of pre-entry engagement deliver an integrated strategy of fair access to, and success in, higher education.

STUDENT TRANSITION AND RETENTION

Despite increased attention to transition strategies and improved awareness of issues affecting student retention, the main reasons for voluntary withdrawal have changed little over the years. The National Audit Office reports (2007 and 2002) highlighted students of similar types are not evenly distributed across the sector, and those less likely to continue may in part be a reflection of the practices of the institutions that tend to recruit those students as well as reflecting the characteristics of the students themselves. Many students leave for a combination of reasons, but the most common reasons for voluntary withdrawal cited in the National Audit Office reports were:

- personal reasons, including homesickness (especially among young women and students from rural areas) domestic obligations (e.g. childcare or elder care)
- lack of integration, including absence of positive ties and cultural isolation (especially among students from deprived areas)
- dissatisfaction with course/institution, including course not leading to the professional accreditation sought
- lack of preparedness, including unexpected course content, lack of appropriate study skills, late application for disabled students' allowance
- wrong choice of course, including not enough research of choices, channelling into inappropriate subjects (especially working class men), lack of information about higher education (especially students from disadvantaged areas)
- financial reasons, including limited funds and fear of debt, unrealistic lifestyle expectations
- to take up a more attractive opportunity, including late realisation of academic interests or career goals.

The report *Rethinking working-class 'drop out' from higher education* published by the Joseph Rowntree Foundation (Quinn et al., 2005) found that choosing the wrong course was given as the main reason for leaving by many of those involved in their research: 'leafing through a prospectus with no real sense of what they should be looking for ... with little guidance from family, university or schools'.

To provide better pre-entry engagement there needs to be a shift away from the passive mentality of making information, advice and guidance available, and not knowing how or even if it's used. This would enable a more interactive approach of informing, advising and guiding potential applicants. Such an approach requires greater integration of practice and more coordinated use of the large volumes of applicant data potentially available internally and externally.

CONCLUSION

Working together on widening access, admissions and transition into higher education within HEIs is vital for a good applicant experience for the applicant and the institution. The many areas that this involves are increasing exercising senior planners, recruiters and managers in institutions as high demand for places, developing competition between institutions and a period of financial constraint converge. If the applicant experience is to be a good one, integrated working with, and awareness of, the roles of internal colleagues – from widening participation and outreach to first year teaching staff – and externally with those in schools, colleges, careers and HE advisors and others will be increasing important, it underpins the student experience and student success in the changing HE environment in the United Kingdom.

NOTE

The SPA was set up in 2006 as a result of recommendations in Fair Admissions to Higher Education: Recommendations for Good Practice (The Schwartz Report, 2004). SPA is a central shared source of expertise and advice for higher education provider institutions on strategy, policy and practice on a wide range of admissions issues that is free to institutions. SPA is the United Kingdom's independent and objective voice on HE admissions, and leads on fair access, and is believed to be unique in the world. It works with stakeholders, providing an evidence base and guidelines for good practice and in helping universities and colleges maintain and enhance excellence and professionalism, share good practice, develop fair admissions and recruitment processes, in order to widen access to higher education (http://www.spa.ac.uk/).

CHAPTER 5.1

GETTING THE HIGHER EDUCATION X-FACTOR

Michelle Gammo-Felton

ABSTRACT

Purpose – *This case study explores how higher education institutions can help develop the social and cultural capital of students who come from non-traditional backgrounds. It aims to examine how selective performing arts institutions can ensure that they widen participation and develop their student body to represent the social make-up of the United Kingdom, when there is such strong competition for places and real focus on quality.*

Methodology/approach – *It is a case study, which simply illustrates the practices and policies for widening participation (WP) at the Liverpool Institute for Performing Arts (LIPA).*

Findings – *There are no real findings as it is not a research project*

Social implications – *It discusses how social and cultural capital can have an effect on the progression of WP students and how access to such capitals can support their progression to higher education.*

Originality/value of paper – *It is an original case study about the LIPA.*

Keywords: Arts; education; social justice; university; access; equality

Institutional Transformation to Engage a Diverse Student Body
International Perspectives on Higher Education Research, Volume 6, 169–177
Copyright © 2011 by Emerald Group Publishing Limited
All rights of reproduction in any form reserved
ISSN: 1479-3628/doi:10.1108/S1479-3628(2011)0000006017

INTRODUCTION

This case study explores access to higher education (HE) performing arts training at the Liverpool Institute for Performing Arts (LIPA) for widening participation (WP) students. These are defined as students from low socioeconomic backgrounds, low participation neighbourhoods, ethnic minorities, disabled students and students who are in care and young people who are 'NEETS' (not in employment, education or training). Traditionally we have a low conversion from application to acceptance for these groups of students. The case study considers access to social and cultural capital, and the development of skills and aspirations. It explores the methods we use to attempt to widen participation to our courses and the challenges involved.

Liverpool Institute for Performing Arts

The LIPA was co-founded by Sir Paul McCartney and Mark Featherstone-Witty and opened in 1996. It is one of the UK's leading HE institutions for performers and those who facilitate performance. There are currently over 700 students studying a range of performing arts degree subjects: Acting, Dance, Community Drama and Music, Design, Technology and Management.

As a young institution, commitment to WP became a focus in the past five years. One of our key goals is to maintain and develop inclusive recruitment of talented students. We want to ensure that students, who meet the entry requirements, have the chance to develop and thrive regardless of background. As a selective institution, our challenge is to ensure that we are not putting any barriers in place, which may prevent talented WP students gaining places on our courses.

OUR APPROACH TO WIDENING PARTICIPATION

We want to encourage applications from students from WP backgrounds; however, successful progression into HE courses in performing arts can be due to students having access early in their lives to high-quality training and cultural activities, which involve financial commitment. Some students from low socioeconomic backgrounds may have a 'raw' talent, but may not have had the opportunities to develop it because of a lack of appropriate training, and they may not have the confidence to pursue their dreams.

These students generally lack reserves of middle-class social and cultural capital, which can help them access and succeed in HE.

Students need to develop a certain amount of social and cultural capital to successfully access HE (Gamarnikow & Green, 2000). Social and cultural capital is rooted in Coleman's idea of rational action theory (Gamarnikow & Green, 2000). His idea was to bridge the gap between the macro and the micro, and how rational actors in society make choices by drawing on the social structures and resources available to them (Gamarnikow & Green, 2000). Social capital is developed through our networks and experiences and cultural capital is developed through, cultural experiences, such as attending galleries, theatre shows and through the knowledge of those who surround us. Although students from WP backgrounds may have valuable social and cultural capital from their own experiences, what is valued at a HE level is more of a middle class, privileged perspective (Reay, 2001).

We plan to support students from non-traditional backgrounds, to develop their cultural and social capital to help them to progress in performance-related disciplines. For example, some boys are excellent street dancers but have never done ballet so they may benefit from having their horizons broadened. We have developed a strategy to help harness their existing talents, develop them, and create greater equality. The strategy is currently being revised due to changes in fee legislation.

We are also developing our strategies and polices in the institution to accept and value the cultural and social capital that the students come to us with. Rather than always trying to change the student, we are looking at how we can develop the institution, by for example, exploring how our audition process may create barriers for some students and by engaging our academic staff in WP projects. If we can enable staff to understand more about the social and cultural capital the students come with they can make informed decision about their progression to HE, rather than using their own expectation of what social and cultural capital the students should have.

Strategy and Policies

The focus for the WP strategy is very much on how we engage with the community outside of LIPA and how we source and develop emerging talent, rather than how we transform the institution. Although in 2011, we will be revising our strategy to have a stronger focus on how we can change some of the practices and progression routes to the university, including foundation courses and compact arrangements. In the past there has been some resistance to these types of changes, partly because in 2009 we received 4,445 applications from UK students for 174 places, so less than 4% of students applying achieve places with us, we therefore have the advantage of being able to take the most talented of the students who apply. There is also the perception that talent is something, which is inherent and does not matter where you come from; if they are talented, we take them regardless of their education or background. This however, shows a lack of understanding of the role that social and cultural capital plays in developing talent.

We are a selective institution, which makes it harder to explain and justify the importance of WP to sceptical colleagues, especially as there is concern over the quality of students from WP backgrounds. In 2011, the anticipated white paper will provide guidance on fees and WP. The subsequent legislation is likely to require us to meet WP targets to charge higher fees. This has opened up the discussion on WP across the institution and raised the profile of WP.

Currently the UK students we admit are generally not from WP backgrounds. There is a low conversion rate between applications and admission. In 2009, 30% of the students who applied came from the two lowest participation neighbourhoods by postcode (POLAR2), and 20% were admitted from the same postcodes. Similarly, 14% of Black and Minority Ethnic (BME) students apply and only 9% achieve places. Our WP work therefore focuses on finding and developing talent and, crucially, converting applications to successful admissions. This work will become more intensive when we reach the new fee arrangements in 2012. Our current WP strategy has three strands: profile raising, the progression programme and partnerships. This is currently being developed and the new strategy will focus much more intensive interventions which talented individual students and defined progression routes.

a) Profile raising

Working with community groups, schools, colleges and national networks, we seek to engage hard to reach and disengaged groups, including care leavers, NEETs and those at risk of becoming NEETS, to inspire them to progress in education. The goal is to not necessarily to get them to progress to LIPA, but to refocus them in education and/or to help them gain confidence through performing arts training. We felt it was important to raise the profile of LIPA as an institution that is interested in WP and working with challenging groups. We sometime experience criticism for not doing enough locally so these projects were about supporting the local community and raising our profile.

b) Progression programme

This consists of partnerships with schools in the North West. In these schools, we work with young people from year 7 to 10 (age 11–15) from disadvantaged backgrounds, who are talented in performing/creative arts. We identify these young people through audition, school recommendations and applications. Students are selected for various reasons: they would benefit from a programme of interventions that will keep them engaged in school; it would build their confidence; or because they show raw talent. The common factor is that they all must show an interest and commitment to performing arts. We provide a programme of interventions for the young people to develop their skills, confidence and knowledge, in school, at LIPA, summer schools and after school clubs. We hope to provide these students with the skills and abilities to compete with other students who apply for performing arts courses who have had the benefit of private training. The programme is currently in 10 schools with a plan to extend this over the next two years.

The schools were selected based on the fact that they are Aimhigher Schools in disadvantaged areas, and they have performing arts status. This programme of intervention was the first we put in place with the new strategy. It was something that the institution fully accepted, because it followed the model of our own courses and entry procedure, as it included audition for a place and although these auditions are not looking for talent, more for commitment and interest, there is a clear selection process. We felt it was the only real way to get to know talent and potential in the North West.

One criticism has been that it is not in more schools. This would be unsustainable because of the commitment required from session teaching staff and the costs involved. Therefore, we had to focus our work on schools, which we felt would benefit. We feel it will benefit us in that we can find real talent in the city and nurture and train that talent to our standards. In 2011 entry, we should see several students who we started working with in 2008 coming through our audition process, and we hope several of them will be successful. By, having these students who know us well coming to the auditions and hopefully getting places, we should retain them through the course as they know exactly what we do, and as a result, we should hopefully get better and more committed students.

c) Partnerships to widen participation

We have developed partnerships with three Further Education Colleges. These partnerships are in-depth relationships and involve staff at the colleges and students. We are working with staff in these centres to develop excellence in teaching, learning, advice and guidance in the performing arts sector. We are also delivering regular interventions for talented young people to aid progression. Interventions include information, advice, guidance and intensive skills development and interaction with our students and exposure to our spaces and shows. There was an expectation that our staff would get involved in these partnerships and would learn about level 3 qualifications taught at colleges and start to understand where our students come from by working with teachers in our partner colleges. This however has been less effective due to the demands on staff time and has therefore had less of a transformation effect on the institution than we expected.

The majority of WP work is linked to build partnerships between internal departments and external stakeholders and interested parties (Action on Access, 2005). Internally these partnerships have included linking with knowledge transfer and HE departments to develop a range of teachers short courses.

Externally, we have developed partnerships with key schools. We have joined up with Rainhill High School and St Helens College to set up the Rainhill learning village trust. We are involved as trust governors and work together with the school and college to develop opportunities for young people in St Helens to develop their knowledge, skills and talent. We have also started to explore with the trust how we as an institution can become more engaged, but firstly we are exploring shared services and IT platforms. We are also represented on the board of governors at Lysander High School in Warrington.

Admissions and Barriers to Entry Research

We are currently carrying out an in-depth research project, which is exploring any barriers to admission. This has predominately focused on our audition and interview processes. This research has only recently started but has already begun to have a transformational effect on the institution. We have discovered through the research with people who apply to us but do not come to audition that the costs of attending an audition along with the audition fee can be a barrier. Therefore, we are exploring how we can change this. As a result of this research we are also changing our audition guidelines, how we communicate with applicants, the possible times of auditions and the way we do auditions. This is one of the first projects that has started to have a transformational effect on the institution. This research in to barriers to admission continues this year and will expand to include any barriers to application.

EVIDENCE OF EFFECTIVENESS

In the short term, an indicator of success is that the students we are working with in the schools and colleges are attending our activities regularly, stay in school and are improving in their subject. In the long-term we want to see more students applying to us from non-traditional backgrounds. However, as we are generally working with younger students to help develop their abilities, we will not see them applying to our courses for several years. We will also be tracking the students we work with through their educational journey to see where they end up, if they do not apply or come to us, we are interested in seeing if they have progressed on to HE as we feel that is a strong indicator that we made some impact on them. We also regularly run focus groups with the students we work with to determine how their confidence and attitude have changed through working with us.

Since 2007, we have seen a slight increase on the number of applications and admissions from students from non-traditional backgrounds. We will continue to monitor the number of students who apply and get places on our courses from non-traditional backgrounds and hope to continue to see this increasing steadily over time. We are also closely monitoring the conversion rate with particular courses, which are not converting applications to admissions from WP students, and discussing with these departments what can be changed to improve the conversion rates.

We have not yet put in place mechanisms to measure how effective we are in changing the institution. However, with the new research about barriers, we may see these measures being put in place in the future. This is something we will include in the new WP strategy, which is due to be written this year. We are in the early stages of monitoring how many staff are engaged in WP work; we are aiming to get a WP patron in each department, who will drive the WP agenda, as we have in the Community Drama, Dance and Music departments.

REFLECTION

Through our WP work, we need to develop ways to help support students from non-traditional backgrounds through the audition/interview process. The challenge is that we have students from working class backgrounds with no history of HE and possibly with less experience in performing arts, who are competing with students from middle-class backgrounds who may have the benefits of more support and may find it easier to negotiate a complex and stressful audition process.

This investment in training and family backing however is no substitute for raw talent. Therefore, we need to both recognise raw talent and help get students ready for the audition process. Regardless of backgrounds the students must be able to get through this process at the right standard.

For young people from backgrounds where these opportunities are not readily available, we need to find ways to provide them in the school, college and community. We do this through the progression programme outlined above and through targeted work, which includes audition workshops, skills development weeks and summer schools.

Balancing Aspirations

We have the challenge of balancing any aspiration raising and skill development work with the expectation that we can only take a limited number of students per year on to each of our programmes. Currently, we work with over 1,000 students throughout the year; all these students will have regular access to our training, shows and activities, many of these students may hope to apply to our courses when the time is right. However, their chances of gaining a place on one of our courses are low. Therefore, we need to make sure, when we work with the young people that we manage their expectations for their future prospects. Therefore, we need to support the students in understanding their other options and helping them to consider all possibilities.

Employability and Risk

There are also the challenges of employability in the arts and how students survive when they graduate. The performing arts and related industries often require the graduates to be flexible and self-sufficient when they graduate. They are unlikely to end up in full-time, permanent work positions and are much more likely to have portfolio careers with a range of jobs and activities. It may take them some time to gain experience and well-paid employment in the industry. Students from non-traditional backgrounds may perceive it to be too risky not to be guaranteed regular work, and thus not be willing to train in such a discipline. Students from working class backgrounds often select subjects which appear less risky and more likely to offer employment such as business studies (Archer, Hutchings, & Ross, 2003; Burke, 2002, 2005; Bowl, 2003; Reay, 2001; Reay, David, & Ball, 2005).

Moreover, in all subjects, research shows large inequalities in graduate earnings. Class still impacts on graduate progression, and simply owning a degree does not necessarily guarantee increased earning potential for working class students (Archer et al., 2003). Therefore, promoting arts-based degrees to working class students can be a challenging concept. We therefore have to work with families and students to reassure them of the future potential earnings, whilst informing them of the reality of the performing arts sector.

THE FUTURE OF WP

We are currently evaluating our WP activities and assessing which interventions have made the most impact and what is the most effective way of engaging young people. We are exploring how we can be more focused in our interventions and how we can put in place true progression routes to our courses, which may include foundation courses. We expect to be facing some funding challenges in the next few years; therefore, we are exploring ways to make the most of the funding we have available. We will also be exploring how as an institution we can make changes to our practices, particularly with the barriers to entry research. Our transformation as an institution may be slow, but it is developing in the very early stages.

CHAPTER 5.2

BALANCING MISSION AND MARKET IN CHICAGO: AN ENROLMENT MANAGEMENT PERSPECTIVE

Brian Spittle

ABSTRACT

Purpose – *This chapter aims to provide an overview of the use of strategic enrolment management at DePaul University in Chicago.*

Design/methodology/approach – *A case study approach is used to provide an analysis of strategic enrolment management (SEM) and its particular use at DePaul University in the context of the university's long-standing commitment to student access.*

Findings – *As the United Kingdom moves to a more market-based system of higher education, universities may need to pay closer attention to strategic enrolment management concepts and practices. While enrolment management has been criticised for reflecting a wider movement toward 'marketisation' in higher education, the experience at DePaul University in Chicago indicates that SEM has played an important role in clarifying the university's commitment to student access during a period of environmental and institutional change.*

Originality/value – *This chapter sets DePaul's experience within the wider development of SEM in the United States and illustrates some of*

Institutional Transformation to Engage a Diverse Student Body
International Perspectives on Higher Education Research, Volume 6, 179–186
ISSN: 1479-3628/doi:10.1108/S1479-3628(2011)0000006018

*the ways in which enrolment managers at the university have been able
to balance a mission-based commitment to student access with other
institutional goals and priorities.*

Keywords: Strategic enrolment management; access; admission;
market position; Chicago Public Schools

INTRODUCTION

The past three decades or so have been tumultuous ones for American higher
education. Colleges and universities have faced – as they will continue to face –
changing demographic patterns, structural shifts in the economy, persistent
and widening gaps in family economic resources and educational attainment,
a growing inability or unwillingness of states to subsidize their public
universities, a rapid expansion of a for-profit postsecondary sector and a
consumer culture shaped by an increasingly pervasive rankings industry.
Such developments have reverberated throughout the higher education
system. Yet nowhere has their impact been more pronounced than on the
patterns of college student aspiration, choice and outcome. As a result,
American colleges have been obliged to pay much closer attention to their
enrolments as determinants of institutional viability and effectiveness. In
doing so, they have been guided to a large extent by the emerging theory and
practice of strategic enrolment management (SEM). While SEM embraces
various perspectives and organizational applications, it is generally understood as a coordinated set of concepts, tools, and practices that harness
institutional intelligence and resources to achieve the optimum mix and flow
of enrolments to support a college's mission and goals.

This brief chapter reviews the emergence of SEM in the United States by
focusing on its development and evolution at a particular institution,
DePaul University in Chicago. The emphasis throughout will be on the
relationship between SEM and issues of college access and attainment
during a time of profound organizational and environmental change.

THE EMERGENCE OF STRATEGIC
ENROLMENT MANAGEMENT

Briefly put, enrolment management emerged in the late 1970s as an
institutional response to the demographic crisis threatening to destabilize

American higher education. After a history of almost unbroken expansion and a decade or two of very rapid growth, American colleges and universities were scarcely prepared for an era of contraction. Private institutions were particularly threatened. Heavily dependent on tuition revenue, many were and remain vulnerable to changes in the market. If they were to survive, let alone flourish, colleges and universities would have to adapt. Business as usual was hardly an option.

What business as usual typically meant was a general lack of connection, both conceptually and administratively, between the principal units and programs having to do with student enrolment, such as admissions, financial aid, marketing or new student orientation. But some individuals and institutions were starting to lead the way toward more coordinated and intentional approaches supported in part by the developing literature in such areas as non-profit marketing, student choice research and retention. Other perspectives drawn loosely from systems theory added to the mix so that by the early 1980s the essential elements of enrolment management were starting to come together. Organizationally this took many forms. At one end of the spectrum, it was little more than a new term for student recruitment. At the other, substantial administrative realignments were effected. But whatever organizational form it took, enrolment management nearly always involved a more tightly coordinated and intentional approach to college enrolments. That it also implied an entirely new mental model was perhaps not widely understood at the time. But it soon would be. While SEM has evolved along a number of lines, David Kalsbeek has proposed that its *strategic* aspect is grounded in a market perspective. What this means, he argues, has less to do with *marketing* and everything to do with how the structure, stratification and segmentation of the marketplace influences institutional thinking, planning and action (Kalsbeek, 2006). As Kalsbeek is senior vice president for enrolment management and marketing at DePaul, it is this perspective that has naturally shaped the university's own approach.

SEM AT DEPAUL UNIVERSITY

DePaul University was an early adopter of enrolment management in the early 1980s and since then has developed one of the more distinctive and comprehensive SEM models in the country. A private, Catholic university located in the heart of Chicago, DePaul has long been proud of its commitment to access and its agility in responding to market trends and opportunities. But when enrolments started to decline in the early 1980s, the university faced an uncertain future. Given that revenue from tuition accounted for over 80% of its operating budget, the margin for error was very slim. It was in these circumstances that the university embarked on a bold strategy of enrolment growth, quality enhancement and campus improvement that would, if successful, not only see it through the immediate financial crisis but also put it on a path to long term sustainability. The adoption of an enrolment management model which aligned admissions, financial aid, enrolment research and student retention functions under an associate vice president was a central part of the new strategy though its effectiveness was bolstered by parallel decisions to anchor the university's undergraduate programmes in a strengthened College of Liberal Arts and Sciences and create a residential community by greatly expanding the opportunities for students to live on campus.

The plan worked and within a decade, the university was indeed on a very different footing. Today, with a total enrolment of over 25,000 students (16,000 at the undergraduate level), DePaul is the largest Catholic university and eighth largest private not-for-profit university in the country. Additionally, the academic profile of entering freshmen has improved, socioeconomic and racial diversity have been enhanced and graduation rates have improved. And with substantial investment in facilities and residence halls DePaul is now widely recognized as one of the best urban campuses in the country. It has been a dramatic transformation.

Enrolment management at the university has also been transformed. During the late 1990s its responsibilities were broadened to include marketing, career services and a more substantial commitment to enrolment research and analysis. Today, the division of enrolment management and marketing is the largest administrative unit on campus with a comprehensive range of functions and an important voice in university strategic planning and decision-making. But again, the importance of SEM at DePaul has less to do with its administrative scope than the intelligence and perspective it brings on the higher education marketplace to optimize the university's enrolment, academic and financial profile.

BALANCING MISSION AND MARKET

It is now widely accepted that American higher education has become more stratified and less accessible in recent decades (Kahlenberg, 2010). Whether enrolment management concepts and practices have modified or accelerated these developments is a matter of some debate, however. Certainly, enrolment management has its critics. On the broadest level, they argue, it represents a further indication of the marketisation of American higher education. More particularly, they contend, SEM-based practices such as tuition discounting are focused more on enhancing institutional revenue and reputation than access and opportunity. Defenders respond that the problem lies less with SEM itself than with the broader market context in higher education. It is naïve, they say, to try to make judgments about what is happening in universities independent of the competitive environment in which they operate. Besides, they contend, the tools of enrolment management are essentially neutral and can be used to achieve a variety of institutional goals, including greater student access.

What is demonstrably true, but not always explicitly acknowledged, is that universities look to their enrolments to achieve various goals and that these goals are not always in harmony with each other. This is a situational and contextual reality for most institutions and perhaps points to the essential role for SEM today. As Don Hossler has put it, the primary task of enrolment managers has to do with managing 'the nexus of revenue, prestige and diversity' within their institutions (Hossler, 2008).

How then has enrolment management at DePaul approached the question of access given its central role in advancing the university's strategic agenda to improve sustainability and stature? It is an important question not least because of the university's distinctive and mission-based commitment to educational opportunity and accessibility. For most of their history, Catholic colleges in the United States have been upward mobility institutions having been established for the most part to serve the burgeoning immigrant population in America's cities during the latter part of the 19th century. While Catholic higher education in the United States has changed considerably since that time, its urban roots remain. This is particularly true of DePaul where a mission-based commitment to social and economic diversity in the student body resonates deeply and broadly throughout the university.

There is no question that the university's success in recent years has put pressure on this commitment. Improved market position has led to increases in student demand (as measured by applications for admission) that have outpaced planned enrolment growth. As a result the percentage of applicants accepted for admission has fallen from about 80% in the mid-1990s to under 70% today. Given that the distribution of high school educational provision and attainment tends to reflect underlying patterns of social and economic inequality, this has had real consequences for applicants from low-income families or under-resourced schools. The obvious irony could be that greater academic distinction will lead to a loss of mission distinctiveness.

The danger is real but needs to be seen in broader context. First, DePaul is a selective university. Its commitment to accessibility does not imply a special obligation to enrol students from economically disadvantaged families *independent* of their capacity to succeed. How that capacity is determined in the admission process is a matter that will be returned to below, but the point is an important one because it is sometimes obscured in arguments for greater access. Second, federal and state-aid programmes are not sufficient to make Paul affordable for students from lower-income families. The gap must therefore be met at least in part from institutional resources. At DePaul, as at other tuition-dependent institutions, this involves a substantial commitment of operating funds. In other words, the capacity of the university to enrol low-income students is inherently tied to its ability to attract relatively affluent students requiring little or no institutional subsidization. Third, students value a high-quality education or at the very least a high-quality credential. This is as true for low-income and first-generation college students as it is for everyone else. In this sense at least, student and institutional aspirations need not be inconsistent. Nevertheless, the fact remains that reputational strategies are typically achieved at the expense of student access. Experience at DePaul suggests that an effective balancing of both requires institutional focus and commitment. It does not happen by default.

SEM ACCESS STRATEGIES AT DEPAUL

DePaul's focus and commitment to student access can be illustrated by three closely related enrolment management strategies. First, there has been a considerable investment in research on the profile and performance of low-income, first-generation and minority populations at DePaul. One result has been a more nuanced understanding of these populations as well as a growing recognition that blanket terms such as 'at risk' sometimes betray institution-centric assumptions. This has been accompanied by a reframing of DePaul's approach to student retention including a shift from *persistence* (from year to year) to *progress* (toward academic goals) as a way to think about and improve degree completion.

Second, enrolment management has cultivated partnerships with Chicago schools and community organizations to build more effective pathways to the university. For example, for over a decade, DePaul was the largest university partner with Chicago Public Schools (CPS) in a 'dual enrolment' program that allowed about 150 CPS students a year to strengthen their academic preparation for college and gain early familiarity with the campus environment while still in high school. This has been accompanied by a close partnership with one of the more promising educational projects in Chicago, the establishment of International Baccalaureate programmes in a number of schools serving low-income neighbourhoods. Although their standardized test scores tend to fall below university averages, their retention and graduation rates either equal or surpass DePaul averages.

A third strategy is based on the recognition that the sorts of measures typically used to determine admission have their limits especially when applied to students from poorly resourced schools and neighbourhoods. American colleges and universities rely heavily on 'standardized' college entrance tests such as the SAT (Scholastic Aptitude Test) and the ACT, a more achievement-based assessment that has become a widely used alternative to the SAT. Such tests are not without meaning or utility, but they tend to exert a hold both on admission decision-making and public discourse that is not justified by the evidence. In part this has to do with the role they play in college rankings. In its most extreme form this may lead to a college denying an applicant with a low standardized test score even when it is more than offset by other more powerful indicators such as high school coursework or grades. In such cases, the issue is not whether the student can succeed or not (the ostensible purpose of the standardized test score) but whether he or she contributes to or undermines the college's academic profile. As a result of such concerns, DePaul has started to supplement its application process with short essay questions that focus on 'non-cognitive' indicators of student potential (such as confidence, realistic self-appraisal, leadership and a preference for long-term goals) based on the research of psychologist Dr. William Sedlacek. While it is too soon to assess the impact of these indicators on admission or retention, the project is ample evidence of the university's seriousness in balancing issues of quality and access.

Such moves have been supplemented and institutionalized by the establishment of a Center for Access and Attainment within the enrolment management division to elevate its partnerships with Chicago schools, to link those partnerships more effectively with internal support structures such as the university's grant-funded TRIO programmes that deliver targeted support to low-income and first-generation students and to provide an institutional focal point for research, dialogue and decision-making about future access strategies.

To date DePaul has maintained a strong commitment to access while reframing its strategy in terms appropriate to a vastly changed market position. Looking at the 2010–2011 freshmen class for example, we find that 38% are from low-income families, up from 35% the year before, while 18% are Latino and 6% African American. Additionally, the proportion of freshmen from first-generation families increased to 36% up a percentage point from the previous year. And while 85% of the students in CPS come from low-income families, DePaul continues to enrol a far higher number of the system's graduates than any other private, selective university and by a substantial margin. These are impressive figures for a private university. Whether they are sustainable in the years ahead remains to be seen, of course. But at the very least they suggest that an enrolment management strategy that effectively balances mission and market perspectives need not be at the expense of student access.

CHAPTER 5.3

ACKNOWLEDGMENT OF PRIOR EXPERIENTIAL LEARNING TO WIDEN PARTICIPATION AT THE UNIVERSITÉ LIBRE DE BRUXELLES: THE CHALLENGE OF THE INSTITUTIONAL MESSAGE

Renaud Maes, Cécile Sztalberg and Michel Sylin

ABSTRACT

At the Université libre de Bruxelles (Belgium), acknowledgment of prior experiential learning (APEL) is conceived as a tool to widen participation. We describe the initiatives set up to allow under-qualified, experienced job seekers to access higher education through the APEL process: a network involving the regional offices in charge of employment policies, the universities themselves, but also institutions in charge of education for social advancement and an integrated approach to offer to 'APEL candidates' an adequate support to contribute towards their academic success.

We discuss the interaction between the university and those APEL candidates and, therefore, the efficiency of all those initiatives. We studied

Institutional Transformation to Engage a Diverse Student Body
International Perspectives on Higher Education Research, Volume 6, 187–198
Copyright © 2011 by Emerald Group Publishing Limited
ISSN: 1479-3628/doi:10.1108/S1479-3628(2011)0000006019

the admission files and conducted a series of interviews with APEL students. We show that the inclusion of those specific students is a real pedagogical and institutional challenge. Moreover, the institutional message clearly affects the interaction between APEL students and the university. It is, therefore, necessary to develop a clear institutional message on widening participation that could embrace all institutional initiatives and highlight their common goal to increase their chances of success.

Keywords: Acknowledgement of prior experiential learning; returning adult learners; social stigmata

INTRODUCTION

Unemployment is a major issue in Belgium and, more particularly, in the Brussels-Capital Region. One of the sources of this problem is the generally low level of qualifications held by many workers (almost 25% of the unemployed population do not hold a secondary education diploma) (ONEM, 2008). Concurrently, in some sectors of the labour market – such as, notably, teaching institutions – the National Office for Employment has diagnosed a general lack in numbers of graduate workers. One explanation set forth to explain this situation is that the Belgian education system is strongly inequitable (HIS, 2000) and generally inefficient (OECD, 2006). In particular, although the higher education system has undergone a 'massification process' since the 1960s, students coming from low socio-cultural and socio-economic backgrounds are more likely to terminate their studies after leaving secondary school. Furthermore, when they decide to continue their education at university, their chances of success are dramatically lower than those of the other students (De Meulemeester & Rochat, 1995; Ortiz & Dehon, 2008). As a result, many of those students do not progress to higher education, and those that do are more likely to leave without a qualification.

When the legislator authorized the acknowledgment of prior experiential learning (APEL), the Université libre de Bruxelles (ULB) saw in this new mechanism:

- an opportunity to offer adults who did not follow or succeed in prior university courses, because of their socio-cultural and socio-economic backgrounds, a 'second chance' to obtain a university diploma and
- a tool to fight unemployment of experienced, under-qualified workers.

The ULB, together with the Université de Mons, set up a partnership network to achieve those two goals. The stakeholders involved in this network are the regional offices in charge of employment policies (ROCEP), the universities themselves, but also institutions in charge of education for social advancement (institutions that provide adult-targeted, out-of-hours intensive courses). In parallel, the ULB developed an integrated approach to offer to 'APEL candidates' an adequate support to contribute towards their academic success. This integrated approach combines APEL counselling, psychosocial support and adult-targeted learning methods.

INSTITUTIONAL CONTEXT

In the French-speaking Community of Belgium, the APEL has been authorised since the adoption by parliament of the decree entitled '*Décret définissant l'enseignement supérieur, favorisant son integration dans l'espace européen d'enseignement supérieur et refinançant les universités*' [Decree defining higher education, encouraging its integration into the European Higher Education Area and providing new funding opportunities to Universities] in March 2004. This decree indeed implements the local implementation of the reforms inspired by the Bologna Process and has deeply transformed the higher education system.

The Higher Education System

The higher education system in the French-speaking Community of Belgium has an extremely specific structure, constituted of 'networks' (*réseaux*) and 'types' (Maes & Sylin, 2009). The types relate to the length of the study path (Table 1): the 'short type' is only organized by non-university higher education institutions and the 'long type' is organized by non-university and university institutions.

The three networks are, in the case of university higher education, the state-organized universities, the catholic state-funded universities and the liberal state-funded universities (such as the ULB) (Maes, Sztalberg, & Sylin, 2010). All these universities award diplomas recognized by the French-speaking Community of Belgium and are, therefore, subject to a great number of legal constraints concerning, notably, the organization of their courses.

Table 1. Comparison between the Different Types of Higher Education in the French-Speaking Community of Belgium.

	Short Type	Long Type
Type of contents[a]	Based on the association of theoretical and practical aspects Professionally targeted training	Based on fundamental concepts, experimentation and illustration In-depth and general training
Institutions	Schools of Art High School	Universities
Specificities[a]	Professional or artistic aim Link between education and applied research Strong link with the labour market	Link between education and scientific (pure and applied) research
Number of students 2007-2008[b]	63,642	19,248	70,183
Qualifications[a,c]	Bachelor (EQF 6)	Bachelor 'de transition' (EQF 6) Master (EQF 7)	Bachelor 'de transition' (EQF 6) Master (EQF 7) Doctorate (EQF 8)

[a]Data from the Decree of 31 March 2004.
[b]Data from CREF (2009) and ETNIC (2009).
[c]EQF stands for 'European Qualification Framework'.

Although the majority of study programmes are accessible without applicants having to enter any entrance examination, and that the higher education institutions are widespread throughout the entire geographical area, the higher education system in the French-speaking Community of Belgium is one of the least egalitarian throughout the whole of Europe. More specifically, as the *Eurostudent 2000* (HIS, 2000) study underlined, considering the ratio of fathers of students to all fathers from working-class families (blue collar), it is obvious that working-class families are under-represented in Belgian French-speaking higher education in general (EPI, 2005). Moreover, students coming from lower socio-economic backgrounds tend to choose to follow short type higher education programmes and, more generally, non-university higher education programmes (De Kerchove & Lambert, 2001). University is, therefore, generally the privilege of the upper-stratum in terms of students' orientation (De Kerchove & Lambert, 2001) and probability of success (De Meulemeester & Rochat, 1995; Droesbeke, Hecquet, & Wattelar 2001; Ortiz & Dehon, 2008). This phenomenon of course study tendencies contributes to the dramatically low levels of qualification in the Walloon and Brussels-Capital regions (ONEM, 2008).

The APEL Mechanism

APEL was authorised by parliament in the Decree of 31 March 2004 under the name '*valorisation des acquis de l'expérience*'. This process is similar to the French partial accreditation of experience (*validation partielle des acquis de l'expérience*). In the case of the French Community of Belgium, however, there is no formal recognition of the experiential learning: the process only entitles the 'APEL candidate' to access university and to follow a shorter learning curriculum to obtain his/her diploma. We therefore translated 'valorisation des acquis de l'expérience' as 'acknowledgment of prior experiential learning' to distinguish the Belgian process from the French one.

The public authorities conceived a relatively awkward process: this process allows a person without the otherwise required qualifications to access the master cycle (EQF 7), but access is still not possible for the bachelor cycle (EQF 6) – even though, for the two cycles, APEL allows an overall shorter duration in the curriculum.

In practice, all universities in the French-speaking Community of Belgium conceived a harmonized APEL process, whereby each APEL candidate must overcome five 'initiatory' steps.

The first step concerns 'information and welcome': the future APEL candidate makes his/her first contact with the university. The most frequently used contact points are the university website and orientation services. However, as we discuss later, the ULB and the Université de Mons developed a specific contact point in partnership with the regional organisations in charge of employment policies, dedicated to job seekers.

The second step concerns 'orientation and positioning'. The APEL candidate chooses the programme he/she wants to follow. He/she must also demonstrate that he/she possesses at least five years professional or personal experience, a prerequisite defined by the Decree of 31 March 2004.

The third step is called 'contractualisation'. Despite the inaccurate name of this step, in most universities, the candidate only has to schedule a series of appointments with an 'APEL counsellor' to receive assistance in completing the 'APEL' file. It should be noted, however, that catholic universities tend to confer increased importance to this step than other universities (Maes et al., 2010).

The fourth step concerns 'evaluation': an academic jury considers and evaluates the file submitted by each candidate. This jury is constituted exclusively of teachers involved in the study programme concerned (contrary to the French case, the APEL counsellor is not involved in the jury). Following discussion, the academic jury determines whether or not the candidate can access the second cycle and/or shorten his/her study cycle.

The fifth and final step concerns 'results'. The decision of the academic jury is issued to the candidate. This decision must be well argued by the jury and may be accompanied by comments and advice for the personal attention of the candidate. Refused candidates can be redirected to another level of education or to an institution specialising in education for social advancement, to gain the prerequisites needed to access the university system.

Throughout the entire APEL process, the candidate can choose to be accompanied by an 'APEL counsellor'. This counsellor facilitates the transition between each step, provides guidance and assists candidates in undertaking all of the necessary administrative formalities and to structure, select and organise the adequate documents which duly justify his/her previous experience.

PARTNERSHIPS AND NETWORKS FOR APEL DEVELOPMENT

Since 2004, the ULB has developed an institutional strategy, based on the APEL process, to recruit specific students: the target group includes experienced, low-qualified, job-seekers (including both unemployed workers and employed workers willing to evolve in their careers and therefore enrolled as 'job-seekers' in the databases of the offices in charge of employment policies). To allow this group to gain access to university, it appeared necessary to set-up a network involving both external and internal partners.

External Partners

The first partnership developed was a network involving the ROCEP, universities (the Université libre de Bruxelles and the Université de Mons) but also institutions responsible for education for social advancement. The reason for involving two different kinds of educational institutions can be found in their specificities: in general, university grants access to more advanced, theoretically complex knowledge (Maes & Sylin, 2009). The education for social advancement offers an alternative route to getting qualified to enter higher education through out-of-hours, intensive courses. It should also be observed that the regional offices in charge of employment organize short-duration vocational training programmes. Thanks to this wide supply of education and training possibilities, the network can tackle numerous individual situations.

The ROCEP recruits potential candidates using their databases. They invite selected job seekers who appear to hold a sufficient level of professional and personal experience to a collective information session. After this collective information session, a series of basic personality tests is organized for the interested participants. On the basis of an analysis of their motivations, a first selection is performed at the end of these tests. Those individuals selected are then invited to the university, so as to participate in a further information session where the details of the different programmes on offer at the university are presented.

The ROCEP agreed to participate actively in such a process with the sine qua non that the programmes offered to the selected job seekers would have the objective of increasing the vocational and professional employability of the participants. Those candidates who are not selected by the ROCEP or by universities after the APEL process are redirected to short-term training programmes organised by the ROCEP or by education for social advancement. At the end of their learning programme, following award of their diploma, the ex-APEL candidates benefit from individual coaching organised by the ROCEP to further improve their likelihood of finding a job.

Internal Partners

Even though the external network has undergone development, it quickly became clear that many of the candidates were withdrawing before the end of the APEL process. The Continuing Education Service at the ULB conducted an investigation into the motivations of their withdrawal and found that following a study cycle necessitated, for them, an impossible financial and psychological investment. The ULB possesses a social service that offers individual social counselling (Maes & Sylin, 2009) and several psychological support services for the students, but these were not accessible to APEL candidates, as they were not yet registered students. Thus, an internal partnership was constructed, bridging the student social service, the psychological guidance service, the orientation service and the continuing education service; this internal partnership allows APEL candidates to benefit, before registration at the university, from all these support services. This 'internal network' is also accessible for APEL candidates who were not recruited through the external network.

APEL CANDIDATES

In the previous section, we described the general framework of the APEL apparatus. APEL of course implies the recruitment of older, more experienced students. It is however interesting to go far beyond this basic description and to characterize the motivations of such returning adult learners.

The Typical Profiles of APEL Candidates

To understand who APEL candidates actually are, we studied the files of 98 candidates who chose to be accompanied during their APEL process, during the period between September 2005 and September 2009. In 36 files, the application letters were available. Fig. 1 represents the age pyramid for our target population. It should be noted that males and females are almost equally represented in this population. The 'typical' APEL candidate is 46 years old. The relatively low number of APEL candidates aged between 25 and 35 years old is a consequence of the legal condition requiring at least five years of personal and professional experience.

In 82% of cases, APEL candidates have exclusively professional experience. Only 6% of them have only personal experience (voluntary

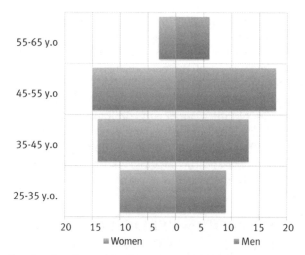

Fig. 1. Age Pyramid of Accompanied APEL Candidates.

work, self-teaching, etc.) and 12% have 'mixed' experience, combining both professional and personal aspects.

The vast majority of candidates decided to follow the master's programme in 'Labour Sciences', a multidisciplinary study programme, offering four different specialisations. This master's programme was selected by the ROCEP as a key-programme to increase employability of APEL candidates. Moreover, two specialisations are organised as out-of-hours study programmes, allowing daytime workers to follow the courses. This contributes to explaining the huge success of this study programme.

The Motivations of APEL Candidates

In our previous publications, we proposed to classify the motivations into four types inspired by the classification outlined by Philippe Carré (1999, 2005): economical, vocational, identity-based and epistemic. In 94% of cases, APEL candidates first and foremost state vocational motivations. They try to pinpoint the correspondence between their curriculum vitae and a 'personal project'. 94% of candidates state identity-based motivations and 72% economical motivations. All candidates mentioning economical motivations also state identity-based motivations. Only 36% of candidates mention epistemic motivations, that is motivations linked with course content. The explanation for such a low level of epistemic motivations and high level of vocational motivations is to be found in a conformation process induced by the enunciation of the external network's strategic goals (Maes et al., 2010): offering adults who have not followed or succeeded in university courses because of their socio-cultural and socio-economical backgrounds, a 'second chance' to obtain a university diploma and contributing to the combat against unemployment of experienced, low-qualified individuals. APEL candidates often express motivations following their understanding of the institutional strategy and the 'ideological' (in a broad sense) positioning of the university where they wish to register.

IS THE APEL PROCESS EFFICIENT? THE NEED FOR AN INTEGRATED POINT OF VIEW

We have already described the two partnerships (external and internal) in addition to some characteristics of APEL candidates themselves. We have also discussed the conformation process that influences the personal motivations of candidates in their APEL file. But what happens after admission through the APEL process? To what extent has the institution adapted in response to the admission of a diverse student cohort?

Stigmatisation and Pedagogical Challenges

In previous work, we have demonstrated that there is a strong correlation between the academic success of candidates and the fact that the study cycle is organized out-of-hours (Maes et al., 2010). Using the testimonies of students admitted through the APEL process, we explained that correlation as follows: older, more mature students attend the programme out-of-hours. In this context, no one can distinguish 'APEL' students from other students. On the contrary, daytime courses are followed by younger, less mature students and in that case, the maturity of the 'APEL students' constitutes a 'social stigma', in the sense of Erving Goffman's stigma definition (Goffman, 1963): 'an attribute that is deeply discrediting'. One 'APEL student' who was interviewed stated that: 'other students sometimes call you "Mister", which reminds you of your old age'. Because of this 'stigma', 'APEL students' fail to integrate themselves into student groups; this is detrimental to the academic success of these students (Coulon, 1997). On the contrary, those

'APEL' students interviewed mentioned the attitude of some teachers as being 'disturbing'. A former APEL student stated that he was disappointed by 'the attitude of those teachers who, despite of the fact that they are the same age as us [the APEL students] and sometimes have even less work experience, treat us like children' (Maes et al., 2010). It is, therefore, clear that a 'mixed' group of 'APEL' and 'non-APEL' students constitutes a particular pedagogical challenge in guaranteeing an inclusive group dynamic that, at the same time, does not make APEL students feel stigmatised.

The Importance of the Institutional Message

'Social stigma' is constructed in comparison with a 'social norm': the adult student is no longer a 'lambda' or an 'ordinary' student and may therefore suffer from social exclusion. The 'social norm' at university can be conceived as the result of the two different processes: a normalisation process, related to the attributes of the majority of students, and a norm-related process, shaped by the rules and institutional discourses.

Even though universities in general, and the ULB in particular, have voluntarily implemented policies to recruit students through APEL, the success of all such initiatives remains moderate in terms of the inclusion of 'APEL students'. This failure can be related to the norm-related processes and the institutional message, here defined as the aggregation of the institutional discourses. For example, the institutional discourses at university in the French-speaking Community of Belgium often focus on 'Excellence' and suggest that institutional policies have a common goal of 'attracting the best students to attend the best courses'. It is quite clear that 'APEL candidates' do not see themselves as fitting into that profile, as many of them conceive the APEL process as a way of remedying a 'youth mistake', and of obtaining a 'second chance to study' (Maes et al., 2010).

The university iconography used for advertising official events often focuses on young, attractive students. In the pictures of students shown on the university website, none of them have wrinkles, grey hair, etc.

The institutional message, here defined as the official discourses and the 'marketing' material, is clearly meant for younger, successful students. It increases the feeling of the APEL students that they do not 'fit in' or 'belong' at the university.

As an APEL student said: 'I know I do not belong here, I am an alien in this university. An old looser who is desperately trying to obtain his diploma'.

CONCLUSIONS

In this chapter, we have attempted to sketch the institutional strategy of the ULB in its recruitment of 'APEL' students. This institutional strategy relies on the constitution of two kinds of partnerships:

• the 'external' partnership, constituted of ROCEP, universities and institutions specialising in education for social advancement and
• the 'internal' partnership, constituted of the student social service, the psychological guidance service, the orientation service and the continuing education service.

Through studying several candidates' motivations, we showed that the institutional message has an important impact on the interaction between APEL candidates and universities.

We discussed the 'social stigma' of being an adult 'APEL student' amidst a younger student group and the subsequent challenge represented by mixed groups. However, there is a clear need to respond successfully to this challenge: splitting the students between younger, less experienced students and adult, more mature student groups could end up in curricula two-tier curriculum. In such a scenario, the risk is that the diploma would be marked by a social stigma.

In this case also, the institutional message clearly affects the interaction between APEL students and the university. In this context, the discourses regarding 'Excellency' could represent an obstacle for widening participation policies. It is, therefore, necessary to develop a clear institutional message on widening participation that could embrace all institutional initiatives and highlight their common goal.

All stakeholders and external partners should be involved at appropriate levels in line with their specificities, in the construction, management and quality assurance of the widened participation policies in general and, the APEL process more particularly. This indeed constitutes one of the main key factors on the path to succeeding in such an ambitious project.

CHAPTER 6

TRANSFORMING THE LEARNING EXPERIENCE TO ENGAGE STUDENTS

Kerri-Lee D. Krause

ABSTRACT

This chapter explores strategies for engaging students in the first year of university study. It draws on a national study of the first year experience in Australia and proposes a model of student engagement, highlighting the multi-faceted nature of the construct. A holistic student life cycle approach to student engagement is proposed as the basis for transforming learning experiences in the first year of university study. This approach includes consideration of the role played by pre-arrival engagement opportunities, the importance of engagement with institutional cultures, practices and communities, along with engagement with disciplinary contexts and cultures. A whole-of-institution approach to student engagement is argued, along with the importance of focussing on shared responsibilities for learning.

Keywords: Engagement; student lifecycle; whole-of-institution approach; student experience; pre-arrival engagement; first year experience; institutional cultures; purpose-designed curricula; disciplinary contexts; quality framework

Institutional Transformation to Engage a Diverse Student Body
International Perspectives on Higher Education Research, Volume 6, 199–212
Copyright © 2011 by Emerald Group Publishing Limited
All rights of reproduction in any form reserved
ISSN: 1479-3628/doi:10.1108/S1479-3628(2011)0000006020

INTRODUCTION

The notion of student engagement in higher education has a distinguished history, particularly in the long-standing student experience research in the United States. For instance, Astin's work on university environments, student involvement and student development dates back to the 1960s (Astin & Holland, 1961; Astin & Panos, 1969). Similarly, Pascarella and Terenzini (1991) first published their scan of the research on student experiences in higher education in the early 1990s, reflecting on a 20-year history of studies in this regard. Likewise, in Australian higher education, Little (1970, 1975) explored characteristics of the university student experience as early as the 1970s. It was not until the late 1990s, however, that Kuh et al. (2001) began to focus on the construct of student engagement through a pilot of the *National Survey of Student Engagement* (NSSE) in 1999. Since that time, the NSSE has drawn considerable attention to the importance of engaging students in a range of educationally purposeful activities. Similarly, the *Australian Survey of Student Engagement* has raised the profile of student engagement across the Australasian higher education sector since its introduction in 2007. These survey instruments provide an instructive means of gathering information about student behaviours and time on task. Yet it should be recognised that they represent just one piece of the puzzle (tool in the toolkit) when it comes to understanding the complex interplay of relationships and experiences that characterise the multi-faceted student body in higher education.

This chapter explores strategies for engaging students with and through the many learning experiences and opportunities available to them in the first year of undergraduate study. The first year represents an important milestone in the lives of university students. It is a time of adjustment as students come to terms with the nature of university cultures, communities and conventions, whether they be online or in face-to-face campus environments. During the first year, identities are typically shaped and re-shaped as students come to terms with new ways of thinking and engaging with people, cultures and knowledge. For many, it is also a time to take stock and decide on whether or not to persist with university studies. These decisions can be influenced by the extent to which students are engaged with their learning and with the university community. This chapter examines the meaning of engagement among diverse first year student cohorts. It considers strategies for transforming first year learning experiences as part of a holistic student life cycle approach to student engagement. The chapter concludes by arguing for the importance of whole-of-institution approaches to student engagement, highlighting the reciprocal responsibilities of students and institutions in building positive, engaged learning communities.

PERSPECTIVES ON THE MEANING OF ENGAGEMENT IN THE FIRST YEAR

A constructivist paradigm underpins the theoretical framing of student engagement. In essence, the construct is based on the assumption that effective educational experiences are those in which students construct their own knowledge. Psychometric validation and statistical modelling has shown that it is a multifaceted construct comprising both behavioural and attitudinal dimensions. It encompasses academic, non-academic and social elements of the learning experience and it includes both behavioural and attitudinal components (Krause & Coates, 2008). For the most part, student engagement is presumed to be a positive state of being, something to which all students and institutions should aspire. However when one investigates more deeply, this is not always the case. Typically, instruments like the NSSE (2010) depict engagement in terms of time spent on a range of educationally beneficial activities such as time devoted to asking questions in class or time spent discussing ideas with faculty members outside of class. Although these may be the behaviours we seek to foster among university students, some may be involved in 'engagements' of an entirely different variety. For instance some may perceive university study as just one of many 'engagements' in their weekly schedule, along with other commitments such as family responsibilities and paid work. Others may find that trying to 'engage' with university study and integrate into the social and cultural context of the institution is like 'engaging' in a battle (Krause, Vick, Boon, & Bland, 2009). For these students, the university culture is foreign and perhaps alienating and uninviting. This may be particularly so for international students, or those who are first in their family to engage in university study.

In the 2010 national study of the first year experience (James et al., 2010), the *Comprehending and Coping Scale* was used to gauge the success with which students perceived they were engaging with their learning, understanding the course material and coping with course requirements. The sample for this study comprised a random stratified sample of 2,422 commencing undergraduate students across 9 Australian universities. The items in the *Comprehending and Coping Scale* were as follows:

I find it hard to keep up with the volume of work
I feel overwhelmed by all I have to do

My course workload is too heavy
I had difficulty comprehending my course material
I had difficulty adjusting to the university style of teaching

Each item was reverse coded and a mean score determined. Table 1 provides details of various student subgroups who scored below the sample mean on this scale. These included students from low socio-economic backgrounds, those for whom English was a second language, those who acknowledged that paid work interfered with their study and those studying in online mode. Arguably, for these students, engagement is in some ways a battle. It should be recognized that these findings make no inferences about students' intellectual ability. Rather, they represent first year students' self-reported assessment of how well they perceive themselves to be coping with university study towards the end of their first year. They have persisted, yet they admit to finding university life a challenge. There may be several explanations for these findings. Linguistic barriers may impede the understanding of students from non-English speaking backgrounds. For those entering higher education from under-represented backgrounds, the approach to learning and coping strategies may not be in place, leaving students feeling isolated and overwhelmed (Forsyth & Furlong, 2003). Those achieving grade averages of less than 70% report greater difficulty engaging successfully, as do those who feel that paid work interferes with their study. First year students who report some instability in their subject or course enrolment patterns also tend to report difficulties in such areas as managing workload, understanding course materials and adjusting to the university style of teaching. Notably, those students enrolled only in online

Table 1.   Student Subgroups Showing below Average Engagement on Comprehending and Coping Scale.

Student Subgroup Descriptor	Below Average Engagement on *Comprehending and Coping Scale*
Socioeconomic background	Low socio-economic status
Language spoken at home	Language other than English
Average end-of-semester grade	Less than 70%
Paid work – level of interference with study	Paid work interferes moderately/severely with study
Mode of study	Online mode with no face-to-face classes
Level of stability in enrolment patterns	Withdrawn from subjects and/or plans to change courses in the new year

modes of study, with no face-to-face contact also tended to score well below average on the Comprehending and Coping scale.

Data such as these challenge universities to find out more about the diverse experiences and engagement patterns of their respective cohorts and sub-cohorts. A one-size-fits-all approach to student engagement is far from adequate in mass higher education contexts. Moreover, the emotional dimensions of engagement – the potential feeling of not belonging, not fitting in – are just as important as the behavioural indicators such as time spent on task. Universities need engagement strategies that recognise the diverse social and cultural capital resources which characterise first year student cohorts.

APPROACHES TO TRANSFORMING THE FIRST YEAR LEARNING EXPERIENCE

In order to understand how we might transform first year learning experiences to engage students, there is merit in considering the various dimensions of student engagement and their potential contributions to enhancing student learning. Fig. 1 presents a model of selected institutional dimensions, people and processes with which we expect first year students to engage when they arrive at university. Together, these facets of engagement offer an opportunity to transform students' learning experiences; equally, they provide scope for disengagement if not proactively addressed. Each dimension will be explored briefly, in turn, though it should be emphasised that their interconnectivity makes for powerful engagement opportunities.

Pre-Arrival Engagement

A student life cycle approach to engagement is key if we are to appreciate the full spectrum of opportunities for engaging students at different milestone points in their learning journey. For instance, before they arrive at university, there is value in engaging with prospective students in home, school and community contexts. This may take place through provision of relevant course-level information, as well as accessible expectation-shaping guidelines on how to be a successful university student. For some students, this information comes via parents, siblings or friends who have been to university before. However, for an increasing number of students who are first in their family to enrol in higher education, there is limited or negligible

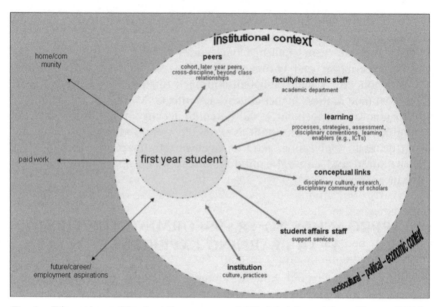

Fig. 1.   Dimensions of Student Engagement: A Model. Adapted from Krause (2006).

pre-enrolment engagement with the university through such means as information booklets, websites or campus-based information sessions.

Pre-arrival engagement also presents an opportunity to connect with students, their families and communities in relation to economic and social factors that may play a role in their decision to come to university. Students need advice on such matters as employability options and how these might influence their choice of study programme. Equally, they need to understand the influence on them of government-level policy and funding decisions with respect to fees and the like.

A coordinated whole-of-institution approach is needed to engage with students, their families, schools and communities before arrival and enrolment. It may involve external relations personnel working with student support services and academic advisors to develop a strategy for making connections with schools and communities using a range of media. It also involves close consultation with academic departments to ensure that course-related information is current and that expectations of students are clearly communicated at every opportunity. The need for a whole-of-institution approach will be discussed in further detail in the final section.

Engaging with Institutional Cultures and Practices

In order to enhance and transform the quality of learning experiences in the first year, it is important to take account of the broader institutional cultures and practices into which students need to be inducted if they are to benefit fully from their learning experience. Often, this dimension of engagement is left to chance. Important opportunities are missed for helping students to understand the mission and goals of the university and the academic departments in which they spend so much of their time.

Orientation and transition programmes provide a good opportunity to introduce students to the university, its history, its values and its cultures. These early opportunities are invaluable for engaging with students and for communicating the message that the quality of the student experience is a high priority for the institution. Krause and Coates (2008) found a strong positive correlation between students' transition experiences and their intellectual engagement and interactions with staff. These dimensions of engagement are pivotal to student success, as outlined in the next section.

Engaging with People in the Learning Environment

First year students have the opportunity to engage with a range of people when they come to university, as shown in Fig. 1. These include peers, academic staff and student affairs staff and prospective employers. Each of these relationships offers an opportunity to learn and develop. The peer group may include those within the first year cohort or it may extend to peers in later years through mentoring programmes and the like. It is most common for students to engage with peers in their own discipline, but powerful, transformative learning experiences are fostered when learning communities are created, comprising peers and purposeful learning activities across disciplines (Smith, MacGregor, Matthews, & Gabelnick, 2004). Some of the most effective peer relationships extend beyond scheduled classes where students take their learning experiences beyond the classroom and build sustaining connections with peers beyond the scheduled classes (Krause & Duchesne, 2000).

Faculty or academic staff and student affairs staff are key players in the learning environment (Tinto, 1998). Building connections with academic and professional staff is a key to successful first year learning. Students value academic staff who are approachable, and who take time to explain tricky concepts and to provide feedback on their progress. In the 2010

Australian study of the first year experience (James et al., 2010), only 29% of students reported regularly seeking advice and assistance from academic staff.

Engaging with Learning in Disciplinary Contexts

Effective engagement with learning in disciplinary contexts relies on the creation of conditions that stimulate and encourage student involvement in learning (Davis & Murrell, 1993). Although students also have a key role to play in engaging with learning opportunities, a significant responsibility rests on the university and its academic and professional staff to ensure that first year students have every opportunity to engage in productive learning experiences.

Ensuing that curricula are purposefully designed to engage students in their first year of university study is a hallmark of an engaged and engaging institution. Appendix presents a quality framework for first year curricula, comprising three quality practice dimensions to guide those committed to enhancing and transforming first year curricula. Although not intended to be an exhaustive checklist, this framework summarises key components characterising intentional approaches to designing first year learning experiences. Each dimension is explored in more detail later.

Strong Partnerships between Academic and Professional Staff Teams

The first dimension involves the development of effective staff teams including academic and professional staff working in partnership to support students in the learning enterprise. Engaged staff are key to successfully engaging students. Engagement strategies may include pre-semester team meetings comprising academic staff teams, including sessional and part-time staff, along with professional staff representing key service areas such as the library, IT services and learning services. It is important for these teams to come together to coordinate efforts and share ideas for supporting students throughout the year, but particularly in the crucially important first few days and weeks of their study programme. Those responsible for timetabling should be integral to these planning sessions to ensure that everything possible is done to prioritise the scheduling of first year classes. Apparently simple steps such as the sequencing of classes and timetabling of lectures, tutorials or laboratory sessions can have significant implications for the quality of the first year study experience.

Purpose-Designed First Year Curricula

First year curricula need to be custom-designed to induct students into the disciplinary conventions and standards expected of them as university students. These learning experiences should not be left to chance. Rather, the curriculum should include learning activities and assessment tasks designed to scaffold students' development as they engage in the process of learning and develop strategies for effective study practices. For instance, depending on the disciplinary context, students may need to learn how to read and synthesise large amounts of scholarly material, they may need to learn how to contribute to small group discussions or work in teams effectively. In order to engage in fit-for-purpose curriculum design, it is important to know who your students are, what their learning needs are and what background information they may bring to the learning environment. This information may come from a variety of sources. For instance, institutional student data may provide information about student demographics. However, in order to understand the range of capabilities among your first year student cohort, some diagnostic tools are required. These may range from informal conversations with students, to informal quizzes on key concepts in the discipline, to opportunities for students to raise questions either in face-to-face or virtual learning environments. These diagnostic assessment activities should be timetabled into the learning design and fit-for-purpose so as to cater for the wide range of abilities that one typically finds in first year undergraduate cohorts.

Assessment is one of the key challenges for students in their first year. Many students are uncertain of the standard of work expected of them and they need guidance in the development of academic skills to assist them in completing assessment tasks. The notion of assessment literacy (see Smith, Fisher, McPhail, & Davies, 2010) is a particularly useful one for those designing first year assessment tasks. It represents a reminder of the importance of explicit instruction in the area of assessment skills. Learning how to interpret assessment items, how to select appropriate references, how to reference scholarly material, how to organise the presentation and how to demonstrate higher level critical analysis and synthesis skills – these are just some of the skills that students need to develop as they prepare for their first assignment. Students are often uncertain about their level of skill development and whether or not they meet the required standard, hence the need for early low-stakes assessment tasks that provide opportunities for feedback on their progress without the fear of failing the subject. Assessment in the first year is also an opportunity to extend students and to motivate them to go beyond the minimum required to pass the subject. Flexibility in the approach to assessment in the first year is key. For the more able students, this may include extension activities in the form of additional assessment items, challenging problem-solving opportunities or further reading. For those students who may be struggling, there is merit in providing additional opportunities to practise skills or to test their understanding through self-review quizzes and the like.

The strategic and effective use of information and communication technologies (ICTs) has the potential to transform students' learning experiences in the first year of study. However, there is a vast difference between approaching ICTs as a 'bolt-on' device and using them as learning enablers (see Fig. 1). Table 2 (James et al., 2010, p.46) suggests that emerging and innovative ICTs such as social networking tools (e.g. Facebook) should be used with caution if one is seeking to enhance the quality of student learning. These findings were reinforced by Kennedy et al. (2008) who confirmed that the assumption that students want to learn with as wide a range of ICTs as possible needs to be questioned. Although students may use a range of social networking tools in their personal lives, these practices do not necessarily transfer to the learning environment, particularly when high stakes issues such as assessment and academic progress are involved. Table 2 also highlights the fact that students value fit-for-purpose ICT use such as online learning management systems and custom-designed online resources; however there is less certainty about the value of online discussion boards for enhancing learning.

In the case of all technologies, the key to success lies in ensuring that: the technologies are integrated into the curriculum with intentional learning-related goals; students derive learning benefits from their use; their use is

Table 2.   Student Mean Ratings of ICT Usefulness for Learning in the First Year ($N = 2,422$).

Form of ICT	Mean (1 = Strongly Disagree; 5 = Strongly Agree)	Standard Deviation
Online learning management system (VLE)	4.4	0.86
Internet-based resources purpose-designed for the course	4.1	0.89
Podcasts of lectures	4.1	1.09
Online discussion with other students	3.4	1.18
SMS alerts or reminders from my university	3.3	1.37
Social networking technologies	2.9	1.36

evaluated; and students are equipped with the appropriate technical and communication skills to be able to engage effectively with these learning tools.

Having planned and implemented the curriculum, it is important to review and enhance it as part of a commitment to continuous improvement. The evaluation process may be informed by a range of sources, including student feedback, self-review, peer review of teaching and curriculum design, and benchmarking with colleagues in other institutions. Formative feedback from students at key milestone points during their first year is particularly helpful for gauging their learning needs, for gaining insights into their views and perspectives, and for monitoring changes in the ways they engage with the course material, with peers and with the institution as a whole.

Student Engagement through the Curriculum

Effective engagement is premised on the fact that students have ready access to accurate program advice before they enrol and during the early part of their first year. Students also need information about available support services such as counselling, support for students with disabilities, financial advice and study skills support. Integrating academic skill development into the programme of learning activities is another way to ensure that students develop the skills they need to engage with learning in higher education contexts. Targeted and explicit approaches to introducing students to the cultures and conventions of the discipline should be a priority in the first year. The first year curriculum is the place where students should begin to develop a sense of belonging to a community of scholars in their chosen discipline (see Fig. 1). They need opportunities to make early, meaningful connections to disciplinary research cultures. In their national study of first year students, James et al. (2010) found that only half of those surveyed agreed that their first year of study gave them an awareness of the latest research in their discipline, whereas less than one-third (31%) acknowledged that they had the opportunity to learn about the research being done in their institution. Engaging students with the research culture of the university and with the discipline may take place in a range of ways. For example, academic staff may talk about their own research during lectures, they may invite colleagues or industry representatives to talk about the application of disciplinary knowledge in real-world contexts. Alternatively, they may design assessment tasks that include discipline-appropriate research skills, such as framing of problems and research questions, opportunities to gather, document and analyse data, and opportunities to work with teams of peers on inquiry-based learning activities.

The first year curriculum is an opportune site for challenging and stimulating first year students. It is never too early to raise their aspirations for further study. Equally important is the need to ensure that students are appropriately prepared for their transition to the second year of study. The first year is often a time of exploration of study options, particularly for those who are uncertain about whether or not they want to remain in their current programme of study. There is value in taking the time to acknowledge these uncertainties when designing curricula and learning support materials. At key decision-points in the study period, lecturers may consider devoting some lecture time talking about pathway options and course choices for students beyond the first year.

In summary, approaches to transforming first year learning experiences are characterised by a team approach involving professional and academic staff and academic staff teams. Complementary to an emphasis on institutional responsibilities is an acknowledgement that students also need to take responsibility for their learning. Transformative approaches adopt a life cycle approach to the student experience. Students move through developmental milestones that need to be recognised and monitored through progressive gathering and reporting of relevant data. First year learning experiences are not haphazard but purposefully designed and framed by quality practices and standards. The first year curriculum should be qualitatively different to the learning designs of later years, taking into account the need to induct students into disciplinary languages, cultures and learning processes.

A WHOLE-OF-INSTITUTION APPROACH TO ENGAGEMENT

Coordinated, whole-of-institution approaches are fundamental in achieving the transformations explored in this chapter. Fig. 1 highlights the interconnectedness of a range of engagement dimensions and the importance of aiming for a coherent experience for the first year student. Engagement of a diverse student body is no longer a cottage industry. Pockets of good practice in engaging students are not sufficient in a mass higher education setting. A whole-of-institution approach comprises several parts including (see also Krause, 2010; Krause in press):

- a coordinated strategy that brings together representatives from across the institution to work together towards a shared and explicitly articulated goal of enhancing student engagement;

- institutional policies and funding models that give priority to student engagement;
- practical support for academic staff teams, including sessional staff in relation to developing of engaging learning designs, whole of programme curriculum mapping to achieve coherence, good practice guidelines for assessment design, skill development in pedagogically sound integration of ICTs to enhance learning, and evaluation skills for the purposes of continuous improvement of curriculum and
- a strong evidence base that represents data on the experiences, perspectives and learning outcomes of diverse student cohorts.

APPENDIX. A QUALITY FRAMEWORK FOR FIRST YEAR CURRICULA: THREE QUALITY PRACTICE DIMENSIONS

This framework builds on the important introductory work of social and academic integration that takes place during Orientation and academic induction programmes.

1. For staff
   Staff teams working in first year contexts are characterised by:
   1. academic and professional staff partnerships to engage first year students, including identifying, assessing and supporting those at risk of failure;
   2. specialised induction and professional development in first year curriculum, pedagogy and assessment design;
   3. supportive peer review of teaching and curriculum design in first year and
   4. whole-of-school, coherent strategies to support students in and beyond first year.
2. For curriculum
   First year curricula comprise:
   5. a whole-of-course roadmap, including early and sustained connections to graduate skills and outcomes;
   6. early assessment tasks in week 2–3 to provide early, formative feedback;

7. step-by-step induction to disciplinary assessment practices and standards;
8. at least one inquiry-based learning activity to engage students with disciplinary inquiry;
9. the best of blended learning strategies to enhance learning and
10. integration of academic literacy skills in disciplinary contexts.
3. For students
   First year students experience:
   11. an integrated first year with accurate program advice and coordinated access to support services as needed;
   12. introduction to university cultures, disciplinary cultures, school cultures;
   13. early, meaningful connections to disciplinary research cultures;
   14. aspiration-raising and intellectual stimulation throughout the first year in preparation for future transitions and
   15. pathway support for those transitioning into second year.

CHAPTER 6.1

TRANSFORMING THE FIRST YEAR EXPERIENCE THROUGH LEARNING COMMUNITIES

Scott E. Evenbeck and Frank E. Ross

ABSTRACT

Purpose – *Indiana University Purdue University Indianapolis (IUPUI) developed learning communities incorporating a first year seminar to serve all entering students in their first semesters of university study to increase student academic achievement and persistence.*

Methodology/approach – *The first year seminars are taught by an instructional team of faculty member, academic advisor, student mentor, and librarian. There is an instructional template for the more than 150 sections of the seminar taught each fall across – academic units rather than a common syllabus. The seminar is often coupled with writing, communication, psychology, or other general education course with students in a cohort group learning together across courses.*

Findings – *Program evaluation results consistently show a 9% positive impact on retention when comparing student outcomes for participants vs. nonparticipants, controlling for background characteristics.*

Research limitations/implications – *This structured approach serving nearly all entering students as a required course reinforces the importance*

Institutional Transformation to Engage a Diverse Student Body
International Perspectives on Higher Education Research, Volume 6, 213–223
Copyright © 2011 by Emerald Group Publishing Limited
ISSN: 1479-3628/doi:10.1108/S1479-3628(2011)0000006021

of mandating interventions on a large scale, in a context of planning and improvement.

Practical implications – *The institution developed the program over 20 years, and revisions to the program have been based on program evaluation. Careful attention to experiences before the learning communities (orientation programs in the summer and bridge programs just before the beginning of the academic year) and after the learning communities when the students move to their second semesters of study is critical.*

Social implications – *Approximately half the students in the learning communities are first generation college students and approximately half are low income students. This intervention has been central to the university's context of widening participation in higher education.*

Keywords: Case study; learning community; first year seminar; program evaluation

INTRODUCTION

Learning communities are a primary educational intervention on many campuses in the United States. The learning community movement has its roots in educational innovations early in the 20th century and enjoyed resurgence late in the 20th century as campuses documented the success of learning communities in enhancing student learning and academic achievement.

Learning communities are defined by students in cohort groups enrolling in two or more courses together. Psychology has long found that attraction is a function of increased exposure. So it is with students, they become more familiar with one another and are more likely to form study groups and otherwise work together as a common cadre of students take several classes together. Learning communities reduce the anonymity that students often experience in their courses, particularly before they enter their majors, and introduce them to other learners who work together with them to enhance their academic and social connections with their learning and with their institutions.

For many years, learning community practitioners paid primary attention to how many courses were linked together, serving a common cohort of students. The focus of conversations was about the inherent interdisciplinary learning that is associated with students taking courses together, sometimes with less attention to the students' learning than to the faculty collaboration in creating and teaching innovative interdisciplinary approaches to social problems or other concerns of inherent interest to students.

Recently, leaders in learning communities have come to stress the integration of learning on the part of students as the defining component of learning communities. Emily Deckard Lardner and Gillies Malarnich of the Washington Center for Improving Undergraduate Education at Evergreen State College in Olympia, Washington, USA, lead the Learning Community Institute each year at which university faculty teams come together to plan, implement, and eventually assess their learning community programs. More information on the Washing Center for Improving Undergraduate Education can be found at http://www.evergreen.edu/washcenter/home.asp.

The emphasis of the American learning community movement now is on student learning (Barr & Tagg, 1995) rather than on faculty teaching. The Association of American Colleges and Universities (AAC&U) has articulated a national strategy for enhancing student learning: Liberal Education American's Promise (LEAP). LEAP is a national initiative that champions the importance of a 21st century liberal education – for individual students and for a nation dependent on economic creativity and democratic vitality (Kuh, 2008). The LEAP initiative articulates the following outcomes for student learning:

- Knowledge of Human Cultures and the Physical and Natural World
- Intellectual and Practical Skills, including
  - inquiry and analysis;
  - critical and creative thinking;
  - written and oral communication;
  - quantitative literacy;
  - information literacy; and
  - teamwork and problem solving.
- Personal and Social Responsibility, including
  - civic knowledge and engagement – local and global;
  - intercultural knowledge and competence;
  - ethical reasoning and action; and
  - foundations and skills for lifelong learning.
- Integrative and Applied Learning, including
  - synthesis and advanced accomplishment across general and specialized studies.

As outlined by AAC&U and the Washington Center, both national leaders in American undergraduate education, learning communities are a primary platform for introducing entering students to integrative learning.

LEARNING COMMUNITIES AT INDIANA UNIVERSITY PURDUE UNIVERSITY INDIANAPOLIS (IUPUI)

IUPUI has had an interesting history with learning communities. The campus, located in downtown Indianapolis, was founded in 1969 when academic units of Indiana University and of Purdue University, located in Indianapolis, were consolidated to form a new urban university. The campus which now has celebrated its 40th birthday has grown to over 30,000 students. Academic schools at IUPUI may be found at http:// www.iupui.edu/academic/schoolsdepts.htm.

At its beginning, IUPUI served entering students though a federally funded program called the "HELP" program for underprepared students and an innovative program called "Guided Studies" where a study skills course was coupled with a general education course to support student learning in the context of a discipline. In the 1980s, the campus attempted to launch first year seminars, but the program was not sustained. Later, in the 1990s, the campus again sought to launch first year seminars and again found that the effort could not be sustained. Teaching was done on a volunteer basis, and a small cadre of dedicated staff rather than faculty offered most of the sections.

University College was founded in 1997. The mission of University College is the following: University College is the academic unit at IUPUI that provides a common gateway to the academic programs available to entering students. University College coordinates existing university resources and develops new initiatives to promote academic excellence and enhance student persistence. It provides a setting where faculty, staff, and students share in the responsibility for making IUPUI a supportive and challenging environment for learning. Collaboration through University College is critical for supporting student learning and success (Ross & Smith, 2010).

University College defined the following principles in achieving its mission, the context for the development of the learning communities:

- promotion of student learning;
- focus on individual student success;
- establishment of its own traditions and recognition of accomplishments;

- provision of a quality first year experience;
- development of strong connections with the degree-granting units;
- commitment to faculty and staff development;
- creation of a community that values diversity;
- implementation of collaborative governance built on individual responsibility; and
- commitment to intentional reflection and assessment.

Joining the Scholarly Community

Indiana University's new president, Myles Brand, launched an innovative program to strengthen campus planning and improvement called "Strategic Directions." Funds for new initiatives were awarded on a competitive basis for the implementation of new programs with high probability of enhancing the university's mission. University College was awarded funds to launch a new course called "Joining the Scholarly Community." That course, developed by seven faculties in the School of Liberal Arts who had release time for a year to develop a course appropriate for IUPUI, became IUPUI's first year seminar.

Since IUPUI has so many schools with varying expectations for engaging students, the first year course was not defined by a common syllabus but rather by a template of expectations for the course, known as the Template for First Year Seminars. Among the distinctive features of the course was having it taught by an instructional team of faculty member, academic advisor, student mentor, librarian, and technical support person.

Roles for each instructional team member are defined in the Template for First Year Seminars. Faculty members play the critical role in the design, presentation, and assessment of learning communities. Academic advisors provide keen insight to new students regarding university rules and regulations, and provide academic and career planning assistance to students weekly in class. Librarians play the critical role of introducing learning community students to information literacy. Student mentors serve as a positive role model for new students and greatly assist in their transition to the university.

The Director of the University Library at IUPUI, Philip Tompkins, brought strong commitment to student learning and engagement within the classroom. A team from IUPUI visited the University of Washington to learn about their instructional teams. The librarians became key members of the teams (Jackson & Orme, 2007). As learning communities continued to develop and expand, the role of the librarian changed from being present at every class to being a member of the team developing the course and then being present in class two-three times a semester. University librarians took the lead in defining expectations for information literacy for entering students.

Reviewing and Revising the Learning Community

IUPUI was invited to participate in the Restructuring for Urban Student Success (RUSS) project funded by The Pew Charitable Trusts, Inc. with Temple University and Portland State University. All three universities had developing learning community programs. Faculty and staff from the campuses visited one another campuses as "critical friends" in reviewing campus efforts and articulating recommendations for enhancing the work.

The campus has revised the template organizing the first year seminar twice. The third revision, approved by the faculty and then adopted in 2010 gives increased attention to the learning outcomes of first year seminars, discussed the importance of active and collaborative learning within the classroom, and gives expanded discussion of the role of instructional team members. This template is located at http://uc.iupui.edu/uploadedFiles/Learning_Communities/LC%20Template.pdf.

Evidence of Effectiveness

Learning communities were developed at IUPUI as the primary intervention in providing students with a context for entering postsecondary education where they would achieve academically and where they would be more likely to persist to the second year and to graduate. IUPUI formed University College as the academic home for all entering students, responsible for orientation, bridge programs, learning communities incorporating a first year seminar, academic advising, and academic support programs, all offered in collaboration with the degree-granting schools of IUPUI.

Extensive research supports that the IUPUI learning community program has had significant impact on student learning, engagement, and persistence. According to Hansen (2010):

- Students participating in first year seminars were retained at a significantly higher rate compared to nonparticipating students, even while controlling for all background and enrollment characteristics.
- First year seminar participants earned statistically significant higher GPAs compared to nonparticipants.

- African American students participating in first year seminars were retained at notably higher rates compared to nonparticipating African American students.

Longitudinal tracking of student success and persistence provides evidence to the effectiveness of learning communities at IUPUI. Data demonstrate both increased graduation and retention rates for participants compared to nonparticipants (Table 1).

Another metric important in evaluating success is student engagement. Student engagement is "a domain of constructs that measures the time and energy students devote to educationally purposeful activities, and how students perceive facets of the institutional environment that facilitate and support their learning" (Kuh, 2001). Students participating in first year seminars at IUPUI were also found to report higher levels of engagement as compared to nonparticipants (Evenbeck, Ross, & Kinzie, 2010) as measured by the National Survey of Student Engagement (NSSE).

REFLECTION

IUPUI's experience with learning communities has provided the following insights into successful implementation.

- The development of learning communities will occur over time. Continuous improvement comes as institutions incorporate assessment and refine expectations of learning communities.
- The learning community must focus on student learning and student learning outcomes.
- Learning communities provide the foundation for comprehensive first year experience initiatives.
- The success of learning community programs is contingent on demonstrating effectiveness. Multiple methods of assessment – both quantitative and qualitative, must be employed. A comprehensive strategy should include analysis of local data and comparisons with national data.
- The involvement of faculty in developing the learning community program appropriate to the university context was fundamental to the success of the program.
- Learning communities are most successful when viewed as an institutional priority supported through collaboration between academic affairs and student affairs.

Table 1. First-Time, Full-Time Cohort Five-Year Retention.

	Initial Totals	1 Year		2 Years		3 Years		4 Years		5 Years		6 Years	
	%	Retained %	Graduated %	Retained %	Graduated %	Retained %	Graduated %	Retained %	Graduated %	Retained %	Graduated %	Retained %	Graduated* %
TLC Participants vs. Nonparticipants													
Fall 2004 cohort													
TLC participants	253	71	0	60	0	52	2	48	11	46	32	46	38
TLC nonparticipants	1833	66	1	54	1	50	2	46	13	44	27	43	35
Total	2086	66	0	54	1	50	2	46	12	44	28	44	35
Fall 2005 cohort													
TLC participants	368	69	0	54	0	50	1	44	9	41	26		
TLC nonparticipants	1826	63	1	52	1	47	2	43	13	42	27		
Total	2194	64	1	52	1	47	2	43	12	42	27		
Fall 2006 cohort													
TLC participants	368	70	0	58	0	53	1	51	15				
TLC nonparticipants	1901	66	1	57	1	53	2	51	15				
Total	2269	67	1	58	1	53	2	51	15				
Fall 2007 cohort													
TLC participants	560	76	0	66	0	61	1						
TLC nonparticipants	1890	69	1	58	1	53	2						
Total	2450	70	1	60	1	55	1						
Fall 2008 cohort													
TLC participants	647	72	0	60	0								
TLC nonparticipants	1904	74	2	65	2								
Total	2551	74	1	64	1								
Fall 2009 cohort													
TLC participants	742	74	0										
TLC nonparticipants	1774	76	0										
Total	2516	75	0										

Note: Graduation figures include bachelor and associate degrees awarded through August of the appropriate year, and certificates awarded through December of the appropriate year. Retained includes students awarded a degree or certificate or students who have re-enrolled.
*Graduation rates of students earning both bachelor and associate degrees.

Bridge Participants vs. Nonparticipants

	N												
Fall 2004 Cohort													
Bridge participants	161	72	0	65	0	57	1	55	11	53	36	55	42
Bridge nonparticipants	1925	66	1	53	1	49	2	45	13	43	27	43	35
Total	2086	66	0	54	1	50	2	46	12	44	28	44	35
Fall 2005 cohort													
Bridge participants	172	78	0	66	0	60	2	54	18	51	39		
Bridge nonparticipants	2022	63	1	51	1	46	2	42	11	41	26		
Total	2194	64	1	52	1	47	2	43	12	42	27		
Fall 2006 cohort													
Bridge participants	196	68	0	58	0	56	0	55	13				
Bridge nonparticipants	2073	67	1	58	1	53	2	51	15				
Total	2269	67	1	58	1	53	2	51	15				
Fall 2007 cohort													
Bridge participants	335	76	0	63	0	58	0						
Bridge nonparticipants	2115	70	1	60	1	55	2						
Total	2450	70	1	60	1	55	1						
Fall 2008 cohort													
Bridge participants	407	76	0	65	0								
Bridge nonparticipants	2144	73	1	64	2								
Total	2551	74	1	64	1								
Fall 2009 cohort													
Bridge participants	389	81	0										
Bridge nonparticipants	2127	74	0										
Total	2516	75	0										

Note: Graduation figures include bachelor and associate degrees awarded through August of the appropriate year, and certificates awarded through December of the appropriate year. Retained includes students awarded a degree or certificate or students who have re-enrolled. Bridge participation for Fall 2006, Fall 2007, and Fall 2008 includes only students who participated in the 2-week bridge program.

Table 1. (Continued)

	Initial Totals	1 Year Retained %	1 Year Graduated %	2 Years Retained %	2 Years Graduated %	3 Years Retained %	3 Years Graduated %	4 Years Retained %	4 Years Graduated %	5 Years Retained %	5 Years Graduated %	6 years Retained %	6 years Graduated %*
Bridge/TLC Combination Participants vs. Nonparticipants													
Fall 2004 cohort													
Bridge/TLC participants	97	76	0	71	0	60	1	58	9	54	35	55	42
All others	1989	66	1	54	1	49	2	45	13	44	28	43	35
Total	2086	66	0	54	1	50	2	46	12	44	28	44	35
Fall 2005 cohort													
Bridge/TLC participants	75	83	0	51	0	57	0	53	13	49	36		
All others	2119	64	1	52	1	47	2	43	12	41	26		
Total	2194	64	1	52	1	47	2	43	12	42	27		
Fall 2006 cohort													
Bridge/TLC participants	104	69	0	57	0	55	0	53	14				
All others	2165	67	1	58	1	53	2	51	15				
Total	2269	67	1	58	1	53	2	51	15				
Fall 2007 cohort													
Bridge/TLC participants	177	78	0	65	0	60	0						
All others	2273	70	1	60	1	55	1						
Total	2450	70	1	60	1	55	1						
Fall 2008 cohort													
Bridge/TLC participants	225	73	0	62	0								
All others	2326	74	1	64	2								
Total	2551	74	1	64	1								
Fall 2009 cohort													
Bridge/TLC participants	235	81	0										
All others	2281	74	0										
Total	2516	75	0										

Note: All others refers to students who did not participate in both bridge and TLC. They could have participated in either one program or neither and Fall 2006, Fall 2007, and Fall 2008 includes only students who participated in the 2-week bridge program. Graduation figures include bachelor and associate degrees awarded through August of the appropriate year, and certificates awarded through December of the appropriate year. Retained includes students awarded a degree or certificate or students who have re-enrolled.

First Year Seminar Participants vs. Nonparticipants

Fall 2004 Cohort												
FYS participants	1789	67	0	55	51	2	47	13	45	29	45	36
FYS nonparticipants	297	61	3	50	43	6	44	11	39	22	37	30
Total	2086	66	0	54	50	2	46	12	44	28	44	35
Fall 2005 cohort												
FYS participants	1841	65	0	52	48	1	43	11	42	26		
FYS nonparticipants	353	58	6	50	46	7	44	14	41	29		
Total	2194	64	1	52	47	2	43	12	42	27		
Fall 2006 cohort												
FYS participants	2018	68	0	58	54	1	51	14				
FYS nonparticipants	251	58	10	53	51	10	49	21				
Total	2269	67	1	58	53	2	51	15				
Fall 2007 cohort												
FYS participants	2164	71	0	60	55	1						
FYS nonparticipants	286	68	6	59	52	7						
Total	2450	70	1	60	55	1						
Fall 2008 cohort												
FYS participants	2359	73	0	63								
FYS nonparticipants	192	76	16	69								
Total	2551	74	1	64								
Fall 200 cohort												
FYS participants	2288	76	0									
FYS nonparticipants	228	65	1									
Total	2516	75	0									

Note: Graduation figures include bachelor and associate degrees awarded through August of the appropriate year, and certificates awarded through December of the appropriate year. Retained includes students awarded a degree or certificate or students who have re-enrolled.

CHAPTER 6.2

INCLUSION AND THE STUDENT VOICE: LESSONS FROM THE TRINITY INCLUSIVE CURRICULUM STRATEGY

Michelle Garvey

ABSTRACT

Purpose – *This case study describes the Trinity Inclusive Curriculum (TIC) strategy, which aims to embed inclusion within Trinity College Dublin (TCD) through the creation of an online application for self-evaluating the inclusivity of academic practices, and a supporting resource website.*

TIC arose in response to the additional needs arising from increasing diversity within TCD, resulting from national and institutional policies aiming to widen participation in higher education.

Approach – *TIC involved three phases.*

Phase I reviewed the academic environment within TCD, primarily through a student survey. Following this review, TIC developed a draft teaching and learning self-evaluation tool, and piloted it within 12 TCD courses in phase II. Pilots involved stakeholder feedback (staff and student), resource review, classroom observation, completion of the draft

Institutional Transformation to Engage a Diverse Student Body
International Perspectives on Higher Education Research, Volume 6, 225–233
Copyright © 2011 by Emerald Group Publishing Limited
All rights of reproduction in any form reserved
ISSN: 1479-3628/doi:10.1108/S1479-3628(2011)0000006022

tool and engagement with the resulting action report. Following the pilot, TIC created an online version of the tool.

Phase III is underway, and seeks to embed this tool within TCD policies and processes, and to promote its use elsewhere.

Findings – *Extensive student feedback has shown that there are common barriers for all students. Common themes include difficulties finding information, and difficulties arising from a lack of coordination between academic, administrative, and service areas. The TIC self-evaluation tool allows staff to reflect on, evaluate, and respond to issues causing student difficulty.*

Value – *TIC is working to embed this tool within TCD and elsewhere. Through the TIC tool, TCD, and other participating institutions can continue to enhance the inclusivity of their academic environments.*

Keywords: Inclusion; universal design; diversity; non-traditional; Ireland; higher education; university; case study

BACKGROUND POLICY AND PLANNING AT NATIONAL AND INSTITUTIONAL LEVEL

Trinity College Dublin (TCD) is Ireland's oldest university with a prestigious 400 year history and approximately 16,000 students (of which one-third are postgraduates). Traditionally, TCD's student base came from a limited range of backgrounds, being overwhelmingly English speaking, non-disabled, middle class, school leavers. However, this has been changing over recent years in line with government and college policies focusing on widening access to third level education.

Over the past decade, the Higher Education Authority (HEA), the statutory planning and policy development body for higher education in Ireland developed a national policy regarding access (HEA, 2004, 2008). The most recent Access Plan (HEA, 2008) included the following targets:

- all socio-economic groups will have entry rates of at least 54% by 2020;

Furthermore, by 2013:

- Mature students will comprise at least 20% of full-time entrants and 27% of all entrants,
- Non-standard entry routes will account for 30% of all entrants,

- The number of students with sensory, physical and multiple disabilities in higher education will double.

TCD responded to the HEA Access Plan by including widening access as a strategic goal (TCD, 2006a, 2009a). TCD has three access services: the Disability Service, the Mature Students' Office and TAP (Trinity Access Programmes, for students from socially disadvantaged backgrounds). Students entering TCD through these services' alternative access routes are subsequently registered with these services. Students using the central applications entry route (CAO) who fulfil appropriate criteria may also register with these services. By 2008, when the Trinity Inclusive Curriculum (TIC) strategy commenced, 4% of TCD undergraduates were registered with the Disability Service, 4% with TAP and 9% were mature students (TCD, 2009b). This will rise as the College Access Plan: 2009–2013 (TCD, 2009c) has set the following institutional targets for 2013:

- 22% entrance rates according to key access criteria;
- 13% entrance rates by underrepresented socio-economic groups; and
- 10% increase in students with a disability (excluding specific learning difficulties).

The Move towards Inclusion in TCD

In 2005, a Disability Service quality review highlighted the need to move towards an inclusive environment and recommended a review of the extent to which disability is considered in course content, teaching and assessment, with developmental proposals being brought forward by the Disability Service and the Centre for Academic Practice and Student Learning (CAPSL) (TCD, 2006b).

At that point, disability support in TCD was considered specialist support, with expert staff devising retroactive strategies to overcome barriers found within the traditional curriculum. This approach was deemed unsustainable and undesirable because:

- The workload and co-ordination necessary to supply supports and adjustments increased as the numbers of students registered for additional supports and adjustments grew.
- This approach failed to cater for those within the university population who, while not registered with an access programme, had difficulty with traditional curricular approaches (e.g. undiagnosed/undisclosed disabilities, students with carer responsibilities, students with English as a second language).

Following on from this review, the Directors of the Disability Service and CAPSL collaborated to create a project proposal that was eventually funded through the national HEA Strategic Innovation Fund. This project was to become the TIC strategy. This case study will look at the methods employed by TIC and the outcomes achieved to date.

TIC STRATEGY: OBJECTIVES AND ACTIVITIES

TIC was set up with the primary aim of responding to the needs of the modern student population post-registration by embedding inclusive practices within the mainstream curriculum to enable all students to participate more fully in the academic life of College. This involved identifying actual and potential barriers to engagement within the academic environment; devising enabling strategies to overcome these barriers; and promoting these strategies through the creation of teaching and learning self-evaluation tools to be embedded into TCD policies, procedures, training and awareness activities. A resource website promoting reflection and understanding of inclusion was also to be created.

TIC received funding for three years. To reflect this timeline, the strategy was broken into three phases, each corresponding to an academic year. At this point, phases I and II are complete and TIC is into phase III. This case study will follow the progression of TIC through phases I and II, and will discuss tasks underway for phase III, which aims to ensure the sustainability of progress and the continued enhancement of inclusion beyond the funding cycle.

Phase I: Reviewing the Context within TCD

When TIC commenced in October 2008, there was limited awareness of the principles of inclusion within TCD, and there was fragmented knowledge of the specific needs arising from the TCD context among those involved in TIC. Thus, the primary aim of this phase was to seek communication between the key stakeholders to enhance mutual understanding and raise awareness.

The key stakeholders were identified as

- staff involved either directly or indirectly in teaching, learning and assessment (e.g. lecturers, administrative staff creating student information resources) who understand the limitations faced in providing an inclusive environment and can offer suggestions to overcome difficulties based on personal professional experience;

- staff working directly to support 'nontraditional' students within the access offices and the International Office who have specific experience of the types of difficulties faced by students entering college from nontraditional backgrounds and
- the student body, who are best placed to understand and report on the needs of students within the academic environment.

A working group was set up involving representatives from each stakeholder group allowing each to have a voice in the overall direction of TIC. Throughout the first year, TIC sought understanding of the varied perspectives and experiences within the TCD context and thus sought feedback from representatives from the college community.

Student Survey
The administration of a student survey was identified as a key task in phase I, aiming to:

- enhance inclusivity and student engagement by identifying good practice in teaching and assessment, and areas for improvement and
- gather feedback on student satisfaction with facilities and services.

TIC identified the target cohort as all students registered with TCD's access services. Major themes were agreed in consultation with key stakeholders (e.g. access services, CAPSL, the Students' Unions and members of the academic community).
The themes were:

- student information resources,
- teaching and assessment methods,
- academic facilities,
- academic support services,
- general academic experiences and
- effects of 'nontraditional' status on academic experiences.

The survey received 493 responses. Due to cross over between cohorts, it is not possible to offer a definitive population size. However, this is estimated as a response rate of approximately 33%.
Key issues arising from the survey included:

- Class timetables and continuous assessment deadlines not organised to ensure maximum engagement. Students urged better notification of timetables, and a more even spread of deadlines throughout the year.

- Inaccurate, out of date information within student information resources cause difficulties.
- The variation in student feedback regarding teaching and assessment methods reinforced the importance of offering a range to suit differing strengths, weaknesses and learning preferences.
- There is a need for clearer communication between disciplines offering single programmes, and between academic and service areas.

Immediately following the survey two audits took place to follow up on feedback regarding information resources. These led to the collation of good practice guidelines for both programme handbooks and reading lists, and the creation of a programme handbook template for use as a resource by programmes as they create or revise their handbooks.

Phase II: Creation and Pilot of the TIC Self-Evaluation Tool

TIC created a draft teaching and learning self-evaluation tool over the summer of 2009. This tool, created using the feedback received from all college stakeholders, aimed to promote reflection on current teaching practice, and to offer suggestions for enhancing inclusion. As such, it aims to play an active role in enhancing student access and engagement post-registration.

The tool was created for use in programme and module design/review, individual lecturer self-evaluation and review of provision to research students. It took the form of a tick box questionnaire, with questions grouped within specific sections.

Sections included:

- Teaching Design,
- Application and Orientation,
- Accessible Information,
- The Physical Environment,
- Specific Teaching Methodologies,
- Assessment,
- Student Research Experience and
- Student Feedback.

The tool is not an auditing system with users scored and benchmarked against others. Instead, it is a reflective aid for users, with questions design to promote discussion and evaluation of their provision for their diverse student populations. Upon completion, users receive a summary report with recommended actions. The tool focuses on the delivery of teaching and assessment. Its scope does not cover the subject matter and syllabus of courses.

Enhancing the accuracy, usability, and effectiveness of the self-evaluation tool and resulting action plan was the central objective of phase II of TIC. To achieve this goal, 12 extensive pilots of individual courses took place. Pilots covered both undergraduate and postgraduate programmes, and all major subject disciplines. Pilots involved the completion of the draft tool by course coordinators, classroom observation, resource review and stakeholder feedback. All information was collated to create action plans for enhancing inclusion within each course.

For feedback, stakeholders were identified as all staff working on, and all students studying within, the pilot programme or module. TIC endeavoured to gather feedback from the student stakeholders via both interviews and surveys. Student representatives for each pilot programme and module were invited to meet with the TIC officer to offer the student perspective on their course. Representatives were asked to confer with their classmates before the meeting to gather feedback on good practices within the course, and areas where difficulties were experienced.

TIC also administered student surveys for programmes and modules within the pilot.

The student representatives' interviews and the data collected from student surveys, showed great similarities across all schools, faculties and levels. Student feedback concerning both good practices and areas of difficulty cohered. Furthermore, the data from phase II surveys and interviews, and the phase I survey of 'nontraditional' students showed a large degree of overlap. This indicates that the needs of traditional and nontraditional students are very similar, though it may be that areas of difficulty affect the engagement of 'nontraditional' students to a greater extent than 'traditional' students.

Student feedback indicated that the key issues considered important by both traditional and nontraditional students when creating an inclusive, student centred, academic environment include ensuring all students have:

- Access to information on the academic environment, supports, facilities, etc. that is proactively circulated (current information was seen as fragmented, hidden within websites and difficult to find, especially for someone unfamiliar with college). This was particularly important to international students and mature students who may be unfamiliar with the college environment and enter college with less initial support from peers.

- Access to clear, reliable, comprehensive study materials that are easily available online.
- Reliable access to facilities within key areas such as IT and the library.
- Consistently clear, productive, constructive feedback that is returned in a timely manner.
- Comfortable and appropriate physical environments with appropriate lighting, acoustics, temperature and layout.
- An even spread of work throughout the academic year. This necessitates clear communication and coordination between programme personnel. This was a particular concern for students studying in multidisciplinary courses, where coordination and communication could be limited.

TIC noted that many of the above issues lie beyond the control of the individual lecturers, and regular module evaluations conducted within the institution, which focus on the lecturers and their classroom practices, do not pick them up. However, these issues can have a significant impact on the academic experiences of students, and their ability to engage equally with their programmes of study. As such, TIC feels that it is important to offer and promote student feedback mechanisms that can take account of the whole student experience.

TIC has created a set of student feedback questionnaires that consider the whole student experience and can be administered as part of the evaluation of teaching and learning.

Phase III: Embedding TIC

Following extensive stakeholder feedback in phases I and II, TIC has launched an online application allowing staff to evaluate teaching, learning and assessment practices for inclusion (www.tcd.ie/capsl/tic/evaluation).

This application is available externally, and in phase III TIC will work with other Irish higher education institutes to evaluate its effectiveness. TIC has been in contact with interested practitioners who are working to enhance inclusion and student engagement within their own establishments, and believe the application could be a useful tool.

Through phases I and II of the strategy, TIC has sought out those within the TCD community who are interested in, and open to, inclusion and widening participation. This has created a ripple effect, whereby inclusion has become a more familiar concept within the college community.

As TIC enters its final stage, it is important that inclusion becomes embedded across TCD. Although direct opposition has been rare, active engagement is also infrequent as staff work in an already demanding environment. To enhance engagement, work is required to embed the TIC tool into current academic processes and to make its completion straightforward and speedy.

TIC is speaking to senior management within TCD to seek methods to embed the tool into processes such as the quality review system, programme design and teaching awards. Progress to date includes the incorporation of inclusion into the 'Provost Teaching Award' application process and the recommendation to use the TIC tool in the guidelines for quality review. TIC seeks to further embed inclusion over the coming academic year.

TIC has also created a series of workshops and presentations to help engage lecturing staff. Emphasis is given to those beginning their academic careers who will be the practitioners of the future. TIC seeks to make the process of engagement with the tool as easy and clear as possible by seeking and acting on user feedback and further developing supporting audio-visual materials. This will continue through 2010–2011.

It is expected that through TIC, staff in TCD, and other participating institutions, will improve their ability to respond to student needs so as to enable all students to participate more fully within academic life regardless of social, cultural or educational background.

CHAPTER 6.3

MAINSTREAMING BLENDED LEARNING TO ENHANCE THE ACCESS, LEARNING AND RETENTION OF STUDENTS FROM EQUITY GROUPS

Violeta Vidaček-Hainš, Blaženka Divjak
and Renata Horvatek

ABSTRACT

In this chapter we present a case study about a bottom-up approach in creating the strategy and action plan for the mainstream implementation of blended learning in one Faculty at a higher education institution in Croatia, and the implications this has on the access and retention of students from equity groups. In previous research the target groups were identified, and the next step was to investigate the specific needs of those groups of students, focusing on creating an effective learning environment. Taking an evidence-informed approach, institutional experts, management and staff developed a strategic framework, covering ICT support, the E-learning system and curriculum development to meet the specific needs of these students. One of the very important goals of mainstreaming widening participation at the Faculty of Organization and Informatics

Institutional Transformation to Engage a Diverse Student Body
International Perspectives on Higher Education Research, Volume 6, 235–243
ISSN: 1479-3628/doi:10.1108/S1479-3628(2011)0000006023

(FOI) is to create an effective learning environment for all students. E-learning is recognized as an important tool in making learning and education more accessible to all students at the FOI. The FOI's Strategy for E-learning contributes to this objective and since FOI is one of the leading faculties in the implementation of E-learning at the University of Zagreb, FOI's approach to E-learning is exemplary within the institution, and it has been taken into account when University of Zageb Strategy was being developed and implemented.

Keywords: Blended learning; access; targeted groups; evidence-informed approach; effective learning environment; strategy of E-learning

INTRODUCTION TO HIGHER EDUCATION IN THE REPUBLIC OF CROATIA AND AT THE UNIVERSITY OF ZAGREB

The higher education (HE) system in the Republic of Croatia includes universities, colleges, polytechnics and schools of higher education, and is governed by the Ministry of Science, Education, and Sports. Following the Bologna Declaration (1999), which was signed by Croatia in 2001, and the subsequent new higher education legislation implemented in 2003, HE has been re-organised to offer bachelors, masters, PhD, and professional programs. The Bologna Process (1999, 2007) enhances the experience of students in HE institutions and it seems to reduce withdrawal rates, which was a driver for HE reform in Croatia.

The University of Zagreb was founded in the 17th century, in 1699, and is one of the oldest and largest universities in South-East Europe, with more than 60,000 full-time and part-time students. The University has 29 faculties, three art academies and the Centre for Croatian Studies. One of the 29 Faculties is the Faculty of Organization and Informatics (FOI) in the city of Varazdin. The FOI spans the fields of Information Science and Information Technology and Business and Management, and contains seven departments: economics, organization, quantitative methods, theoretical foundations of informatics, computing and technology, information systems development and foreign languages and educational disciplines.

MAINSTREAMING STUDENT-CENTRED BLENDED LEARNING IN THE FOI

Developing an Evidence-Base

In the FOI the process of mainstreaming widening participation, equity, opportunity and success began by using institutional data about access and retention to identify student target groups. This was also informed by Croatian national policy on groups that need special support: disabled students, part-time and mature students, international students, students whose parents were war veterans, students from disadvantaged socio-economic background and gender-related issues (Vidaček-Hainš & Horvatek, 2003; Vidaček-Hainš, Horvatek, & Divjak, 2009). In the FOI a key target group is disabled students, as our discipline areas offer suitable graduate employment for disabled people.

Once the target groups were identified the research team at FOI investigated the specific needs for those groups of students, focusing on creating an effective learning environment. In the last couple of years, various surveys have been conducted among students and a lot of suggestions from the students have been collected. This has been supplemented by international comparative studies to identify effective practice which may be suitable for implementation in the Croatian HE context (see e.g. Vidaček-Hainš & Horvatek, 2003).

Taking an evidence-informed approach institutional experts, management and staff developed a strategic framework, covering ICT support, the E-learning system and curriculum development to meet the specific needs of these target groups (Vidaček-Hainš, Divjak, & Horvatek, 2004). In the FOI a number of issues were taken into account to meet the needs of students, but much of the research pointed to the need for a good E-learning system to facilitate blended learning. For example:

- Adapting learning materials-particularly E-learning materials – for part-time female students who have families and children (Divjak, Vidaèek-Hainš, & Ostroški, 2007; Vidaèek-Hainš, Divjak, & Ostroški, 2009).
- The specific needs of students with disabilities (Vidaèek-Hainš, Horvatek, & Divjak, 2009), especially in relation to computer attitudes and computer literacy because this is one of the most important re-entry factors when students with disabilities have to choose their future college or university (Vidaèek-Hainš, Kiriniæ, & Dušak, 2009).

- Student mobility, especially for international students who intend to come and study in Croatia (Vidaèek-Hainš, Divjak, & Ostroški, 2008; Kovaèiæ, Kiriniæ, & Divjak, 2009).
- The importance of creating an effective learning environment and comparing the results with other higher education systems were taken into consideration (Vidaèek-Hainš, Prats, & Appatova, 2009; Vidaèek-Hainš, Appatova, & Prats, 2008).
- Learning outcomes and adaptation of learning outcomes for target groups of students (i.e. students with disabilities) according to their specific needs (Vidaèek-Hainš et al., 2008).

One of the very important goals of mainstreaming widening participation at the FOI is to create an effective learning environment for all students. An effective learning environment (ELE) is "a whole range of variables in the area of psychological, pedagogical, technical, cultural, and pragmatic research" (Jonnassen & Lands, 2002 in Vidaček-Hainš et al., 2008, p. 137). The use of ICT is very important in creating an effective learning environment for specific target groups of students (i.e. mature students, part-time students, students with disabilities, international students, etc.). The use of information technology is enhancing traditional teaching, and blended (mixed or hybrid) learning is more and more popular among students and professors.

A Commitment to Blended Learning

In the FOI we believe that using only a teacher-centred model of education will have little effect on equipping students with the competences, knowledge, and skills required for their successful future. We also believe that it is very important to use technology-enhanced learning, especially when teaching ICT students, who are in general inclined to technology, and to facilitate their participation in a knowledge-based economy and society (Geser, 2007). It means that a shift has to be made toward competency based student-centred education.

According to the research (Begičević, Divjak, & Hunjak, 2007) we undertook with a group of 90 E-learning and higher education experts in 2006, the most important advantages of E-learning implementation are:

- accessibility of knowledge (average rating is 4.68 on the scale 1–5);
- flexibility of learning (4.48);
- preparation of students for lifelong learning (4.28);

- more efficient use of learning/teaching time (4.11);
- collaborative learning (4.06); and
- adaptation to student's learning style (4.01).

All of these advantages of E-learning can be directly related to many underrepresented groups, especially to mature and part-time students.

In the same research, the critical factors for implementing E-learning were identified as:

- organizational readiness of environment;
- development of human resources;
- availability of human recourses, Availability of basic ICT infrastructure;
- legal and formal readiness of environment; and
- availability of specific ICT infrastructure.

Developing a Strategy to Engage Staff to Deliver Student-Centred Blended Learning

Based on these findings we prepared a strategy to engage staff in delivering student-centred blended learning, illustrated in Diagram 1.

(a) Managed and implemented by a cross-faculty committee

The coordination and development of the strategy, as well as the implementation of E-learning at FOI has been conducted by the committee for E-learning that consists of representatives of faculty management, professors, assistants, and supporting staff. This promotes ownership of the strategy by all staff in the Faculty.

(b) Phased approach, based on three levels

At FOI there are three different levels pre-defined for E-courses. The first level of E-course includes basic information about curriculum/topics, learning outcomes, references, forum for communication, and learning materials. The second level of E-course includes learning materials organized according to specific topics, forums for different topics for discussion (i.e. student communication), timetable and calendar for different tasks and obligations, information links to the courses, tests, marks, homework, glossary, etc. The third level improves on the second level in terms of design, the inclusion of audio and video materials and online evaluation.

Diagram 1. FOI Approach to Engaging Staff in Developing Student-Centred
Blended Learning.

(c) Contractual agreement to provide level 1 in all courses

The FOI made a commitment to ensure all courses reached a minimum
E-learning standard. All teachers signed contracts to implement the first
level of blended learning in their courses.

(d) Compulsory technical training and pedagogical development for staff

Technology should be used to improve the quality of teaching, to ensure
the achievement of learning outcomes, with pedagogical needs always kept
in mind rather than the imperativeness of the application of modern
technologies. Internal staff development workshops and training sessions
help professors, assistants and staff to manage new technologies, but there
is also training sessions covering psychological and pedagogical topics
to develop understanding of communicative and educational principles of

higher education. Staff training and development covering technical and pedagogical aspects of E-learning has been continuously offered and it has been expected that all teaching staff must participate.

(e) Specialized staff to support materials development

The Moodle system is a course management system designed to help educators who want to create quality online courses. This is a Modular Object-Oriented Dynamic Learning Environment and it is a free and open-source E-learning software platform. The University Computing Centre (SRCE) gives support to the learning management system (LMS), but FOI has its own Centre for supporting E-learning tools and development. For technical support and development of learning material specialized staff are dedicated to assist academic staff.

(f) Innovative case studies to enhance practice

The collection of innovative case studies concerned with the execution of E-learning to enhance the implementation and evaluation of learning outcomes is becoming increasingly important. The examples of best practices are opened inside Moodle for others to see them and analyze and benchmark their own achievements against.

(g) Institutional awards for best practice

In relation to the innovative case studies we specially emphasize the competition across the University for the best E-learning course. All winning courses were presented with their award on the special one-day E-learning event and professors received their awards from the Rector of the University. FOI was ranked top among the 29 faculties of the University of Zagreb receiving two awards, including the best E-learning course. The event was very well disseminated inside the University covered by national media.

Today all courses at FOI have E-learning LMS Moodle and most courses at the FOI are now taught as blended or hybrid courses, which means that we combine face-to-face teaching with an on-line virtual learning environment (VLE). The number of courses in E-learning in the academic year 2009/2010 are as follows: (1) undergraduate study – 72 (100% of courses) + 21; (2) graduate study – 30 (100%); (3) doctoral study – 17 (63%); (4) post-graduate specialist study – 23 (43%); (5) Professional study – 48 (80%); and (6) entirely online – 1 course. In total there are 212 E-courses for students available at the Faculty.

CONCLUSIONS: ENABLERS AND CHALLENGES

Within the FOI we have taken a strategic approach to transforming the learning experience to improve the access and success of students from targeted groups. The approach we have taken has been described earlier, and is summarized in Diagram 2.

The Bologna process and the laws, regulations, resolutions, strategies, and guidelines that have been published in the past few years in Croatia to harmonise our educational and employment system to the EU regulations are among factors that assisted the FOI institutional development considerably.

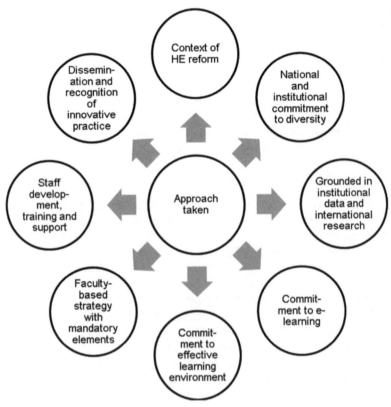

Diagram 2. Approach to Mainstreaming Blended Learning to Enhance the Access, Learning and Retention of Students from Equity Groups in the Faculty of Organization and Informatics, University of Zagreb.

They have provided an opportunity to re-organize provision and review practice, and this has been complemented by the ombudsman for people with disabilities, which is responsible for the law enforcement and implementation of strategies for equal access and equal employment opportunities after finishing tertiary education.

On an institutional level, Article 6 of the Statute (2005), of the University of Zagreb, explicitly says, that "any discrimination on the basis of race, gender, religion, political or other orientation, national or social background, birth, social class, disability, sexual orientation, age etc. is unacceptable." Each faculty of the University of Zagreb has a network of coordinators responsible for the requirements of disabled students. This network consists of teaching staff and students (the majority of which are students with disabilities themselves). This network was established as part of the TEMPUS project Developing University Counselling and Advisory Services (DUCAS). And the establishment of the Office for Students with Disabilities, which is accessible to all students on a daily basis provides a further way of interacting with students.

E-learning is recognized as an important tool in making learning and education more accessible to students at the FOI. The strategy for E-learning at FOI contributes to this objective (Divjak, Begičević, Grabar, & Boban, 2010) and since FOI is one of the leading faculties in the implementation of E-learning at the University of Zagreb, FOI's approach to E-learning is exemplary within the institution.

Collecting and analyzing data is an on-going challenge to the development of evidence-based policies and practice. At the level of the Faculty, the situation is better since the data on students performance is available. At the University level there is an information system that manages students performance but additional services for analyzing and reporting data are required. At the state level the situation is rather confusing because there is no central information system, although a project addressing this issue has been started.

Finally, special attention still has to be given to raising awareness of teaching staff toward the issues of underrepresented groups, their needs and to the dissemination of relevant practices. There are "isolated islands" where the learning environment is designed to be student-friendly but unfortunately they are not widely embraced and standards of teaching and learning quality assurance, even when they are integrated into guidance documents, does not necessarily translate into practice. In the past few months the University committee on quality assurance has taken actions in the right direction and it specially supported a project addressing the learning of students with disabilities. The work in the FOI goes some way to addressing these issues.

CHAPTER 6.4

DEFINING IDENTITY, ENGAGING TEACHERS AND ENGAGING STUDENTS: 'EDUCATION STRENGTHS' IN A FOREIGN BRANCH CAMPUS

Glenda Crosling

ABSTRACT

This case discusses a programme to develop areas of 'education strengths' in the curricula of a foreign branch campus of an Australian university. The programme may be seen as a means for organisational change, enabling academic staff to define their own areas of speciality and foci for curricula development and stimulating them to greater levels of ownership, interest and enthusiasm in their teaching. This program enrichens the curriculum by 'localising' it for the student cohort, it thus impacts positively on student retention.

Keywords: Student engagement; curriculum development; education strengths

Institutional Transformation to Engage a Diverse Student Body
International Perspectives on Higher Education Research, Volume 6, 245–252
Copyright © 2011 by Emerald Group Publishing Limited
All rights of reproduction in any form reserved
ISSN: 1479-3628/doi:10.1108/S1479-3628(2011)0000006024

INTRODUCTION

This chapter discusses curricula development as one way of impacting on institutional transformation. In a transnational higher education institution in the Southeast Asian region, the programme under discussion aimed to identify and develop areas of education in which the campus could specialise. Through these areas conceptualised as 'education strengths', the objective was to develop curricula in terms of content or teaching and learning approach that is relevant to the location and therefore the student cohort.

Student retention in their higher education studies is a complex and many faceted issue. What is known though is that students who are engaged and enthused by their studies are more likely to put in effort, achieve more highly and therefore continue. At the same time, it is well established that the teaching impacts on the approach that students take to their learning and that enthusiastic teachers are more likely to facilitate their students' engagement in their studies.

The programme discussed in this case impacted on the engagement of the academic staff in their teaching and consequently on the engagement of students in their learning, thus assisting their retention in their studies. That is, the intertwined nature of teaching and learning (Biggs, 2005; Prosser & Trigwell, 1999) means that the energy and enthusiasm of engaged teachers impacts on their students' interest in their studies, encouraging them to continue with their studies.

This case study provides an overview of the context for the programme and the rationale. The steps taken to introduce the programme are discussed, as well as the impact of the programme on institutional transformation, and by implication, on student retention. The positive and less advantageous aspects of the approaches taken are also considered.

INSTITUTIONAL CONTEXT

The context for the programme is a foreign branch campus in Malaysia of a large Australian university. The branch campus, in operation for more than a decade, is comprised of six schools, which are a part of the faculties of the wider university. In the Malaysian setting, the university operates as a private higher education institution, but at the same time, it is also a campus of a public Australian university. In the 'offshore' setting, all students are full fee paying, with the Malaysian cohort largely being of Chinese ethnicity.

About a third of the student population is international, emanating from countries such as Indonesia, India, China and Middle Eastern countries.

In the foreign branch campus setting, the curricula offered to the students were originally developed in the 'parent' university in Australia and transposed to the transnational setting. Powerpoint slides of the lectures designed and delivered at the parent university were often used for this purpose. The slides were then delivered in class by the teachers in the offshore setting, at times with limited transformation to cater for the local student cohort and setting. Initially in the early days of the off shore campus, academic staff had limited input into course and subject design and development, tending to be passive and to take roles subordinant to the slides as they delivered the subject content. They had acted somewhat like a conduit for the subject content from the parent university to the foreign branch campus, and this approach had lingered to some degree with some academic staff. Although in many ways, this approach may be seen as appropriate in the establishment stage of a campus as a quality assurance measure, pedagogically and for high quality education, it is not a sustainable approach.

Some teaching staff in the past thus had limited opportunities to transform the programme. From this perspective, such staff could be described as lacking engagement in teaching. From the students' perspective, this situation seems fraught with difficulties. Just as engaged students are more likely to be enthusiastic and motivated in their studies and therefore put in more effort and achieve more highly, it is reasonable to expect the same of engaged teachers: enthusiastic and interested teachers who are reflective of the needs and backgrounds of their student cohort are more effective teachers. Furthermore, the teaching approach shapes the way students go about their studies (Biggs, 2005; Prosser & Trigwell, 1999): a teacher merely delivering information developed elsewhere may be seen as less likely to provide a teaching and learning forum that encourages student engagement and study commitment.

RATIONALE OF THE PROGRAMME TO ESTABLISH THE CAMPUS EDUCATION STRENGTHS

Many institutions worldwide offer broad-based degrees. In the competitive and globalised higher education setting, the challenge is to maintain and increase quality. Differentiating the programme by shaping it to meet the needs of the likely student cohort and setting was seen in the foreign branch campus as an important way of achieving this.

Being designated as an 'education strengths' was not an automatic process, and specified criteria had to be met before a programme could be accepted as an education strength and receive the funding from the central body for implementation. Proposed 'strength' projects were evaluated by the Campus Education Committee against the selection criteria and their requests for funding. The criteria for acceptance as an education strength (and access to the funding) was to develop the curriculum in a way that contributed to the foreign branch campus' branding in the local and regional setting, to the campus strategic plan, and to lead the wider university (that is, to have a focus in an area that is unique in the university). The resultant curriculum is also sound pedagogically as it is highly relevant to the student cohort. From a competitive perspective, contextualised rather than broad-based programs are tailored to meet local and regional needs and so assist the institution to develop an identity which differentiates it from the wider university and assists with its branding. It also appeals more directly to prospective students globally who may be interested in such courses.

The development of curricula as strengths provides a focus for ongoing content development and for staffing, and, by their alignment with campus research strengths that are shaped along the same lines, this potentially deepens the research-teaching link. This approach does not mean giving up areas of teaching with less developed research capability, but that greater research-teaching alignment provides a strong basis for the research-teaching nexus and so contributes to the excellence of the teaching programme.

In a setting where academic/teaching staff's involvement in the development of the teaching programme has been limited, it is not surprising that there was a need for a change in the organisation so as to shape the attitudes of the teaching staff, and eventually as explained previously, to contribute towards learner engagement. Crosling, Edwards, and Schroder (2008) provide a fuller explanation of organisational change in a higher education institution, of which many of the aspects relevant to the education strengths programme are overviewed in this chapter. Overall though, it needs to be remembered that changing staff attitudes and approaches is not simple because, as Toyne (1993) has explained, staff are being asked to operate differently in their teaching. Toyne (1993) also explained that loss of independence and autonomy by staff inhibits organisational change. In contrast to this, the education strengths programme had the distinct advantage of providing staff with increased independence and autonomy in their teaching programmes and so increasing the likelihood of their engagement in teaching.

The education strengths programme as a vehicle to contribute to the transformation of teacher attitudes also aligns with Trowler's (1998) views on organisational change. He explains that a 'bottom up' as well as 'top down' approach enables staff and management to develop a shared vision, thus facilitating commitment to the change. Commitment, according to Trowler (1998) is also facilitated by 'hands on experience' and 'room for experimentation and adaptation' (Trowler, 1998, p. 153) and both of these are hallmarks of the education strengths programme. One of the major stumbling blocks to the development of the programme and teacher engagement may be seen in the fact that organisations tend to be homeostatic (Goodstein & Burke, 1997) and need to be 'unfrozen' (1991) for change to occur. In this context, the funding associated with the strength programme, combined with the opportunity of independence and autonomy it offered, may have acted as stimulators to unfreezing the organisation. Furthermore, the educational strength programme allowed for the three conditions that Carnall (1997) identified for effective change. The first of these, of awareness or understanding the need for change and capability or feeling that they can cope with the change, were met by the programme in that staff were offered the opportunity to initiate, develop and submit their applications for education strength recognition, rather than these being imposed from above. The third of Carnall's (1997) conditions, inclusion or 'ownership' of the change process, was met in that, as with the previous point, staff opted into the programme, rather than opting out. Furthermore, the programme by nature encapsulated ownership, compared with the delivery of a teaching programme designed and developed by others elsewhere. It thus complies with Dirks, Cummings, and Pierce (1996) perspective where the degree of 'psychological ownership' that individuals have for an organisation are self-initiated, evolutionary and additive. Schools and staff nominated to put forward initiatives for approval as strengths. They were evolutionary developments of the curricula in the context of the evolution of the foreign branch campus in establishing its own identity in the region, and were additive in that funds were available to implement the programmes.

PROGRAMME IMPLEMENTATION

The programme to evaluate the education strengths submissions was inclusive, again supporting the spirit of ownership and commitment. Schools submitted applications for education strengths programmes, and were assessed by a taskforce of the members of the campus education committee in relation to the approval criteria. Included on the taskforce was a senior member of the advancement unit, which, among other roles, is responsible for promoting the institutions and attracting prospective students. All of the proposed strengths had a team leader and a team, assisting a sense of collaboration and commitment to the project and its development. Following a rigorous evaluation process, five education strengths were awarded from three of the campus schools (one large school had three strength approvals). The programmes all reflect a focus on the local and regional context.

For example, the strength 'Tropical Biology', is the focus of the School of Science. It responds to the local setting and indeed draws students to the campus from other campuses of the university, and from other universities. This experientially based programme draws on the local context in a way that cannot be achieved in other settings of the university, being a focus specific to the off campus setting. The extended trips to tropical forests mean that students are interacting at a close level on a topic of mutual interest and experience. Students get to know other students from their own campus and from other campuses and universities, assisting their social engagement, deepening and increasing the relevance of their campus studies, and widening their international horizons as they mix with students from other countries.

Islamic Economic Development is again an ideal theme for a strength, with the foreign branch campus being located in a country with a large Muslim population. The strength complements the Islamic studies focus in other sections of the university on Australian campuses and therefore leads the university in this regard. Again drawing students from other educational settings, this approach in the Malaysian setting makes real for students the issues of study, as well as providing an enriching educational experience, again facilitating students' interest and encouraging students to continue with their studies. The School of Arts and Social Sciences strength is on social transformation in Southeast Asia, again a theme highly relevant to this developing region. Including aspects such as cinema studies in the region, a focus is provided for both teachers and students as they engage in teaching and learning, requiring input from their experiences and understandings of the local context and engendering meaning. The School of Business also has a strength named Asian Business Strategy, providing a forum for the interaction of agents and factors for organisational vibrancy, including industry partners. These initiatives again make relevant to the local and global economy the studies that students undertake in the school. Such an industry focus provides a platform that teachers can draw on in their teaching and a context. A further School of Business strength named Capital Market Behaviour again increases the effectiveness of the student experience in the school through developing curriculum and teaching approaches, including foci on internationalisation and research-led teaching.

All of the strengths have reached their first 12 months of operation and all have been approved for a further 12 months. Further strength proposals are emerging, indicating the value of these projects for the campus and the schools, as well as for the staff that participate in them. As a significant indicator of the value of the education strengths programme, the university overall has also adopted the programme, requiring faculties to develop their own strengths.

Hypothetically, it may be argued that a disadvantage of such a programme is that it may divide the staff in a school, leading to an exclusive rather than an inclusive climate. However, in a climate where staff may have become disengaged to some extent because of limited opportunity to engage in curriculum development activities, some competition for engagement in education projects may be valuable, stimulating all staff to new levels of teaching, for the betterment of the educational programme overall, including the students.

CONCLUSION AND COMMENTS

In addressing the complex issue of student retention in their higher education studies, it is known that students who are engaged and enthused by their studies are more likely to put in effort, achieve more highly and therefore continue. It is also well established that the teaching impacts on the approach that students take to their learning and that enthusiastic teachers are more likely to assist their students to engage in their studies. In the setting of a foreign branch campus of a university which is developing and contextualising itself increasingly in the region in which it is located, the evolutionary path may be seen as similar to the maturation process of a child within a family. Initially, the child needs to be guided and supported to learn how to function effectively. In the later years of childhood, as the child hungers for independence, it needs to find its identity in a way that differentiates it from the family, which at the same time adds richness to the family experience. The organisational change in an institution such as that explained in this chapter may be seen as a similar process. Moving from the initial focus on effective operation to greater independence and autonomy, the university overall and the region in which the institution is located can be enriched by its contribution. The education strengths programme addresses these issues.

The need for teaching staff to move away from dependence on the parent institution and take responsibility for their teaching is facilitated by this process. Not only is the unique contribution of the institution to the wider university and local area identified and developed, it provides a sense of pride and achievement for the campus staff overall and particularly for the members of the strength development teams. This adds to confidence, enthusiasm and commitment to teaching in the ways explained previously. The scene is thus set with teachers who have a sense of ownership over their programmes to engage their students in their learning. Furthermore, the exciting educational approaches that emanate from the education strength programme in themselves are engaging for students. Although it is difficult to pin it down, it seems that these developments create a vibrant teaching setting that motivates students to continue with their studies rather than dropping out.

CHAPTER 7

ENGAGING STUDENTS TO ENHANCE PROGRESSION BEYOND THE FIRST DEGREE

Liz Thomas

ABSTRACT

Purpose – *This chapter argues that institutions should take a strategic, integrated approach to enable all students to progress successfully beyond their first degree, to additional education or training or to the labour market.*

Methodology/approach – *The chapter reviews the literature about the progression of students from equity groups to the labour market and postgraduate study and the explanations for lower rates of success. The remainder of the chapter explores what institutions in England are doing to facilitate equality of outcomes for graduates from equity groups, based on analysis of the Widening Participation Strategic Assessments (WPSAs). Each WPSA was coded, and query reports were read and re-read to identify common approaches and themes.*

Findings – *Literature finds that graduates from diverse backgrounds and equity groups have poorer progression outcomes than other students. The WPSAs show that the majority of institutions are addressing employability but not progression to postgraduate study. On the basis of mainstream approaches to engaging students and developing their employability, the*

Institutional Transformation to Engage a Diverse Student Body
International Perspectives on Higher Education Research, Volume 6, 253–269
ISSN: 1479-3628/doi:10.1108/S1479-3628(2011)0000006025

chapter presents a seven-point strategic approach to enhancing the progression and success of graduates from a diverse student body.

Research limitations – *There are limitations associated with analysis of the WPSAs and that there is so little consideration of progression to postgraduate study.*

Practical implications – *This chapter proposes that institutions adopt an integrated and strategic approach to enhancing the progression and success of students.*

Social implications – *This approach addresses progression inequalities.*

Originality/value – *This chapter provides original insights into progression to postgraduate study for diverse students.*

Keywords: Progression; employability; access to postgraduate study; strategic and integrated approach

INTRODUCTION

This chapter argues that institutions should enable all students to progress successfully beyond their first degree. Progression may be to additional education or training (e.g. a top-up degree, postgraduate study, vocational or professional learning), to the labour market or to pursue other personal or professional objectives. Progression is the final stage of the student lifecycle model (see Chapter 2); however, in relation to widening participation, it receives less attention than earlier stages of the model (Thomas et al., 2005), and progression to further learning has largely been absent, the emphasis being on employability and progression to the labour market.

Drawing on and extending Yorke's (2004) definition of employability, progression can be defined as institutions preparing and enabling students to develop the capacities, understandings and personal attributes to make an informed, chosen and successful transition from their current programme of study into further learning, employment or to pursue other objectives. Institutional efforts to inform and enable successful progression need to be integrated into activities across the student lifecycle, including the early stages, and crucially, embedded into the core curriculum.

PROGRESSION OF STUDENTS FROM DIVERSE BACKGROUNDS AND EQUITY GROUPS

Research finds that graduates from diverse background and equity groups have poorer progression outcomes than other graduates. Table 1 presents a brief summary of the labour market and postgraduate progression trends for specific groups.

Explanations for Poorer Progression in the Graduate Labour Market and Postgraduate Study

Research studies suggest that barriers to equivalent success in the labour market for graduates of lower socio-economic status and from other equity groups are due to both direct and indirect barriers (Blasko et al., 2003). The following discussion draws on evidence about progression to the labour market and relates it where possible to evidence about progression to postgraduate study.

Indirect effects relate to educational opportunities and choices, such as poor schooling or institution attended, which in turn influence a graduate's experience in the labour market or access to postgraduate study. Employers systematically favour graduates with certain educational characteristics such as good A level grades, attending high status higher education institution (HEI) (Brown & Hesketh, 2003; Chevalier & Conlon, 2003), preference for some subjects over others (Pitcher & Purcell, 1998) and a good degree classification, (Purcell & Hogarth, 1999). Each of these employer preferences tends to privilege middle-class students and disadvantage working class students (e.g. Machin et al., 2009; Keep & Mayhew, 2004). Wakeling and Kyriacou (2010) report similar biases in relation to postgraduate research degrees, in particular, degree classification, institution attended and subject studied.

Direct effects refer to those where students from certain backgrounds are disadvantaged in the labour market or access to postgraduate study compared to contemporaries with similar educational achievements and experiences. Thus, graduates from non-traditional backgrounds do less well in the labour market and access to postgraduate study, even when other variables such as entry qualifications, institution attended, subject studied and degree classification are controlled for (see, e.g., Hogarth et al., 1997). Working class male graduates in particular experience more disadvantage in

Table 1. Summary of Research Evidence about Progression into the
Labour Market and Postgraduate Study, by Specific Target Groups.

Target Group	Progression Experiences
Graduates from lower socio economic groups (SEGs)	For people from SEGs being a graduate offers labour market advantages compared to non-graduate peers, especially for males (Dearden, McGranahan, & Sianesi, 2004). But SEGs are disadvantaged compared to traditional graduates in terms of gaining full-time employment and/or salaries, particularly in the long term (Purcell & Hogarth, 1999; Smith, McKnight, & Naylor, 2000; Machin et al., 2009). Graduates from professional families/higher socio-economic backgrounds are more likely to be involved in further study (HEPI, 2004, 2010; Machin et al., 2009). Those from families who have no previous higher education experience are less likely to progress to taught postgraduate study (Stuart, Lido, Morgan, Solomon, & Akroyd, 2008). Lower socio-economic status (SES) does not have a *direct* and *immediate* effect on access to postgraduate research, i.e. when factors such as institution attended, subject studied and degree classification are taken into account (Wakeling & Kyriacou 2010). Institution attended is strongly influenced by SES (Machin et al., 2009). Financial circumstances (Anderson, Johnson, & Milligan, 2000) and attitudes towards debt also impact on progression to post-graduate study (Stuart et al., 2008 and Wakeling & Kyriacou, 2010).
Disabled graduates	Disabled graduates are less likely to progress to full-time employment than peers and have lower earnings than non-disabled graduates (Hogarth, Purcell, & Wilson, 1997; Machin et al., 2010), but they are more likely to progress to further study (Croucher, Evans, & Leacy, 2005; Machin et al., 2009). The difference is less pronounced for graduates with unseen disabilities (Croucher et al., 2005).

Table 1. (*Continued*)

Target Group	Progression Experiences
Black and minority ethnic (BME) graduates	Ethnic minorities experience more difficulty in securing employment after graduation than white graduates (Connor, Tvers, Modood, & Hillage, 2004; Blasko, Brennan, Little, & Shah, 2003; Machin et al., 2009), and men in particular are more likely to be unemployed. Once they have secured employment there is evidence of parity or better with majority graduates (Connor et al., 2004; Blasko et al., 2003; Machin et al., 2009). Different minorities have different trends, and there is some disagreement about these.
	BME students are more likely to progress to a taught postgraduate programme than white students (Stuart et al., 2008) and less likely to proceed to a research degree (Connor et al., 2004), however some BME groups are over represented and some under-represented in research degrees (Wakeling, 2009a).
Mature graduates	Male and female mature graduates experience greater disadvantages in the labour market than younger graduates (Conlon, 2001). In part this is due to discrimination by employers, especially in some fields. Stuart et al. (2008) found no age group effects on intentions to progress to taught postgraduate study.
Women graduates	Women graduates earn less than men (Hogarth et al., 1997 and Metcalf, 1997), and this difference is greater if they have a family and a career break. However, being a graduate is an effective way of redressing gender inequality in comparison to non-graduates. More recent data (Machin et al., 2009) finds a broadly similar pattern.
	Women are more likely than men to progress to taught postgraduate programmes (Stuart et al., 2008), but men are more likely than women to progress to research degrees (Wakeling & Kyriacou, 2010).

Table 1. (*Continued*)

Target Group	Progression Experiences
Vocational sub-degree qualifiers	Data are very limited about this group. Vocational students progress to further study and employment, while unemployment appears to be very low. There are however distinct subject variations. Labour market returns are significantly lower than for first degree graduates. (Little et al., 2003).
	Students who study more practical or applied courses at undergraduate level are less likely to progress to postgraduate study (Stuart et al., 2008). Institution attended and subject studied have a strong bearing on progression to research degrees (Wakeling & Kyriacou, 2010). These factors suggest that vocational students in general are less likely to progress to postgraduate study.
Part-time graduates	Part-time students have different labour market expectations, as the majority are in employment while they are studying, but many do report labour market gains. This is mediated by subject, gender, age and ethnicity. (Brennan, Mills, Shah, & Woodley, 2000).
Non-traditional groups and multiple disadvantage	Some studies do not delineate specific under-represented groups, or look at multiple disadvantages. These studies show that non-traditional graduates experience disadvantage in the labour market compared with their traditional counterparts, and these are related to both personal characteristics and educational choices. It should be recognised that particular characteristics are not experienced in isolation, and each individual combines different diversity characteristics as discussed in Chapter 1.

the labour market – such as periods of unemployment – and are less likely to be in managerial or professional posts than middle-class counterparts. This is in part because the recruitment process is often designed to bring out the personal qualities of graduates, and thus the social, cultural and economic backgrounds of candidates are exposed. According to Brown and Hesketh (2003), it is very difficult for those from disadvantaged backgrounds to demonstrate the 'personal' capital required to gain elite employment. These reasons may also influence the allocation of research council funding, which Wakeling (2009b) found was more likely to be awarded to students from higher socio-economic groups than lower ones.

Furthermore, students and graduates from lower socio-economic status groups may have access to limited amounts and quality of information, advice and guidance about HE in general (Quinn et al., 2005b; UCAS, 2002) and access to comparatively low reserves of cultural capital (i.e. knowledge relating to HE and graduate employment) that can be called upon from family, school and other spheres (UCAS, 2002). This may reduce their confidence to enter and engage in HE processes and hinder them further when they make the transition beyond undergraduate education. Students from non-traditional backgrounds may also lack social capital – that is, networks of contacts to provide 'hot knowledge' about postgraduate education and labour market opportunities. In addition, a lack of economic capital makes many non-traditional students, especially those from working class families, more reliant on part-time employment while they are studying in HE, which hinders their engagement in academic and extracurricular activities, further reducing their opportunities for acquiring additional social capital. Hills' (2003) research in one HEI suggests that non-traditional students either do not know where to look for information to assist their job search or they are not using it. She also presents some evidence that suggests that working-class students can disqualify themselves from particular professions as they believe they will not fit in or would not be recruited. This relates to self-confidence and a caricature about some employment fields. Furthermore, Caspi, Entner Wright, Moffitt, and Silva (1998) find that personal and family characteristics begin to shape labour market outcomes years before people enter the labour market, and they remain significant even when educational duration and qualifications are taken into account (the effect is found to be less significant by Bond & Saunders, 1999, however).

Although there is very limited research about access to postgraduate education, it is reasonable to anticipate that many of the same issues come into play as well as the obvious barrier related to the cost of postgraduate education, which is borne substantially by students themselves. In summary, the barriers to progression to postgraduate study are likely to include the following:

- Poor early educational choice (e.g. institution or subject) may limit postgraduate progression opportunities as some institutions or courses or funders prefer more selective institutions, and some subjects have more limited progression routes.

- Lower degree classification or participation in fewer extracurricular activities due to other commitments while studying (e.g. employment and caring responsibilities) may have an impact on postgraduate progression opportunities.
- Selection bias against students from certain social and educational backgrounds who do not have personal capital to be accepted at elite institutions.
- Lack of economic capital to pay for postgraduate education.
- Limited access to information, advice and guidance about postgraduate opportunities due to lack of family or educational cultural capital and social networks.
- Lack of confidence to apply to postgraduate study and a belief that 'people like me don't go to postgraduate study', derived from lower family or educational cultural capital or family expectations or not knowing people who progress to postgraduate study (more limited social capital).

INSTITUTIONAL APPROACHES TO IMPROVING GRADUATE PROGRESSION

HEIs can and should play a fundamental role in improving the future opportunities of graduates from equity groups. This should involve looking at both how they prepare students for progression beyond a first degree and reviewing and challenging employment and postgraduate selection processes, which directly or inadvertently disadvantage students from equity groups. The latter is an area in particular which institutions can have a significant impact as they are the organisations that admit students to postgraduate programmes.

The remainder of this chapter explores what institutions in England are doing at the later stages of the student lifecycle to facilitate equality of outcomes for graduates from equity groups. This is based on analysis of the Widening Participation Strategic Assessments (WPSAs). The request for WPSAs, the method of analysis and its limitations are discussed in Chapter 3.

HEIs were expected to include key information about WP across the student lifecycle, including employability (HEFCE, 2009, §. 10). It is therefore unsurprising that the WPSAs demonstrate widespread commitment to the student lifecycle approach to widening participation. Consequently, the majority of institutions (112, 87%) mention employability and 76 (59%) provide detail about their processes. Conversely, the majority of institutions (over 85%) do not refer to progression to postgraduate study, and only 18 institutions (14%) detail how they are addressing widening participation to postgraduate study.

However, as discussed, there are likely to be commonalities between the issues that restrict the progression of graduates from lower socio-economic and other 'non-traditional' groups to the graduate labour market and those that limit their progression to postgraduate study. The analysis of the 76 HEIs (59%) that provided detail about how they are addressing employability issues identified a number of different approaches, including the following:

• separate provision such as an autonomous careers service, which all students can make use of;
• targeted interventions for specific groups of students who have poorer experiences in the graduate labour market;
• co-curricular programmes to engage students in activities to develop their CVs and enhance their employability;
• partnerships between careers professionals and faculty staff to deliver integrated and tailored learning to develop the employability (or future opportunities) of all students/graduates;
• integrated curriculum approach, embedding the development and recognition of employability skills and confidence across the curriculum and delivered by mainstream academic staff; and
• a strategic and integrated approach to enhancing the progression of all students, which is discussed in the next section.

Developing a Strategic and Integrated Approach to Enhancing the Progression and Success of Graduates

The following discussion about developing a strategic and integrated approach to enhancing the progression of all students draws heavily on the WPSA analysis of institutional approaches to employability, as the work in the area of progression to postgraduate study is very underdeveloped. It is proposed here that this strategic approach could and should be applied to progression more generally and not just to progression to the labour market.

A strategic approach, which includes a strong commitment to integrated provision, is most likely to involve institutional transformation, but also to have the greatest impact on the progression experiences of all students, and especially those from specific equity groups, who are less likely to engage with additional professional services and extracurricular activities than their more traditional peers (Dodgson & Bolam, 2002; Hills, 2003). This is particularly true for students who are not located on the HEI site (perhaps because they live at home, study at partner institutions or are work-based or distance learners), and for those who have other commitments and spend less time on site, and those who do not recognise the importance of accessing these services, or who lack the confidence to do so. The importance of such an integrated approach is articulated clearly by one HEI in its WPSA:

> There was a clear recognition that employability was not just the responsibility of the individual student and the careers service, but was a collaborative venture between our students and the institution. This involved students as individuals, and in groups, staff from faculties and services, alumni and employers ...

> Each faculty in the University has prepared their individual employability plans. These plans have enabled the institutional commitment to employability for all, to reach down to the learning environment in which most students' perspective is focused – that of the faculty and programme ... .

> This mainstreaming approach to supporting employability for those most disadvantaged in the labour market has been developed to help avoid the danger that support services in the field of careers and employability often focus on the most able and motivated rather than those most in need. By embedding activities in the curriculum it is easier to reach those with significant part time and vacation employment commitments, who are often those from under-represented groups. All students are embraced by the faculty employability plans, and in the first year... an estimated 2500 students engaged in explicit support activities.

Analysis of the WPSAs suggests that a strategic and integrated approach includes the following elements, shown also in Diagram 1:

(i) Linking together interventions to improve the progression of all students.

(ii) Addressing progression issues throughout the student lifecycle, including pre-entry.

(iii) Ensuring all faculties and programmes enhance the progression and success of their students.

(iv) Integrating progression into the core curriculum through a direct or partnership approach to ensure that all students benefit from it.

(v) Providing additional, complimentary interventions targeted at specific groups of students who experience challenges in the graduate labour market and accessing progression study and funding, and

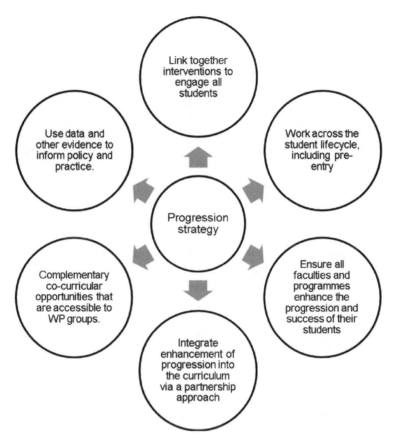

Diagram 1. A Strategic and Integrated Approach to Engage Students and Promotes Progression and Success. *Source*: Adapted from Thomas et al. (2010a, 2010b)

ensuring that all co-curricular opportunities are accessible to equity target groups.

(vi) Underpinning interventions with analysis of data, for example, to understand differential experiences of graduates from equity groups in the labour market/postgraduate access or identify differential take-up and impact of services and interventions.

The ways in which institutions are addressing these key elements of a strategic employability (and progression) policy to support diverse students to be successful is discussed now.

(i) Linking together a range of interventions or approaches to ensure that all students are engaged to improve their employability (progression).

In developing an institutional approach to employability, some institutions recognised that this involves bringing together or linking up a series of interventions and approaches to ensure that the employability needs of all students are met. This is illustrated in this quote from one institution:

> The development of employability skills is a key aim of higher education programmes and the University is committed to enhancing these through provision of a range of opportunities. In fulfilment of this objective the University is already planning to review the undergraduate programme with a view to incorporating more extensive vocational training; increase opportunities for student volunteering; introduce a system of personal development planning (PDP); develop a mechanism for supporting campus employment opportunities for students; and improve the range and quality of transferable skills developed by postgraduate students.

It is interesting to see that in this example, taken from a pre-1992 university, the strategic approach extends to developing the employability of postgraduate students but does not directly address the progression of undergraduates to postgraduate study.

(ii) Addressing employability (progression) across the student lifecycle, including pre-entry work.

It is recognised that progression is not just something that needs to be considered at the end of a programme of study, but rather people's knowledge, expectations and capacities should be developed throughout. This should apply equally to progression to further learning as to employabilityment. This includes working with students at an early stage to help them make informed choices about HE courses and to form expectations about their chosen programme and how it will enable them to fulfil their career aspirations. One institution notes how they have built careers guidance into their pre-entry work and target additional support on learners who have less access to social capital, which will inform their understanding of HE courses and graduate careers:

> Pre-entry HE Careers Guidance is available for all, but "intensive" resources (impartial face to face/one to one guidance) is targeted to WP profile populations (e.g. care leavers/ foster parents; access to HE students/adult returners; compact students; new diploma students). This takes place on campus and in other learning institutions (target schools; community settings; colleges of FE).

(iii) Creating mechanisms to ensure that all faculties and programmes enhance the employability (and progression) of their students.

An institution-wide progression strategy needs to ensure that all faculties, departments and programmes are developing the progression and success of their students across the whole student lifecycle, as this quote suggests,

> Ensure that all academic programmes focus on employability, including careers advice and skills development (e.g. interview techniques and CV development) within a clear strategy for personal development for graduates.

(iv) Integrating employability (and progression) into the core curriculum through direct or partnership approaches to ensure that all students benefit.

To enable as many students as possible to enhance their progression, it is necessary to take an integrated approach, with delivery taking place in the core curriculum. Some institutions have developed a direct approach, involving discipline staff in the delivery of employability, which is integrated into core course learning. This could include the development of skills valued by employers, real-world problem-based learning and team working, which simulate the world of work and work placements and could be extended to assist students to develop their capacity for progression to postgraduate study. For example,

> Graduate employability has an extremely high priority in [our] strategic plans and all academic provision at undergraduate level, whether full-time or sandwich, provides employability pathways for all students. These enable students to acquire the knowledge, personal and professional skills and encourage the attitudes that will support their future development and employment. Additionally the School is committed to providing all students with opportunities to engage in real and relevant work experience whether that be placement, work based learning or work related learning. Both the pathways and the work experience opportunities provided are monitored to assess their effectiveness for both WP and non WP students and enhanced as necessary.

Some institutions have developed partnerships between careers profes-sionals and academic faculty staff and students in the institution to deliver an integrated approach to employability. A range of approaches can be identified across the HE sector, including the provision of training for academic staff, the co-development of learning materials and the co-delivery of sessions. For example,

> Careers Advisers spend between 60-80% of their time on programme delivery and planning with programme teams and between 20-30% on one to one services, face to face or on-line ... Curriculum contacts have increased by 28% from 2006/07 to 2007/08. In semester 1 2008/09 [name of careers service] has delivered employability embedded in the curriculum to 4354 students. Additional careers adviser time and support would facilitate the developments and extend the practice of partnership working with faculties.

Again, such an approach could be extended to also consider issues and skills relevant to progression to postgraduate study.

(v) Providing complimentary extracurricular activities, which are accessible to all students to enhance progression and success.

Participation in voluntary work, clubs and societies, relevant work placements and overseas studies improves students experience in the graduate labour market, whereas participation in part-time employment is generally detrimental (Blasko et al 2003; Stuart, Lido, Morgan, & May, 2009). Institutions have developed a range of co-curricular programmes to engage students in activities to develop their CVs and enhance their employability. A common approach is the development of an institutional award, which provides recognition and credit for students who participate in these types of activities. For example,

> The [name of university] Award is an achievement award for undergraduate and taught postgraduate students at the University. The Award is designed to enhance the employability of [name of university] graduates by providing official recognition and evidence of extra-curricular activities and achievements. These include: attendance at skills sessions and training courses, active participation in sporting and musical activities, engagement in work experience and voluntary work.

Another institution notes the value to existing students of contributing to WP outreach activities and is formalising this for students:

> Our own students and graduates play a vital role at all stages in the delivery of our Widening Participation Strategy. We have developed our programmes to formalise this involvement, which includes rigorous selection and training and, for many, the opportunity to acquire important employability skills and to receive accreditation and academic credit for their involvement.

It should be recognised however that participation in these types of extracurricular activities is shaped by student characteristics (Stuart et al., 2009). Many students from diverse, non-traditional backgrounds are unable or unwilling to participate in co-curricular activities. Stuart reports the link between engagement and widening participation:

> There are a number of groups of students who are not engaged in university activities, which co-relates with the categories often broadly defined as 'widening participation' students: working-class students, ethnic minority students and mature students. This is for a variety of reasons but all of which 'disadvantage' students in obtaining what is considered to be the traditional student experience. These widening participation students spend more time studying, are more involved in their families, whether they are mature or not, and are involved in more paid part-time work so unable to spend as much time at university. (Stuart et al., 2009, p. 3)

Ensuring that all co-curricular opportunities are accessible to equity groups is challenging. Institutional responses include identifying and promoting the benefits for students, offering incentives and measuring take-up by specific types of students and acting on data. Benefits and incentives include academic accreditation and financial reward. Some institutions are offering paid opportunities to students from widening participation groups to develop their employability skills:

> There are specific Earn and Learn opportunities available for WP profile students on course which help them to finance study and to access enhanced support to develop their employability skills and experiences whilst in HE. There are opportunities, particularly targeted to WP profile students, to work as a Student Ambassador, Mentor, Lead SA or Mentor, Project Leader, Residential Helper, Student Enabler etc. All posts have formalised recruitment/selection processes and training programmes with sessions to explicitly link the student experience to careers analysis, confidence building and employability when completed.

In addition, institutions provide a raft of interventions targeted at specific groups to address some of the challenges they face with progression (especially into the labour market). The groups targeted include students with disabilities and mental health issues, Black and Minority Ethnic (BME) students, low-income students, first-generation entrants and students with no family experience of graduate employment and students over the age of 30 on commencing a degree. By far, the most common form of support is coaching and mentoring of these specific students, sometimes making use of institutional alumni. Other interventions include raising awareness of employer requirements, internships and work placements. Efforts to target students to encourage and facilitate progression to postgraduate study are few and far between and not well developed (Thomas et al., 2010b).

(vi) Underpinning interventions with analysis of data

It is important to ensure that a progression strategy and related interventions and approaches are informed by data analysis, both in terms of planning the strategy and interventions (e.g. to understand differential experiences of graduates from equity groups in the labour market) and to identify differential take-up and impact of services and interventions, and then act upon this information. The following two examples illustrate these two approaches to data collection:

> We will collect and analyse employability data of under-represented groups of students against comparable Universities to inform the development of faculty and programme level action plans to improve the employability of all students.

A new online events management system will allow the Careers Service to develop a clearer picture of who is attending specific events and where the gaps are in terms of courses where students are being less proactive in their career planning.

The use of data in relation to postgraduate progression is uncommon, and the references suggest that institutions are only starting to think about the issues, and the first challenge is to identify the groups they should be targeting and monitor their performance. One institution reported,

Initial work will involve identifying existing undergraduates or recent graduates from under-represented backgrounds, using their home postcode data on entry to under-graduate study as an initial identifier. Much work on this objective is yet to be refined, therefore the development of reliable methods of identification will be an early focus.

CONCLUSIONS

HEIs in England have largely embraced the challenges of working with students to enhance their employability (this may of course be influenced by university league tables such as the Complete University Guide, which examines 'graduate prospects' as a measure of employability, see http://www.thecompleteuniversityguide.co.uk/single.htm?ipg = 7281). The approaches reported in the 2009 WPSAs show a move towards a more integrated approach to developing student employability than previously (see Thomas & Jones, 2007). This is in stark contrast to institutional approaches to facilitating progression to postgraduate study: over 85% of institutions do not refer to postgraduate access or the postgraduate learning experience in their WPSA (Thomas et al., 2010b). Institutions do not have in place more than the odd intervention to promote and enable progression to postgraduate study. Often it is not explicit whether they relate to taught or research degrees, or both. Furthermore, issues about targeting and identifying students are embryonic, and strategies to engage these students in postgraduate study are thin. Interventions include analysing institutional data to understand who is and is not participating in postgraduate study and creating ways for targeting students, offering taster sessions to overcome a lack of knowledge or exposure to postgraduate study and the provision of financial support. There is however an emerging recognition of the need for institutions to engage with the issue of widening access to postgraduate provision. For example, one institution writes,

Currently, widening participation thinking is predominantly focused on full-time undergraduates and pre-HE/youth work but it is recognised that we need to refine our understanding of the issues around access to postgraduate study in the next period.

The strategic and integrated approach to student diversity and progression, which is proposed and discussed earlier, would enable institutions to embed progression to postgraduate study into much of their work on employability. This would involve institutional transformation to engage students in developing their capacities for progression in the core curriculum, and it could have a positive effect on graduate progression and institutional postgraduate recruitment.

CHAPTER 7.1

TRANSFORMING LEARNING: ENGAGING STUDENTS WITH THE BUSINESS COMMUNITY

Sandra Hill

ABSTRACT

This study explores the role of social capital in the development of employability skills and attributes of first-generation undergraduate students in a business school.

The research, based on the reflections of graduates, examines the impact of social capital on participation in higher education and investigates the conditions within the learning environment, which enhance or inhibit the development of bridging and linking social capital, as students connect with networks within the institution and with the wider business community.

The findings suggest that the ability to recognise and activate bridging and linking social capital is an important determinant of employability. The analysis illustrates that when students have opportunities to connect with and work within a variety of networks, they build a range of employability skills and capabilities, particularly the interpersonal and social skills valued by employers.

Institutional Transformation to Engage a Diverse Student Body
International Perspectives on Higher Education Research, Volume 6, 271–277
Copyright © 2011 by Emerald Group Publishing Limited
All rights of reproduction in any form reserved
ISSN: 1479-3628/doi:10.1108/S1479-3628(2011)0000006026

Students, who are confident and have the necessary skills to participate in a variety of networks within the immediate environment and with the wider business community, are not only able to access a greater range of resources but are more able to recognise the potential benefits that these activities have to offer. The reflections of the participants also illustrate that the skills and competencies that enable them to network effectively need to be developed deliberately. By supporting students in recognising the relationship between bridging and linking social capital and employability, and giving them the opportunity to reflect upon the achievement of interpersonal skills and affective capabilities, their understanding and acknowledgement of employability is enhanced.

Keywords: First-generation entrants; employability; social capital

INTRODUCTION

This case study describes an approach taken within a business school to transform the learning experience of students undertaking a business studies degree. The students, many of whom were the first generation to participate in higher education (Thomas & Quinn, 2006), were successful in their academic studies, but still appeared to lack confidence and self-belief in their own ability to achieve success as capable business graduates. A lack of experience in connecting with the business community in which they would seek employment meant that they lacked skills and confidence in accessing resources that would inevitably be useful as they sought graduate employment.

Although the development of employability skills was written into their programme of study, there was little evidence to suggest that the social and interpersonal skills, valued by employers and necessary to make connections with diverse others, were being addressed within the curriculum or that their value was recognised by students.

A new approach had to be devised, which encouraged students to acknowledge the importance of these skills and attributes, and greater attention had to be given within the classroom to encourage students to reflect on the transferability of skills. Furthermore, opportunities had to be sought to enable students to practice these skills within the business environment.

THE CONTEXT

The University, located in the west of Scotland, is a new institution formed after the merger of an established modern university and a small college of higher education. The institution serves areas of the country, which have low participation rates in higher education (Tysome, 2007). Striving to be the 'University of Choice' for local students, a number of initiatives to improve employability have been introduced.

The University states in its vision that it seeks to develop confident, enterprising, creative graduates who are able to fully contribute to Scotland and the West's economic growth. Initiatives to support this aim include the launch of an Employability Link, which has specific responsibility for creating more opportunities for students to develop employability skills and be able to access relevant work placements as part of their studies. The Link provides workshops to help strengthen employability skills with students and specialist advice to academic programme teams. Extra funding was made available to provide additional contact hours within core modules of programmes specifically to address employability and personal development planning. However, despite such measures and programme descriptions detailing the employability and personal development skills that would be achieved within the curriculum, recognition of the attainment of these was still not happening for a significant number of students. There appeared to be a missing link between what happened in the internal learning environment and what is required and valued in the business community.

Research undertaken with graduate recruiters (Kelly, 2002; Archer & Davidson, 2008) has consistently highlighted the fact that there remains a degree of concern with the ability of graduates to demonstrate key employability skills, specifically interpersonal and social skills. Too often, graduates are unable to recognise that these skills had been achieved and have difficulty demonstrating their attainment to potential employers.

This may be because students have had little time to reflect upon how and where these capabilities are developed within programmes. The measuring and assessment of their achievement can be difficult and not compatible with traditional assessment methods. Indeed, some academic staff may believe that such activities are outwith the realms of their responsibility (Harvey, 2003; Honeybone, 2002) and may feel uncomfortable or unskilled in identifying and developing such skills (Mason, Williams, Cramer, & Guile, 2002; Layer, 2004).

A different approach needed to be taken to help students in identify those external connections, which would enhance the skills and attributes that make up the personal competencies and transferable skills of employability.

DEVELOPING SOCIAL CAPITAL

Catts and Ozga (2005) describe bonding social capital, the ties between people in similar situations, as the ability to 'get by'; bridging social capital, the more distant ties between similar people, as the ability to 'get on' and linking social capital, reaching out to those outside the immediate community, as 'getting around'. The learning environment had to provide opportunties for students to 'get on' and 'get around'.

Discussions with students had revealed a lack of experience in identifying, accessing and mobilising networks within the business community, which could give access to valuable information and resources. The importance of social capital has been increasingly recognised as an important skill in education (Dika & Singh, 2002; Thomas, 2002a, 2002b) and business (Shaw & Carter, 2004; Halpern, 2006). It was relevant that students who were expected to be enterprising, confident and creative should be able to access and mobilise valuable social capital within their immediate communities and beyond the business community.

A module was designed to provide a range of experiences to develop bridging and linking social capital and to practice the skills and capabilities needed to use these skills confidently in a range of different settings. The assessment task involved students developing a business plan for a new product or service, testing the idea with potential customers and seeking advice from sector experts.

To make the task realistic and ensure exposure to new resources, students were required to present their plan not only to academic tutors but also to external organisations with responsibility for business start-up funding such as Business Gateway and the Prince's Scottish Youth Business Trust (PSYBT). Using personal contacts, staff approached organisations to support the students and to provide guidance and feedback on the feasibility of their plans and information regarding funding opportunities. More importantly, these contacts provided access to valuable networks that enabled students to expand linking social capital.

It became clear early on that although students had some experience in working in groups, the skills and confidence needed to work with new and diverse individuals needed considerable development. A lack of information of potential sources of support and information and a lack of confidence in approaching those who were regarded as more powerful presented barriers for many of the participants. Some students also faced difficulties in their work groups ranging from a lack of experience in organising tasks and workloads to dealing effectively with conflict.

This raised the question of how well we were preparing students for working in teams in the learning environment and ultimately the workplace and that if we were truly using group work as a means of developing employability skills then far greater preparation and reflection on the development of these skills and competencies had to be incorporated into the programme.

It is too often assumed that the skills that are required to participate in groups and teams already exist within the student group and that the very act of getting students to work in a group is enough to give them the skills that are required to demonstrate them to employers. This module demonstrated that students needed to practice the social and interpersonal skills that employers value and be given feedback on performance and opportunities to become more confident and capable in utilising these skills with a range of people.

EVIDENCE OF EFFECTIVENESS

Following participation in the module, students were asked to reflect upon the development of employability skills and attributes. Using the Council for Industry in Higher Education (CIHE) employability competencies, they were able to cite a significant number of instances where they recognised an increase in skills and capabilities.

One participant, now in employment, recognised her learning in the module.

> I did not get on with one of my group but I just had to tolerate them. Now at work there are some people I don't like but you have to learn to deal with it and have a working relationship with them. I learned that in the module even though I did not know it at the time.

Another valued being able to work with different people

> It is good to work with groups you don't know to get different ideas. It helps your confidence. You also realise different things about yourself when you are away from friends.

Others described an increase in confidence in their ability to connect with a wide range of people effectively. Importantly, they also began to realise that they now had access to and were able to contribute to a range of networks, outside their immediate community, which could offer access to new resources and information.

A participant reflected on her experience of meeting with funders from the local enterprise agency.

> It was a great experience. I felt really proud that they liked my idea. I never thought I could speak to people like that. If I wanted to take my idea further I would definitely go back to them.

Another described his experiences of attending a business start-up event,

> I was looking, listening and learning from all the different people. I thought, that is where I want to be in 10 years time. It was really inspiring.

Overall, the participants related a positive experience where exposure to the business community had resulted in an appreciation of the skills and attitudes that were valued. That experience resulted in better acknowledgement of skills development, improvement in motivation in the learning environment and indeed provided role models for those who previously had little exposure to the business community.

> It was good to get someone else's viewpoint. Especially when it takes your project from being a university project to being a real project that could work. Taking it up in front of people like that gives you confidence, makes it more realistic.

REFLECTION

As well as the significant improvement in levels of confidence, having opportunities to connect with a diverse group of people resulted in changes to attitudes towards others and the recognition of the benefits of working with a wider range of people, rather than familiar friends. There was also acknowledgment of the development of other key employability skills, which are often neglected in academic programmes, such as self-knowledge and self-awareness, self-management, the development and articulation of values, including trust and respect, personal and work ethics, care and empathy towards other group members and tolerance for different approaches. These attributes are highly relevant in today's business environment and highly valued by employers.

By reflecting on their interaction with others, students were able to develop resilience and adapt to changing circumstances as they managed and, on occasion, struggled to manage the group task.

There is little doubt that engaging with others improves communication skills, and if those others are dissimilar in terms of background and values, there are opportunities to access new ideas and behaviours, to trigger creativity and to develop and share new values as well as providing potential access to resources and information relevant to employability and graduate employment.

Curricula design and delivery needs to take account of the fact that if employability skills are to be developed within programmes, then better connections need to be made with the communities in which graduates will be employed. Students need to be prepared to connect with these communities with confidence, and deliberate efforts should be made within the learning environment to enable this to happen.

For this approach to be successful, staff need to be able and willing to identify potential resources within the business community and make use of these in creative and imaginative ways. As well as being instrumental in providing space for reflection and support to develop these skills and personal competencies, staff need to put in place the structures to enable bridging social capital; they are the key nodes at the hub of activating linking social capital.

CHAPTER 8

ENABLING INSTITUTIONAL TRANSFORMATION TO ENGAGE A DIVERSE STUDENT BODY: NECESSARY CONDITIONS AND FACILITATING FACTORS

Liz Thomas

ABSTRACT

Purpose – *This chapter draws on the previous chapters and institutional case studies to identify and discuss the necessary conditions and facilitating factors which contribute to institutional transformation to engage a diverse student body.*

Methodology /approach – *This chapter is based on thematic analysis of the previous chapters and institutional case studies. It utilises national contextual information, details of changes undertaken and reflections on the process of change. The key ideas are illustrated by quotes from the case studies.*

Findings – *The following necessary conditions and facilitative factors are identified and discussed:*
i. *Commitment to a transformational approach*
ii. *Sharing understanding and meaning*

Institutional Transformation to Engage a Diverse Student Body
International Perspectives on Higher Education Research, Volume 6, 279–291
Copyright © 2011 by Emerald Group Publishing Limited
All rights of reproduction in any form reserved
ISSN: 1479-3628/doi:10.1108/S1479-3628(2011)0000006027

   iii. *Institutional strategy for change: senior leadership, policy alignment, creating a facilitating infrastructure across the student lifecycle and co-ordinating change*
   iv. *Engaging staff and creating an inclusive culture*
   v. *Developing students' capacity to engage*
   vi. *Taking an evidence-informed approach*
   vii. *Linking change to other institutional priorities and developments*
   viii. *An enabling policy and funding context*

Research limitations – *It is based on the chapters and case studies presented in this book rather than a wider analysis.*

Practical implications – *This chapter offers institutions insight into the conditions and factors that enable and smooth institutional transformation.*

Social implications – *This chapter is designed to support the promotion of social justice in higher education.*

Originality/value – *This chapter draws on international research and institutional examples and identifies common conditions and factors which contribute to managing change to engage a diverse student body. Its value is practical insights into change from an international perspective.*

Keywords: Institutional change and transformation; enabling factors

INTRODUCTION

The early chapters of this book explored the ideas of student diversity, engagement to improve retention and success and institutional transformation. Chapter 3 presented a framework for mainstreaming diversity, which was then exemplified by reference to English higher education institutions. Further chapters then developed the notion of student engagement and institutional transformation in relation to specific parts of the student lifecycle (awareness raising and pre-entry preparation in Chapter 4, admissions and transition in Chapter 5, on course experiences in Chapter 6 and progression beyond the first degree in Chapter 7). The practice of institutional transformation has been further illustrated, reflected on and critiqued through a series of institutional case studies from around the world (although it should be recognised that they are predominantly from high and middle income countries rather than poorer ones). These case studies and the mainstreaming framework in particular indicate a range of necessary conditions and facilitating factors that contribute to institutional transformation to engage a diverse student body. This chapter discusses these issues in more detail. It makes reference to the case studies throughout the book and four further case studies that explicitly discuss these enablers.

Jacqueline Stevenson reflects on the need for a 'golden thread' of understanding and commitment to widening participation (WP) and diversity to be woven into everything the institution does. Marit Greek discusses the necessity of engaging staff in a process of change in relation to their pedagogy, the challenges involved in this and presents the strategy that is being used at Oslo University College to achieve this. Vicky Duckworth provides a narrative about an institution that has social justice at its core and how this is reflected in the institutional culture, including structural issues and staff practices. Tony Hoare and colleagues chart the development of institutional approaches to WP and student diversity at two contrasting universities in Bristol: the University of Bristol and the University of the West of England. They identify the similarities of the paths followed and note the differences, and they focus on institutional drivers and enablers, which include the English policy and funding context, senior leadership, institutional commitment and strategy, and the role of data and research.

This chapter considers the following necessary conditions and facilitative factors:

   i. Commitment to a transformational approach
  ii. Sharing understanding and meaning
 iii. Institutional strategy for change: senior leadership, policy alignment, creating a facilitating infrastructure across the student lifecycle and co-ordinating change
 iv. Engaging staff and creating an inclusive culture
  v. Developing students' capacity to engage
 vi. Taking an evidence-informed approach
 vii. Linking change to other institutional priorities and developments
viii. An enabling policy and funding context

COMMITMENT TO A TRANSFORMATIONAL APPROACH

A number of the case studies point to the importance of the way in which the institution responds to student diversity. Severiens et al. examine how Dutch institutions in urban areas are facilitating the entry to higher education (HE) of students, particularly ethnic minorities, who have followed the vocational route through secondary education. Their research finds that on the whole institutions are expecting students to change to fit into HE provision, rather than considering how their provision may need to be altered to engage a new student cohort. Similar experiences are reported by Maes et al. in the Belgian context and Cooper and Ismail in the South African context. In both examples the institution has extended access to adult learners, but there is a general reluctance by the institutions to undertake significant cultural change. It is noticeable in the example by Gammo-Felton about a specialist performance institution in the United Kingdom that there is a reluctance to challenge institutional perceptions about the relative value of different cultural experiences. Thus, one aspect of the widening participation (WP) strategy is to broaden the (high) culture experiences of the local working class students (e.g. to ballet), but there is not an equal appetite to initiate the more classically trained students into more popular culture (e.g. street dancing). This position is summarised by Greek talking about her own institution: 'to a great extent [this] is caused by the fact that the resources they [i.e. non-traditional students] are offering are considered as irrelevant and worthless in a Norwegian academic environment', and this would appear to have broader applicability to some institutions outside of Norway.

SHARED UNDERSTANDING AND MEANING

Commitment to institutional transformation needs to be underpinned by shared understanding and meaning about what this implies. The case study from Leeds Metropolitan University (Stevenson) indicates how a shift in institutional commitment to embedding WP and making it the responsibility of a much wider staff group quickly resulted in confusion:

> Many staff were no longer sure what widening participation meant within the institution, or whether it even existed as a distinct term, or whether it had been subsumed under generic activity such as marketing. Staff were also unclear as to who might be responsible for widening participation and the types of activities, and for which target groups, they were supposed to be putting in place, if any, to widen participation.

Greek, writing about Oslo University College, also identifies the challenge of helping staff to understand what is required of them, especially to overcome deficit views of non-traditional students:

> Taking diversity into account does not imply a lowering of standards or educating less qualified professionals. It is about reaching the same goals in different ways... The

challenge is to render this visible and contribute to positive experiences among the teachers.

Hoare et al. recognise the challenges of persuading staff to accept an institutional commitment to WP, particularly in an institution, in this case the University of Bristol, that 'does not *need* more high quality applications to fill its courses'.

Thus, institutions have to be explicit about how they intend to respond to student diversity, in terms of both which students they are seeking to attract and how they will develop and change to engage them in HE learning to be successful in their studying and beyond. It is also prudent to make explicit how diversity benefits an institution, perhaps drawing on the drivers for change identified in Chapter 1. Stevenson concludes in her case study:

the institution needed to make its definition of widening participation, and its position in relation to it, clearer to all...the institution needed to be more specific about what WP activity comprises, and what kinds of initiatives should be taking place in the name of WP; crucially the university needed to establish a 'golden thread' of WP that runs through all other initiatives across the university so that it would appear in all key planning, monitoring and reporting documents/publications.

INSTITUTIONAL STRATEGY, LEADERSHIP, POLICIES, INFRASTRUCTURE AND ORGANISATION FOR CHANGE

The case studies imply that in addition to having a commitment to transformation and a shared understanding of what is to be achieved, there needs to be an institutional approach to change. This incorporates a deliberate strategy, senior leadership, policy alignment, a facilitative infrastructure across the student lifecycle and staff with responsibility for co-ordinating change.

The case studies from La Trobe University (Ferguson) and Aston University (Ingleby) both chart the developmental journeys the institutions are engaged in to create more inclusive campuses. Both of these involve a deliberate, high-level strategy for institutional change, led by a pro vice chancellor in each institution. The importance of senior staff is re-iterated by Hoare et al. in the context of the University of Bristol: 'An early buy-in from senior management was also crucial in winning hearts and minds within the University'.

Furthermore, in many of the case study institutions, there is an alignment of the institutions' corporate values and plan, and alignment of major institutional policy areas towards the objective of engaging a diverse student population to access and succeed in HE. Ingleby notes:

> At Aston, widening participation is embedded within the University Corporate Plan, the Learning and Teaching Strategy, and the Employability Strategy. Strategically, community engagement is on an equal footing with teaching and research, and the principles of widening participation, equity and inclusion are core institutional values.

Similarly, Ferguson notes about La Trobe University:

> The core values of the University include responsibility, for Social Justice, Equal Opportunity, Cultural Diversity and Environmental Sustainability and Relevance, ensuring education is a lifelong and interactive experience that produces responsible global citizens.

Both Ingleby and Ferguson discuss the process of aligning policies. Aston created three hubs focusing on outreach, learning and support and employability; and the Widening Participation Strategy was embedded within the Learning and Teaching and Employability Strategies. The hubs became operational working groups with a broadened remit to include an institutional focus on diversity, inclusive practice for all, student success, and preparing students for the global workplace. La Trobe is currently undertaking a review of policies and procedures as part of its quality enhancement work which has inclusion at the heart of it:

> each policy is mandated to address issues of inclusion and equity. Each area of governance that has responsibility for developing policies and procedures must review and amend in accordance with the quality framework for progressing through the University's senior committees.

It is important that institutional policies and procedures reinforce and enable engagement. For example, the University of Cape Town is oriented towards full-time undergraduate study. Ismail and Cooper report that part-time adult students find that administrative offices and student facilities such as computer services, canteens and the Writing Centre are not available when they are usually on campus. This suggests that the Estates policy should be informed by the needs of diverse students. Similarly, some adult students struggle to pay fees up front at the start of the year, and in the past have not had access to institutional financial support; this indicates that the systems of financial support and payment of fees are not informed by the needs of this student group. It is equally important that staff recruitment and development policies reflect the expectation that all staff have a role to play in actively engaging students in learning across the student lifecycle.

Writing about Edge Hill University, Duckworth notes the importance of 'a solid infrastructure' that 'permeates across the three faculty structure' and in each faculty WP work is led by 'a nominated senior manager' who works together and with 'staff from services and support areas'. The processes of policy alignment and co-ordination help to create institutional processes and organisation which enable institutional transformation to engage a diverse student population. It is important that procedures reinforce and enable engagement and that senior staff have responsibility for managing and co-ordinating work in this area, especially when it is dispersed across the institution and is dependent on the contribution of all staff. A fully dispersed model (Thomas et al., 2005) may mean that no one takes responsibility for diversity and the institution loses its way (as Stevenson implies). Indeed, Stevenson suggests that it may be important to have a WP strategy to provide overall direction to the WP activity of the institution, and a central strategic unit to guide the process.

To sum up the key issues relating to institutional strategy, it is instructive to review the list of common features that Hoare et al. identify in the approach of the two universities in Bristol to mainstreaming WP:

- A University-wide Widening Participation Strategy
- A dedicated and sizeable unit tasked with leading and managing its delivery
- Expectations placed by the Strategy 'horizontally' across all faculties and student-facing central services
- A 'vertical' structure of supporting, reporting and accountability stretching to senior management, deputy vice-chancellor (DVC) level
- A reflection of WP principles in other policy and strategy domains, notably admissions, equality and diversity, education and the overall mission statement.

ENGAGING STAFF AND CREATING AN INCLUSIVE CULTURE

Active staff engagement is at the heart of a transformed institution that engages a diverse student body, and this in turn creates an inclusive culture. However as May and Bridger observe, the hearts and minds of staff have to be won over. Crosling reminds us that changing staff attitudes and approaches is not simple because staff are being asked to teach differently, and this may lead to a loss of independence and autonomy and thus change will be resisted (Toyne, 1993). Furthermore, staff must understand the need for change, feel that they can cope with the change and own the change (Carnall, 1997). Crosling discusses an approach to develop the curriculum that is based on staff research interests, because she argues, 'a teacher merely delivering information developed elsewhere may be seen as less likely to provide a teaching and learning forum that encourages student engagement and study commitment'. This approach builds on staff expertise and thus encourages understanding, commitment and ownership of the change process.

Other case studies also work from the bottom-up to engage staff in the process of change (e.g. Greek and Vidacek-Hains et al.). Both case studies work with academic staff in a single faculty to develop their learning and teaching practices to be more inclusive and engaging for a diverse population. Vidacek-Hains et al. use a number of strategies to engage staff, including:

• Involving staff in the management and implementation process
• Using a phased approach to change based on three levels
• Contractually requiring all staff to operate at least at the first level
• Compulsory technical and pedagogical development and training
• Providing specialist staff to support the development of new materials
• Offering innovative case studies to inform and inspire staff
• Making institutional awards for best practice

This combination of mandatory and enabling elements within the change process exemplifies the notion of combining top-down and bottom-up approaches, while offering space for development and experimentation.

Staff need space to become aware of alternative approaches and to understand them and gain expertise and confidence to apply them. Thus, a number of case studies recognise the importance of support and development for staff to create a more engaging HE experience for students. The success of the project coordinated by the Centre for Educational Research and Development in the Faculty of Nursing at Oslo University College is, at least in part, due to its active engagement of staff in understanding and developing new pedagogical approaches. Greek writes:

> One cannot suppose the academic staff to change their attitudes and pedagogical approaches, rethinking old habits and convictions because we tell them to. In one way or another, everybody has to experience it themselves.

The work in the FOI at the University of Zagreb is facilitated by the provision of technical training and pedagogical development and specialist support to assist with the development of new materials. The Trinity

Inclusive Curriculum (TIC) project at Trinity College Dublin (TCD), (Garvey) is designed to understand the barriers to student engagement and enable staff to create more appropriate curricula through 'teaching and learning self-evaluation tools' that are 'embedded into TCD policies, procedures, training, and awareness activities'. At Edge Hill University, Duckworth argues that an inclusive culture is facilitated by staff development and support:

> The Human Resources and the Inclusion Team support staff (and students) to develop positive individualised approaches to learning and teaching by providing direct support for both general and specialist information to different staff groups on policies, procedures, services, provision and student entitlements; guidance to staff on individual student issues relating to handling of complex support issues, leadership for equality and diversity, disciplinary, complaints and fitness for practice.

DEVELOPING STUDENTS' CAPACITY TO ENGAGE

Students' capacity to engage is central to the process of change. It includes developing understanding of the value of engagement in all spheres of the university or college and developing the skills and knowledge to engage.

Bland demonstrates how an intervention based at the University provided an opportunity for school students to challenge their negative perceptions about higher education and to develop wider understanding, knowledge and skills, and resulted in progression to HE. More generally, Hatt and Tate (Chapter 4) explore the importance of developing students' understanding of higher education and their capacity to engage. They note that this is a cumulative process taking place through sustained interventions over a period of time. Furthermore, students need different types of interventions and interactions at different stages of the student lifecycle. Hill focuses on the other end of the lifecycle and demonstrates how learning and teaching can facilitate the development of skills and confidence to enable first generation entrants to successfully progress beyond the first degree and engage in the labour market. A focus on developing social capital in the learning sphere enabled this progression, with positive outcomes for students.

TAKING AN EVIDENCE-INFORMED APPROACH

A number of the institutional case studies identify the importance of an evidence informed approach to change, including the value of student voice. An evidence-informed approached includes: understanding the issues, using data, evaluation and research findings to inform the development of policy, practice and interventions; monitoring the experiences and outcomes of diverse groups; evaluating the impact (or likely impact) of policy, practice and interventions on engagement, retention and success; and using data and research to inform decision-making.

The reasons why students do not progress to higher education or are not successful there should not be assumed. Institutions' approach to change should be informed by evidence, including student and staff perspectives. Bland describes the transformational effect that a students-as-researchers project has had on the progression of young people from one school to HE. The student researchers were disengaged young people biding their time to be old enough to formally leave school, who engaged in research ostensibly to explore their peers' perspectives of factors relating to low aspiration for and access to university. They produced a DVD to address unrealistic perceptions of higher education study, which had a powerful effect and over a number of years contributed to a significant increase in the number of students from the school progressing to HE. Within HE the TIC project at Trinity College Dublin (Garvey) invested time in understanding the barriers to engagement within the academic environment and used this understanding to inform its curriculum-based interventions.

There are a number of examples of how institutions have taken learning from research and evaluation and used it to inform the development of practice. This is identified as an important feature of the strategic approach developed by the Open University:

> Much work is taking place to embed the learning from specific initiatives. For example, all Faculties are currently developing Widening Participation Action Plans, which will draw on the lessons learned through the Openings Programme. The Marketing function is drawing on images and lessons from the Community Partnerships work to inform its wider campaigns. And the quality and robustness of equality action plans across Faculties has improved as a result of greater engagement achieved through informal networks.

Collaboration and learning from others are beneficial approaches identified in the case studies by Evenbeck and Ross, Duckworth and Hoare et al.

At Aston University Ingleby points to the importance of being able to use institutional data and to track the experiences of students from equity groups:

> In 2004 the University appointed a Widening Participation Data Officer... This post was critical to the early institutional research for Widening Participation, and continues to perform a vital role in providing planning and management information to support equality and diversity. From a Widening Participation perspective it is possible to monitor student recruitment, progression and achievement and to identify any performance issues at institutional and local level.

Indeed Aston and the Open University have taken action as monitoring has identified that students from Black and Minority Ethnic (BME) Groups are achieving less well in HE than White peers.

A few case studies provide evidence of the impact of interventions on specific student groups, for example 'at risk' students at Temple University (Andrews and Drake) and students participating in First Year Seminars at Indiana University Purdue University Indianapolis (Evenbeck and Ross). This type of data is influential and can be used to lever support for further change. At the University of Bristol (Hoare et al.) an internally supported and funded WP research cluster has examined 'educational disadvantage' with the intention of facilitating the entry of students with the necessary academic *potential* irrespective of background: 'The University of Bristol has evidence of an "educational disadvantage" gap between prior attainment and degree potential. This evidence provides "a robust defence against 'social engineering' charges, while ensuring applicants are still treated holistically, as individuals"'. Research evidence of this nature has informed decision making at the University Bristol, and 'also chimes with UoB's wider self-portrayal as among the sector's research elite'. If universities do not use evidence to inform decision making, it undermines their claims to be knowledge institutions.

LINKING CHANGE TO OTHER INSTITUTIONAL PRIORITIES AND DEVELOPMENTS

Although some institutions have an integral commitment to student diversity (e.g. University of Bedfordshire, University of South Australia, Edge Hill University), for others it may not be so central. It is therefore important to link student engagement and institutional transformation to other institutional agendas and 'piggy back' on to other institutional priorities and emerging opportunities. For example, the case studies from Temple and Zagreb Universities have been facilitated by linking diversity, pedagogical development and institutional change to institutional concerns about student retention. Drawing from the work of Blythman, Orr, Hampton, McLaughlin, and Waterworth (2006) to bring about change it is necessary to:

- Operate at a range of levels, including the institution, department and individual.
- Identify where formal and informal *power* lies at different levels.

- Link change to dominant discourses, such as institutional mission, concern about student retention, student satisfaction (especially when measured nationally and published in league tables, as in the United Kingdom), quality assurance processes, domestic and international student recruitment and financial returns.
- Couch changes in the language of the powerful.

AN ENABLING POLICY AND FUNDING CONTEXT

Institutional transformation to engage a diverse student body is more effective when it takes place within an enabling policy and funding context. Hoare et al. reflect that:

> All significant WP developments at Bristol's universities can ultimately be traced back at least to, if not before, the national agenda initiated by Dearing. Subsequent political imperatives, WP financial provisions and reporting obligations framed their management of WP affairs.

A number of countries have addressed diversity from a national policy perspective (e.g. Australia, England, Ireland), and this has often been accompanied by additional funding. Indeed, change in Australia is currently being invigorated by funding to the sector as a result of the Bradley review.

Internal funding can also enable change. For example, the case studies presented by Crosling and Evenbeck and Ross were both enabled by institutional funding. In both instances colleagues secured resources from funding available for broader institutional change to develop work to engage diverse students in their learning.

CONCLUSIONS

The book has explored institutional transformation to engage a diverse student body. Institutions have employed a range of approaches to change, and some have focused on specific parts of the student lifecycle and/or the institution, while others have undertaken wider change. In some institutions there has been a top-down approach to implementing and managing change (e.g. Aston and La Trobe universities). The Open University in the United Kingdom has responded to increasing student diversity through ongoing developments in strategy, governance and practice, underpinned by a developing evidence base that explicitly seeks out the student voice. In contrast committed staff from the Faculty of Informatics at Zagreb University in Croatia used 'spaces' created by the changes resulting from the Bologna process to implement changes in learning and teaching to engage a more diverse student population – and this has required the development of an evidence base and staff engagement. Similarly, staff at Oslo University College have responded to increased student diversity as a result of more migration to Norway and have worked to engage colleagues to move away from a utilitarian approach to a more transformative approach. Staff at the University of Cape Town were so frustrated by the lack of institutional change to facilitate WP to adult learners they came together to form the Adult Learners Working Group (ALWG) and have undertaken research, advocacy and lobbying work to bring about changes to support adult engagement. There are therefore a range of approaches to change represented in this book, and no blueprint is advocated. The early chapters provide a rationale and framework for change, while the later chapters explore these changes in more detail. The case studies provide a rich body of evidence and experience about the realities of implementing change, including the vision, the tactics, the challenges and the successes.

Postscript

Since this book and associated research was started, it has been announced that Aimhigher, a major vehicle for WP in England, will not be funded beyond July 2011. Furthermore, there will be significant increases in the cost of higher education to students in England, which are likely to be accompanied by a requirement for institutions to promote the admission of students from lower socio-economic groups, and to ensure their success. This makes the embedding of effective practice into institutions and collaboration at the local and regional level even more important than before, and it provides an opportunity for institutional transformation to engage diverse student population to engage and succeed in HE.

CHAPTER 8.1

ESTABLISHING A 'GOLDEN THREAD': THE PATH TO ENSURING INSTITUTIONAL TRANSFORMATION

Jacqueline Stevenson

ABSTRACT

Purpose – *This case study identifies, from a personal perspective, the essential conditions for institutional transformation that will ensure the effective mainstreaming of widening participation (WP).*

Methodology/approach – *This case study is a personal commentary reflecting on 10 years working as both a WP practitioner and an academic member of staff at Leeds Metropolitan University. The case study also draws on empirical research into WP policy and practice undertaken at the university between 2008 and 2009.*

Findings – *Research undertaken as part of the Action on Access programme 'Mainstreaming and Sustaining Widening Participation in Institutions' and as part of an institutional Quality Enhancement Audit found that whilst there were many examples of excellent WP practice, many staff were no longer sure what WP meant within the institution. In addition, whilst members of the management team felt that the institution still had a strong commitment to WP, other staff were less convinced. The research also highlighted that the relative incoherence in terms of WP*

Institutional Transformation to Engage a Diverse Student Body
International Perspectives on Higher Education Research, Volume 6, 293–300
ISSN: 1479-3628/doi:10.1108/S1479-3628(2011)0000006028

definitions and practice meant that people were drawing solely on their own local and personal values and were blaming others when these peoples' practice was contradictory to their own.

Practical implications – *The case study outlines the conditions needed to effectively mainstream and sustain WP, including establishing a 'golden thread' of WP that runs through all key policy and strategy documents across the university.*

Social implications – *Whilst the principles of mainstreaming WP are sound, strategies need to be put in place to ensure that actual practice is not in danger of privileging some students at the expense of others.*

Keywords: Mainstream; sustain; equality and diversity; research

This institutional case study is a personal commentary, reflecting on 10 years working as both a widening participation (WP) practitioner and an academic member of staff at Leeds Metropolitan University ('Leeds Met'). Aside from my own reflections I also draw on the empirical research into WP policy and practice that I undertook at the university between 2008 and 2009, initially as part of the Action on Access 'Mainstreaming and Sustaining Widening Participation in Institutions' programme and, building on this work, as part of an institutional Quality Enhancement Audit (Stevenson, Clegg, & Lefever, 2010).

Leeds Met is a post-1992 university with the one of the largest number of students in Britain. In the academic year 2008–2009, it was ranked as the 14th largest HEI in the United Kingdom with 27,800 students (HEFCE, 2009). Including all students at all levels (offsite and onsite, overseas, exchange, home, EU and Regional University Network students) brings the figure as of October 2010 to 42,187 (including, at all levels of study). The university has a strong commitment to equity, inclusion and WP and a good track record in attracting students from a wide range of under-represented groups. For example, 94% of young, fulltime, first degree entrants are from state schools (above the overall UK average of 88%) and are 13% from low participation neighbourhoods, compared to the UK average of 9.7% (HESA, 2009). In addition the university has international students from over 70 countries as well as students studying through the Regional University Network – a network of 24 further education colleges who between them have over a third of a million students. Outside the network, the university also validates awards from Norwich and Westminster and from Croatia to India and Hong Kong to Zambia.

The university has a longstanding commitment to WP and is recognised throughout the HE sector as being pioneering in WP practice having been awarded a range of accolades over the last ten years.[1] In the years to 2005 much of the work that took place under the WP banner was centralised, the responsibility of a specific team of staff whose role was, primarily, to raise the expectations and aspirations of under-represented students. The work of the 'Get Ahead' team, the primary provider of outreach activity within the university, was, and still is, regarded as being particularly innovative during this time, with the team implementing a range of projects (which are still ongoing) such as the UJIMA Summer School which introduces African and African-Caribbean boys to higher education; Larkia, a creative arts summer school for Asian girls; 'Reaching for A*' for students at schools in low participation neighbourhoods and the Leeds Met Progression Module.[2] In addition the team works closely with looked after children (i.e. children and young people in the care of the local authority) and, in recognition of their commitment and dedication to facilitating aspiration raising activities amongst young people in care, was awarded the Frank Buttle Trust Quality Mark.[3] During this period the institution had a specific WP strategy (Leeds Met 2005), the implementation of which was the responsibility of the Get Ahead team supported by smaller teams and/or individuals within each faculty.

In 2005, however, the Higher Education Funding Council for England (HEFCE) ceased its requirement that the WP allocation to institutions needed to be ear-marked for specific WP activity. In addition, institutions were no longer required to formulate either WP strategies or action plans or report back on them to HEFCE. This change in policy, alongside a national drive to disperse, embed and/or mainstream WP activity resulted in Leeds Met significantly changing the direction of its WP activity. Over the next few years, strategies were put in place to make WP the responsibility of a wider group of individuals and teams across the institution, with each faculty and service having responsibility for WP, creating what Thomas et al. (2005) have termed a 'dispersed organisational structure' (p. 171).

In addition to devolving WP responsibilities, the previous vice-chancellor was responsible for the development of a range of external partnerships with for example Yorkshire County Cricket, Black Dyke Band, West Yorkshire Playhouse, Northern Ballet and Leeds Museums and Galleries. These partnerships were designed not only to raise awareness of and aspiration to Higher Education in under represented communities but also to offer diverse sporting and cultural opportunities to the university's students. Leeds Met also developed a thriving schools links programme, a cross-university group that continues to work to develop key strategic partnerships with schools. Alongside this activity, to support and retain students once at the university Student Liaison Officers were recruited to offer a first point of contact for students within faculties. In addition, in 2006 the Equality and Diversity Unit was set up to manage the development of equality schemes and supporting infrastructure to enable the University to meet its vision and statutory obligations under the range of new and existing equality and diversity legislation.

By 2008, an institutional decision had been taken not to renew the university's WP Strategy. Not only was it felt that both the objectives and the activities of the strategy had largely been achieved but that taking this final step would ensure that WP was seen not just as the responsibility of a small minority of specialist staff but of the whole staffing body of the university. With this decision, the university's WP action plan and WP evaluation strategy also became obsolete and, at the same time, the WP Practitioners group stopped meeting.

In the same year, however, an institutional team participated in the Action on Access programme 'Mainstreaming and Sustaining Widening Participation in Institutions'. Research conducted as part of the Action on Access programme, mapping the provision and location of WP activity across the institution, highlighted that there had been significant changes as to how 'widening participation' is conceptualised, and therefore implemented in practice, at Leeds Met since its inception, with the term 'widening participation' appearing to increasingly have different meanings to different internal stakeholders. Building on these findings an institutional Quality Enhancement Audit was undertaken in the following year. The aim of this research was to evaluate what claims were being made in relation to WP in the university's key policies and strategy documentation; assess how far these stated ambitions were being achieved, through interviews with university staff and identify areas of good practice as well as areas for improvement/ enhancement.

The audit highlighted that many staff were no longer sure what WP meant within the institution, or whether it even existed as a distinct term, or whether it had been subsumed under generic activity such as marketing. Staff were also unclear as to who might be responsible for WP and the types of activities, and for which target groups, they were supposed to be putting in place, if any, to widen participation (Stevenson, Clegg, & Lefever, 2010). Although members of the management team interviewed as part of the research felt that the institution still had a strong commitment to WP, the majority of other staff were significantly less convinced, with some questioning whether WP still needed to take place since the institution had been 'so successful' in attracting a diverse student body, despite being unable to back this up with any evidence, other than that they 'felt' it was, or saw lots of 'diverse students walking around the institution'.

In terms of WP practice, the research highlighted how, in some areas of the university, almost all students who were not white, male or middle class were now regarded as WP students; in other areas it was believed that those support mechanisms available to all students (e.g. financial services) were WP activities, regardless of whether WP students were accessing them or not. In addition, some staff believed there had actually been an overall decline in WP-related activity simply because staff were no longer clear where they should focus their efforts (Stevenson et al., 2010). Whilst much good practice in WP was still taking place across the institution, staff were increasingly unaware of this. In addition, the relative incoherence in terms of WP definitions and practice meant that people were not only drawing on their own local and personal values but were blaming others when these peoples' practice was contradictory to their own (*ibid.*). These findings mirror Greenbank's (2006) research, which found that a culture of WP was often not embedded and that 'widening participation policy formulated at the senior management level is likely to be reinterpreted, revised – and in many cases even undermined or ignored – as it migrates down the organisational hierarchy' (p. 209).

The conclusions from the institutional research team were that, whilst the principles of mainstreaming WP were sound, a number of prerequisites were not in place that needed to be. First, the institution needed to make its definition of WP, and its position in relation to it, clearer to all. This included reconsidering whether there should be a specific WP strategy and policy, and how the principles and good practice of WP could specifically be embedded in other strategy and policy documents. In addition, the institution needed to be more specific about what WP activity comprises, and what kinds of initiatives should be taking place in the name of WP; crucially the university needed to establish a 'golden thread' of WP that runs through all other initiatives across the university so that it would appear in all key planning, monitoring and reporting documents/publications; alongside this a 'framework for success' and/or measures for success relating to WP needed to be developed, within a specific institutional context, with ongoing reporting and dissemination of performance outcomes against these measures. Finally the team argued that although the faculties would retain responsibility for WP, there needed to be a dedicated, senior member of staff to help facilitate developments and collaboration across the university, what

Thomas et al. (2005) have called a 'dispersed with centralised co-ordination structure'.

As the institution, with its new vice-chancellor, moves into a new decade various changes are being put in place to facilitate this new centralised coordination structure. The university's public commitment to WP is now enshrined in its Strategic Plan (Leeds Met, 2010a), which states that Leeds Met is committed to 'providing a supportive, inclusive and welcoming environment, and preparing students for employment and lifelong learning'. The plan also outlines the university's key performance indicators (KPIs) of which the most specific relating to WP is that 'the percentage of students from under-represented groups to match or exceed the Higher Education Statistics Agency (HESA) performance indicators'. In addition the university is in the process of developing a new WP Strategy that will be closely linked into and cross-reference the institution's other policies and strategies. In the run up to the development of this new strategy staff and students from across the have been asked to contribute to discussion exploring what they feel 'widening participation' actually means; what the university's WP objectives should be; who the WP target groups should be; what different strands of WP activity the institution should be undertaking (or not undertaking) and how the institution can better ensure that WP activity is integrated, monitored, evaluated and best practice disseminated.

Alongside this research into WP, a review of Equality and Diversity at Leeds Met during 2009–2010 also indicated the need for a more robust and embedded approach to equality and diversity activities across the university. Consequently the university has now established a Equality and Diversity Committee with formal reporting lines (a 'golden thread') from Committee to the Corporate Management Team and the Board of Governors (Leeds Met, 2010b). The committee is chaired by a deputy vice chancellor who will act as the executive champion of equality and diversity issues. In addition, local advisory groups have been established in each faculty/service area to review policy implementation, with a senior equality and diversity champion chairing the advisory group and leading on equality and diversity issues at a local level. The existent equality and diversity fora have been integrated into the overall equality and diversity structure, and links to the Student Union's equality and diversity structure and fora have also been established. Through the development of such a wide range of equality and diversity advisory groups the engagement and participation of staff and students on equality and diversity issues has been assured.

REFLECTION

The past 10 years of WP at Leeds Met have been exciting, invigorating, innovative, challenging and, at times, frustrating. I have never doubted that the majority of staff across the institution are highly committed both to WP and to supporting the success of all our students. At times, however, a lack of communication between staff and, in my opinion, an over-emphasis on celebrating our successes, rather than an honest analysis of our weaknesses, has meant that our WP practice has been somewhat unfocussed and unstructured. This has resulted in a level of confusion and uncertainty and, as a consequence, a lack of requisite action.

It may be argued that the changes that are now taking place at Leeds Met are in response to the (re)requirement from HEFCE, following the National Audit Office report of 2008, that HEIs should have WP strategies that they report back on. It may also be argued that HEFCE's requirement, from 2009, that HEIs must submit annual Widening Participation Strategic Assessment is a key driver for these changes. I hesitate to be so cynical. I genuinely believe that Leeds Met has learned from what I would term its 'well-intentioned mistakes' in trying to mainstream WP-without putting in place the pre-conditions needed to make this successful.

The effective mainstreaming of WP demands that institutions have a shared understanding of WP across the whole institution, and at every level; that good practice is identified, is evidence based rather than anecdotal and is shared with others; that the institution has a WP strategy that has clear and achievable aims and objectives and that both policy and practice are regularly assessed and interrogated. Despite the financial challenges we face, as Leeds Met moves into a new decade, with a new vice chancellor, I believe that these conditions are being firmly put in place and, as a consequence, we will now truly be able to mainstream, and sustain, our WP activity.

NOTES

1. These include Highly Commended in national Training Awards (2004) for work in widening participation of adult learners; Winner of Times Higher Award (2006) for 'outstanding contribution to the local community'; Frank Buttle Trust Quality Mark; 'Champion of Diversity' in West Yorkshire Award (2010).

2. The Progression Module is a rigorous programme of exploration, encouraging students in the first year of advanced level study to develop their skills and investigate

progression routes into HE. The module is divided into four assessed units and delivered by tutors in schools and colleges.

   3. Established in 2006 lin recognition of Higher Education institutions 'who go that extra mile to support students who have been in public care' (http://www.buttletrust.org/quality_mark/).

CHAPTER 8.2

REVERSING FRAMES: INSTITUTIONAL DEVELOPMENT AT OSLO UNIVERSITY COLLEGE

Marit Greek

ABSTRACT

Purpose – *This chapter addresses how pedagogical innovations can promote changes in the culture of an Academic institution. The overall aim is to develop pedagogical methods that are suitable for teaching and learning in a diverse environment across the institution and implementing these in the institution.*

Methodology/approach – *The project is organized as a cooperation between Centre for Educational Research and Development, the Faculty of Nursing at Oslo University College and The Police Academy. Members of the academic staff are engaged as part-time project workers and are co-responsible for developing a language and communication course for immigrants applying for HE. They are also responsible for rendering their knowledge and experiences visible to their colleagues.*

Findings – *The developmental project has revealed a great ignorance among the academic staff, when it comes to taking advantage of the diversity in tutoring. The academic staff generally is unable to notice and to make use of the resources in diversity among the students. They also have great difficulties in understanding Norwegian second-language*

Institutional Transformation to Engage a Diverse Student Body
International Perspectives on Higher Education Research, Volume 6, 301–310
ISSN: 1479-3628/doi:10.1108/S1479-3628(2011)0000006029

students. Reluctance understanding that the linguistic minority students are in many cases caused by the feeling that the resources they are offering seems irrelevant and worthless in a Norwegian academic environment.

Research implications – *The interfaculty cooperation has been mutual stimulating and contributed to an extended effect of the work. The project has resulted in an increased awareness of multicultural learning environments. In the wake of the project, a number of new projects have started up, and they are now linked to the main developmental project.*

Keywords: Educational developmental; development project; interfaculty cooperation; institutional development

INTRODUCTION

This case study considers how a developmental project in the Faculty of Nursing at the Oslo University College (OUC) is being used to create a diverse learning environment that promotes equity and success of all students. The project is organized as a cooperation between Centre for Educational Research and Development (CERD), the Faculty of Nursing at OUC, The Police Academy (PHS) and the Faculty of Nursing at Akershus University College (HiAk). It has engaged academic staff in reversing institutional, pedagogical and individual frames (or ways of doing things) to shift the institution from a deficit approach to minority students towards a more inclusive culture, and consequently improving the quality of the learning experience for all students.

Education in Norway

Norway has an egalitarian model of schooling, which has resulted in a great equality of participation in higher education, and fewer differences between students entering HE than in many other countries. This is due to the unitary school system and the fact that the Norwegian society has been relatively homogeneous. Thus, until relatively recently, higher education has not had to respond to student diversity. However, there has been a radical change in the student population over the past 10–20 years, especially in Oslo where every fourth citizen has an immigrant background. It is no longer possible to assume that all students have the same educational, cultural and linguistic backgrounds.

Oslo University College

OUC has a long history of working on issues of multiculturalism and internationalization, and it has positioned itself as a university with competence and experience in these areas. In the wake of an increasing heterogeneous student population, diversity and multicultural challenges are focussed at OUC. The emphasis is however on how to help the non-traditional linguistic minority students to adjust to the existing provision rather than on the implications of diversity for the learning environment, the curriculum and the academic culture.

Thus OUC appears self-contradictory; on one hand it seeks diversity, while on the other hand it does not want to face the consequences of this plurality. Adapting students to fit in is hardly an appropriate strategy for the future. There is a need for development in the institution itself, towards a culture that appreciates diversity and takes advantage of the wide range of perspectives.

This case study illustrates how sustainable change in an institution has been achieved through a development project carried out by academic staff and thus implemented in the faculty.

REVERSING THE FRAMES

My concern is to improve the quality of teaching and learning at OUC by nurturing a multicultural and inclusive learning environment, which allows all students to be successful. A change of policies and practices to better adapt to our students requires new ways of thinking. Themes such as intercultural communication, tutorial skills, managing diversity and creating a diverse learning environment must be given attention.

To succeed, one has to combat structural and personal constraints at all levels of the institution: the institutional and pedagogical frames, pedagogical approaches, curriculum contents and the individuals within the institution. Consequently one has to concentrate on both students and the staff, on the majority and the minority at the same time.

The Starting Point: A Preparatory Programme for Applicants

The starting point was a preparatory programme for applicants in some of the bachelor's degree programs at OUC. Communication skills are crucial to successful learning outcomes, especially when collaborative learning activities are the focal point. With this in mind CERD has, since 2004, as a part of a longitudinal study, offered a voluntary preparatory study course to all applicants for OUC. The aim was to support applicants and future students of OUC by preparing them for collaboration in diverse cultural and language groups and thereby enabling them to succeed as students at OUC. We also aimed to assist students to develop confidence in themselves and their own resources and encourage them to persevere even when challenges might seem overwhelming.

Over the three-year period, approximately 250 individuals have participated in the preparatory course, 40–50 per cent of them as Norwegian second-language speakers. The evaluation shows that all the participants, irrespective of their Norwegian language skills, dared to take the risk to express themselves, to fail and to try again. We also found that the participants embraced the challenges of intercultural communication and really attempted to seek the meaning behind spoken words. Student evaluations of the programme were consistent and positive. Some students stated: 'The course has made me think differently'. When interviewed during their final year, most of the students who had participated had a positive attitude to cooperating in different projects and believed that it had a positive impact on their learning. Participating in the course had reduced their fears about being a student and helped them to be active participants in higher education.

Next Step: Engaging Staff

To succeed in creating a multicultural university college, promoting non-traditional students success implies managing linguistic variety. This presupposes interaction between the participants, characterized by willingness to listen actively to each other despite the differences. Even though this knowledge is evident and acknowledged, it seems to be most difficult for the academic staff to practise. The majority of the academic staff have great difficulties being open-minded and understanding Norwegian spoken and written in an unusual way – in a second-language way.

The project has revealed that reluctance to understand the linguistic minority students to a great extent is caused by the fact that the resources they are offering are considered as irrelevant and worthless in a Norwegian academic environment.

Our experience with the preparatory course demonstrates that it is possible to create an inclusive learning environment that is optimal for all students, in which diversity is valued and makes a positive contribution to learning. The question is how to use knowledge gained from the preparatory programme and institutional research to improve the pedagogical approaches used across the different faculties at OUC. This has been, and still is, the great challenge for CERD. One cannot suppose the academic staff to change their attitudes and pedagogical approaches, rethinking old habits and convictions because we tell them to. In one way or another, everybody has to experience it themselves.

Taking diversity into account does not imply a lowering of standards or educating less qualified professionals. It is about reaching the same goals in different ways. Institutional and pedagogical frames and practices need to be flexible to accommodate students from many different social, cultural and educational backgrounds. The challenge is to render this visible and contribute to positive experiences among the teachers. Therefore CERD has, together with the Faculty of Nursing, initiated a project for educational development.

The Successful Educational Practices Project

The overall aim of the project is to develop pedagogical methods that are suitable for teaching and learning in a diverse environment, independent of specific faculties. The project is based in the Faculty of Nursing, but knowledge gained through it is then generalized across OUC as well as PHS. Pedagogical principles and approaches are meant to be useful in any faculty; however, the concrete subject matters will of course differ depending on the specific faculty and discipline.

The underpinning principle is to address teaching practices rather than the shortcomings of the students. The project is framed by the national and institutional quality assurance systems. For example, the Quality Assurance System at OUC clearly identifies diversity and learning by cooperation as two of the main goals. Research at OUC however reveals a significant gap between the objectives and the experiences of adult immigrants.

Competence in cooperating with fellow students is essential to success in the Faculty of Nursing: the students are expected to participate actively and contribute professional knowledge to joint projects. One of the three main goals is to identify successful pedagogical approaches that promote a culture for collaboration, including both native and non-native speakers and giving them the opportunity to improve their communication skills.

We have found that non-native speakers are disadvantaged in the learning context; thus, the project has emphasized:

- consideration of the linguistic minority students' individual experiences and communicative skills in all learning and teaching methods;
- utilizing cooperation and interaction among the students to develop intercultural communication skills;
- serious consideration of the guidance about cooperation and communication;
- ensuring the participation of all students and
- focusing on the content of the students' contribution rather than the writing itself when guiding the students in written assignments.

In addition, a number of non-native speakers at OUC need to improve their communication skills, using Norwegian in new contexts to further their learning and enable professional practice. We have therefore developed a course covering academic, professional and collaborative learning language and communication skills to address this shortfall. But in addition to the challenge concerning the students' language and communication skills, we have to face the challenge of the institution itself – the framework, the curriculum and the underlying pedagogy that emphasises collaboration on professional issues with fellow students and jointly written assignments. This indicates the necessity to increase awareness and competence in 'managing diversity' amongst the academic staff in the faculty and heighten interest in these issues.

This project has therefore sought wider staff engagement to contribute to challenging institutional norms. This is happening as a consequence of the way in which the project is organized, as shown in Diagram 1.

Faculty-Based Management
The project is based in the Faculty of Nursing, who therefore own the project and have responsibility for its implementation. This contributes to increasing commitment to achieving positive results.

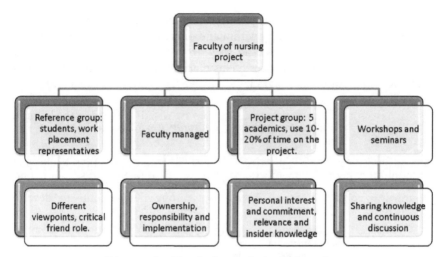

Diagram 1. Developing Inclusive Pedagogies.

Academic Staff as Project Workers

The project involves academic staff from the different faculties involved. All Faculty staff involved in the project continue being members of academic staff in the faculty, and work part-time on the project. This builds on their personal interest and generates commitment to be successful. It also facilitates the flow of knowledge and experience in both directions.

By being responsible for developing the course, the five collaborators, who are all assistant professors, will gain competence and it is hoped that the ideas and pedagogical approaches slowly, but surely, will be implemented in the faculty, in ordinary programmes.

Broad Reference Group to Act as Critical Friend

Students and external stakeholders, such as work placement representatives, bring a diversity of perspectives to the project, and question priorities and approaches and fulfil a 'critical friend' role, helping to improve the project.

Engaging Other Staff across the Institution through Dissemination

The overall aim is to develop pedagogical methods that are suitable for teaching and learning in a diverse environment across the institution. Essential to this is engaging other faculties.

In the wake of organizing the project, there has been an increasing interest in this topic. Different faculties within and outside OUC have made contact, developed individual projects, and they are all linked to the main project 'Successful educational practices'. This engagement beyond the Faculty of Nursing is illustrated in Diagram 2.

Network for a Diverse Learning Environment

The project has developed a network, which is a centre of resources, a colloquium where the members participate in a focused discussion and

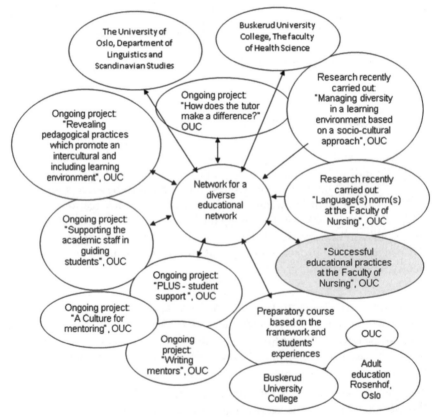

Diagram 2. The Wider Engagement of Staff in Projects Intended to Reverse Frames at OUC.

contribute their experiences and knowledge. Participants from different university colleges in Norway, different faculties and with different roles in the institution ensure that various perspectives are taken into consideration. Engagement from different faculties will also contribute in spreading knowledge and new perspectives in the institution.

Research Recently Carried Out

The qualitative research 'Language norm at the Faculty of Nursing' and 'Managing diversity in a learning environment based on a socio-cultural approach' are carried out by Jonsmoen and Greek (CERD). They address the phenomenon of interaction that takes place in the bachelor program at The Faculty of Nursing, in the field, between professionals and between professionals and students and in small learning communities at school, between students and between students and the lecturers.

The main project, 'Successful educational practices' are to a great degree based on what the research revealed.

The Different Projects Linked to the Main Project

The different projects are all about how to manage diversity and promote intercultural communication at OUC. Greek and Jonsmoen (CERD) are connected to all projects, either as supervisors or as member of the project group.

The voluntary preparatory course is now offered at other institutions, Buskerud University College and Rosenhof, Oslo, as a result of these institutions participating in the Network.

CLOSING COMMENTS

This project has demonstrated that interfaculty cooperation is mutually stimulating and has contributed to an increased awareness of multicultural learning environments; how to meet a heterogeneous student population and how to activate and make use of students' individual resources so that the whole learning community will gain from it. Furthermore, the engagement from different faculties really has facilitated the flow of knowledge and experience in both directions and has contributed to a growing recognition for the need of change in the institution. As a result of this, a number of new projects have started up and are linked to the main developmental project and more still coming.

Attaching the academic staff at The Nursing Faculty to the project, in a part-time engagement, has turned out to be a success. They have participated actively in spreading knowledge and positive, personal experiences among colleagues and initiated discussions and seminars for the academic staff. Being members of the faculty, they have managed to influence the staff more than what is possible for CERD, as a centre outside the faculty itself. They have all become personally committed to creating diverse learning environments and will continue this work after this project is finished.

CHAPTER 8.3

DEVELOPING AN ORGANISATIONAL CULTURE WHERE SOCIAL JUSTICE AND COLLABORATION RUNS ALONGSIDE WIDENING PARTICIPATION

Vicky Duckworth

ABSTRACT

This case study explores the organisational culture at Edge Hill University (EHU), seeking to identify how practitioners operate to provide equitable opportunities for access and participation in community engagement and higher education.

EHU works within a governance model, where there is shared responsibility for the widening participation (WP) agenda. This is promoted across and within its three faculty structure of Education; Health; and Humanities, Management, Social and Applied Sciences (HMSAS) strengthened by the WP service. Innovative, collaborative and pro-active approaches to WP are encouraged with staff inspired to take ownership of decisions and have autonomy. This allows the freedom to

Institutional Transformation to Engage a Diverse Student Body
International Perspectives on Higher Education Research, Volume 6, 311–317
ISSN: 1479-3628/doi:10.1108/S1479-3628(2011)0000006030

engage in institutional and community projects for example, incorporating pre-entry experiences such as taster sessions, as well as post-arrival teaching, and providing access to guidance and student services.

There is no doubt that educationalists can play an instrumental role in the academic and personal development of students with whom they interact, this interaction is in part governed by the institutional culture. This may be empowering or disempowering both on them and the local and wider communities they serve. Social justice in education requires active work by the whole of the institution allowing 'communities' to change both within and out of the university, where environmental circumstances may negatively impact on shaping the learning journey (LJ) of students.

The study presents an argument which drives the WP agenda forward encouraging engagement of educationalists, policy makers, social justice activists and communities to collaborate in pushing forward innovative, flexible and pro-active ways to develop meaningful knowledge.

Keywords: Case study; collaboration; social justice and learning cycle

OVERVIEW

Edge Hill University (EHU) in the North West of England has been delivering higher education (HE) for 125 years. Initially EHU provided teacher education for women; it received full degree awarding power in 2006 and research degree awarding power in 2008. Runner up in the Times Higher Education Award 2010, EH is a university with a vision, ambition and a determination to push forward working in collaborative, participative and interdisciplinary ways that bring together academics, practitioners, managers and policy makers, interested in widening participation (WP) and other aspects of educational equality.

INTRODUCTION

HEFCE (2008a) describes WP as a tool to address disadvantage of access to HE between different social groups. How this WP tool is applied differs institution to institution (Shaw, Brain, Bridger, Foreman, & Reid, 2007). At

EHU it is understood to mean taking an anticipatory, pro-active and whole institution approach to widening access to HE and promoting student retention and success within HE and beyond. To support this University adopts a lifecycle approach (HEFCE, 2001a). An important facet of this approach is the idea that WP has to be addressed throughout students' interaction with HE, not just before entry or at the point of admission. As such, effective engagement and communication between staff from across the institution, when sharing student knowledge, is crucial. This includes teaching staff working closely with other services, for example, the Inclusion Team when sharing information on how best to develop and implement effective support packages for students with learning and additional needs arising from physical or sensory impairments, mental health or other complex needs. This is in contrast to some higher education institutions (HEIs) that focus primarily on the pre-entry phases of the student lifecycle and who do not engage staff in WP from across the institution.

INSTITUTIONAL APPROACH, ORGANISATION AND INFRASTRUCTURE

To support the student life-cycle model, a central tenet of the university is the shared responsibility for achieving WP participation and student success. The networks that flow in, out and within EH working within a governance model based on the principle of dialogic accountability whereby there is a shift of WP policies, processes and practices from the peripheries to the forefront. This shift includes more authentic engagements and shared responsibility. Thomas (2005) identifies 'an integrated model of academic and pastoral support that enables all students to achieve their potential' (p. 108). This model may be viewed as shifting from deficit discourse, and instead embracing a philosophy of partnership, with structures, roles, processes and ways of working to match, and which move us towards a WP strategy based on the premise of inclusivity, diversity and transformation. This application is driven by a solid infrastructure which encourages WP initiatives, whilst recognising and reflecting on the challenges this brings in terms of the teaching, learning and assessment as well as the cultural and social experiences of students and staff. The solid infrastructure permeates across the three faculty structure of: Education; Health; and Humanities, Management, Social and Applied Sciences (HMSAS) as well as each faculty having a nominated senior manager (Associate Dean) with responsibility for WP and these staff work together as a team with nominated staff from services and support areas to form the University's Widening Participation Group (a sub-committee of equality, opportunity and student success committee).

SHARING RESPONSIBILITY

At EH there is a focus that embraces a commitment to nurture staff to drive forward academic development and take ownership of decisions. This ownership is strongly bound in working in innovative, collaborative and pro-active ways across departments, the university, locally, nationally and internationally. To facilitate this, the human resources and the inclusion team support staff (and students) to develop positive individualised approaches to learning and teaching by providing direct support for both general and specialist information to different staff groups on policies, procedures, services, provision and student entitlements; guidance to staff on individual student issues relating to handling of complex support issues, leadership for equality and diversity, disciplinary, complaints and fitness for practice. Further to this, to work towards social justice and inclusion, we have embedded WP into the learning and teaching strategy. The aim is to drive forward equitable opportunities for access and participation in HE. Part of this access and opportunities mean ensuring a wide range of programmes that enable people to engage in courses that are relevant to their context and situations. For example the undergraduate framework has been designed, validated, implemented and evaluated to actively address the students' diverse needs. This includes offering flexible approaches to teaching and learning, such as e-learning and blended learning. This offers a wide range of learners the opportunity to study at a time, place and pace suitable to them. The virtual learning environments (VLEs) have also proved successful in supporting a growing number of further education (FE) students in HE. For example, it offers trainee teachers in the lifelong learning sector (LLS), who are often in-service, have heavy teaching loads and are taught in their place of work a dedicated VLE space they can access in their own time to link with other practitioners and share practice and reflections (see Wenger, 1998).

WORKING IN COLLABORATION

We recognise that learning journeys (LJs) are not always linear and smooth and that the field of HE, and education as a whole is one of flux, particularly with a new government in office. But with our real passion for and commitment to WP at strategic and operational levels, we are equipped to drive the WP and the effective collaborations forward. Indeed, schools and colleges play a pivotal role in shaping a student's life chances and as such the partnerships forged are vital to raise aspirations where necessary and, especially, improve attainment levels and rates and to overcome those situational barriers wherever possible. EHU work closely and effectively with schools and colleges through activities targeted at students and through activities aimed at teachers as well as at staff who deliver advice and guidance on future careers and HE options. Involvement in the HEFCE project Mainstreaming and Sustaining Widening Participation during 2008 helped consolidate our thinking on raising achievement. As a result we have developed a new range of pre-entry preparation for HE programmes to improve academic skills, critical thinking and the transition experience with the intention of improving student success. These are cross institutional developments. 'Evolve' for Year 12 and 13 pupils is one example of the new innovations offering an out of hours, supplementary programme, with a learning, teaching and assessment experience at Level 4. There has also been collaborative approaches in the development of Foundation Degrees in partnership with FE colleges with a high level of employer support and engagement has been the focus of our developments. The number of partnerships has grown from a handful of college partners in 2006 to 10 in 2008/2009 and 15 partners validated for delivery in September 2009. More significant has been the increase in programmes delivered at partners with 24 in 2008/2009 rising to 45 validated for 2009/2010.

SOCIAL JUSTICE AND COMMUNITY ENGAGEMENT

Driven by the senior management, EH works within a transformative discourse, based on the premise of education and social justice being strongly linked (see Jones and Thomas, 2005). As such there is a keen recognition that the purpose of education should be to empower people to take agency and have increased control over themselves, their lives and the environments and communities they live. The strong drive for social justice is shaped by the management culture and in turn shapes the operation of the organisation. For example, as an educationalist and community activist, I have been supported by the dean of faculty to play an active role in community initiatives. These have included working on projects such as

Write About ..., a voluntary initiative established to promote writing, by ordinary people, about social issues that have impacted on their lives, and to publish collections of the most inspiring writing as Easy-Readers to help teenagers and adults in basic skills education come to terms with their own experiences and to overcome their personal barriers to education (Gate-house Books, 2008, 2009). Further to this, in 2008–2009 together with students at EH and partnership colleges and schools I was provided with funding from the dean of education to develop the I teach ... project (Duckworth, Gelling, Sheridan, & Shiel, 2010). This is a collection of LJs written by students at EHU. Their LJs have not always followed a conventional path, with many of the students having to overcome significant barriers along the way. Typically, the writing conveys a passion to teach and, because of their personal experiences, displays an under-standing of the issues faced by students from a variety of backgrounds. The aim is to encourage people from various backgrounds to enter HE and the teaching profession.

CONCLUSION

Offering professional development programmes to support academics in their awareness of the barriers that WP students face and addressing negative stereo-types is vital. We must be aware that engagement in the WP agenda by some may be mixed and often ambivalent (Trowler, 1995). Indeed, by virtue of their roles as academics in HE, a number of tutors are initially wary of opening their classrooms and indeed their minds to non-traditional students whose trajectories into HE and world picture are far removed from their own traditional LJs. A way to address this includes academics with 'insider' knowledge of marginalised communities working with other individuals to promote positive attitudes and changes to practice. For example, my own life-history that includes being the first generation of my family to enter university and my subsequent trajectory has greatly influenced the commitment I have for finding opportunities to enable others to take agency and aspire to reach their potential (Duckworth & Taylor, 2008). This can include learners voicing their stories at educational conferences (Johnson, Duckworth, McNamara, & Apelbaum, 2010). Individuals and their passion and drive can play a quintessential role in shaping and influencing the development of WP. Indeed, in these challenging times, it will continue to be essential that educationalists, researchers, policy makers and the communities we serve work together in flexible and pro-active ways to develop new knowledge that drives the WP agenda forward. We have to remain resolute to reach across the boundaries, build bridges and sustain communities where people work together in ways that contribute to meet challenges to social justice in HE, addressing the barriers to HE engagement and participation in the knowledge development cycle.

CHAPTER 8.4

WIDENING PARTICIPATION BRISTOL-FASHION: EMBEDDING POLICY AND PRACTICE AT THE UNIVERSITIES OF BRISTOL AND THE WEST OF ENGLAND

Tony Hoare, Betsy Bowerman, Chris Croudace and Richard Waller

ABSTRACT

Purpose – *The chapter reviews, compares and contrasts the experiences of two neighbouring universities, the University of Bristol and the University of the West of England, in the introduction, pursuit and institutional embedding of widening participation (WP) policies and programmes.*

Methodology/approach – *Comparative analysis of, and commentary on, the historical and ongoing experiences of the two universities' WP activities.*

Findings – *Contextual differences in the missions and roles played by the two universities inevitably mean their experiences have different underlying logics, but in terms of the practical drivers at work and outcomes more subtle similarities are also evident.*

Institutional Transformation to Engage a Diverse Student Body
International Perspectives on Higher Education Research, Volume 6, 319–326
ISSN: 1479-3628/doi:10.1108/S1479-3628(2011)0000006031

Practical implications – *Making direct comparisons between the parallel experiences of universities sharing a common geographical setting can be illuminating, as can examples of their joint working and collaboration. Other neighbouring universities could follow suit.*

Social implications – *The 'takes' on WP by different universities inevitably reflect the types of institutions they are and aim to be, but successful WP practices and policy embedding is not the prerogative of any particular university type.*

Originality/value of paper – *The direct inter-university comparison of WP policy offered here is rare within the literature.*

Keywords: Comparative analysis; widening participation; Bristol; actions; drivers; effectiveness

INTRODUCTION

Like many British provincial cities, Bristol houses two very different higher educational institutions (HEIs). As their responses to the national widening participation (WP) agenda show obvious differences, the temptation to regard them separately as 'case studies' is strong. But we prefer to explore them comparatively, stressing similarities and the inevitable differences. Not only do their students live as undergraduates in the same city environment, seeking accommodation in the same housing market, term-time employment in the same local economy and share leisure and entertainment facilities, the WP trajectories of Bristol's HEIs intersect in other ways too. This is especially so when considering how each has 'mainstreamed' WP into its institutional fabric, and set about delivering WP among existing and potential future students, effecting substantial changes in their practices and ethos.

INSTITUTIONAL CONTEXTS

Four miles separate the University of Bristol (UoB) campus, amidst city centre buildings, from the University of the West of England (UWE), mostly on a greenfield city-fringe site. In many ways, in their history and teaching structure, they typify the national 'binary divide' of pre- and post-1992 institutions. UWE, previously 'Bristol Polytechnic', has nearly 30,000 students, 80% of them undergraduates of whom 20% are part-time, taught across about 600 programmes [see Evans (2009) for a historical account of UWE]. Its neighbour, founded in 1876 (see Carleton, 1984), is smaller (approximately 13,000 undergraduates) and more dependent on full-time students, especially for its undergraduate programmes (over 98%). It teaches fewer programmes (about 400), specialising in a more 'traditional' academic diet, while UWE has relatively more 'applied' subjects. UoB belongs to the Russell Group of research-led universities, UWE to the University Alliance, those with both a research and business focus.

The social composition of the two HEIs' 2007/2008 intakes are sharply different, with UoB's drawing 62% from state schools (UWE 89%), 14% from low social class households (28% at UWE) and just 3% from low participation neighbourhoods (LPNs) (UWE 9%). In common with such 'elitist'-intake universities, UoB's retention rates, at approximately 98%, are among the highest nationally (UWE's are about 93%). So Bristol's HEIs also typify the stereotypical 'old' and 'new' WP landscape, one with a traditional intake mostly staying the course, the other a more socially-representative intake, suffering greater subsequent attrition.

To support their WP work, both institutions have established a raft of key performance indicators (KPIs), targets and 'milestones' too numerous to detail. UoB has more of these milestones than any other UK university [unpublished survey of university access agreements by one of us (AGH)] and now distinguishes between those for students it initially attracts and those it eventually recruits. With its somewhat lower entry standards, retention rates and more regionally focussed mission, UWE's KPIs include entry tariffs, and targets for subsequent progression to first employment and recruitment from the South West region.

ACTIONS

Both universities offer a persuasive case for firmly embedding WP in institutional missions and practices. While the fine print is inevitably varied (and detailed UWE's recent HEFCE WP strategic assessment runs to 71 pages plus 14 appendices!) both can support such claims by:

- A university-wide WP strategy
- A dedicated and sizeable unit tasked with leading and managing its delivery

- Expectations placed by the strategy 'horizontally' across all faculties and student-facing central services
- A 'vertical' structure of supporting, reporting and accountability stretching to senior management, deputy vice-chancellor (DVC) level
- A reflection of WP principles in other policy and strategy domains, notably admissions, equality and diversity, education and the overall mission statement.

Both universities also support the institutional embedding of WP through research activities. UWE colleagues led a major investigation into LPNs of south Bristol (Raphael Reed, Croudace, Harrison, Baxter, & Last, 2007), and the co-ordination of that report's umbrella 'Four Cities' study for its funder (HEFCE, 2007b), while work by Harrison and Peacock (2009), Hatt, Hannan, Baxter, and Harrison (2005) and Waller (e.g. 2006) further illustrate a diverse and vibrant WP research agenda. At UoB corresponding research has been triggered by questioning the University's own WP experiences. So Paton and Surridge (2005) surveyed the on-course experiences of different 'WP' student groups, while the Sociology Department twice investigated the reasoning of candidates turning down offers of a place at the university (Levitas, Fenton, & Guy, 1991; Levitas, Guy, Fenton, Fenton, & West, 2006). In the *2004–0909 WP Strategy* such research was placed on a firm institutionally supported and funded footing through establishing the WP Research Cluster (WPRC), dedicated to provide an evidence base for UoB's WP policies and practices. The WPRC has hosted two national research seminars and peer-reviewed publications (e.g. Hoare & Aitchison, 2009; Hoare & Johnston, 2011). It led the university's 2008/2009 review of WP milestones, now based on empirically verified evidence of 'educational disadvantage'. The university's rationale here is that WP facilitates the entry of students of the necessary academic potential from whatever background, as captured by the strap-line of the *2004/0909 Strategy* – *'Quality through Diversity'*.

The two university WP chronologies have also been similar. UWE can trace WP mainstreaming to the establishment of its Community Action Centre in 1995. UWE's first WP strategy was approved in 2001, and the Outreach Centre (which oversees its WP activities) began in 2005. UoB also recognised the need to respond swiftly to Dearing's WP agenda (National Committee of Inquiry into Higher Education, 1997a). Its first 'Participation' strategy was published in 1999, with further iterations in 2001 and 2004, leading to the current (2009–2016) *Strategy*. Its WP Office was established in 2000.

Today, each university's involvement in WP activities touches every faculty and most academic departments in some way or other. Both universities are heavily involved in outreach, admissions processes and on-course support, with UWE also supporting WP students seeking employment.

Finally, we should note some important collaboration. The two HEIs jointly deliver much of their local outreach, from contacts in primary schools to parents' evenings and the Aimhigher roadshow. And since 2006/2007, academics and WP managers have met regularly to compare experiences and launch joint research projects, including one funded by a substantial Leverhulme grant, tracking the longitudinal experiences of 'matched pairs' of new students from Autumn 2010. This chapter is another such output.

EFFECTIVENESS

As we have seen, using the qualitative criterion of significant and widespread institutional impact, their WP agendas have been effective agents for change in both Bristol's universities. What if their more publicly visible success on the quantitative measurements widely used within the HE sector? As the percentage of undergraduates drawn from WP groups has steadily risen nationally, attributing any university's KPI improvements solely to its WP endeavours is over-simplistic. However, UWE's achievements are still impressive and consistent with raising WP's three 'As' of *awareness, aspiration* and *attainment*. Since the first (1999) set of such KPIs, UWE has seen a steady increase in the diversity of its intake, in the take-up of student bursaries and growth of many other WP activities.

UoB has fewer such quantitative markers of success, though can point to growing enrolments on its summer schools and local 'Access to Bristol' programmes. However, it has been less successful on its nationally benchmarked KPIs and self-generated milestones. The university's fine-grained (down to department level) annual profiling of achievements against its WP milestones produces a wealth of detail. Results have inevitably been varied, but fewer clear and consistent trends to increased diversity are apparent. As its HEFCE strategic assessment (UWE, 2009) noted, while the 2008/2009 admissions' cycle saw a slight rise in Black and Minority Ethnic and low social class students, mature student recruitment remained static and LPN, state school and low-performing school intakes were lower. An over-arching review of these milestones led to a more sharply focussed and evidence-based set of revisions: that for intake (rather than applications) now concentrates on mature students and 'school performance'. For the latter,

UoB now has evidence of an 'educational disadvantage' gap between prior attainment and degree potential, with appropriate information on applicants provided to admissions' tutors at the point of decision making. As noted in the recent national 'Harris' report on WP in selective universities, UoB's pioneering methodology and rationale has sector-wide application, providing, for the first time, a robust defence against 'social engineering' charges, while ensuring applicants are still treated holistically, as individuals (OFFA, 2010).

REFLECTIONS

All significant WP developments at Bristol's universities can ultimately be traced back at least to, if not before, the national agenda initiated by Dearing. Subsequent political imperatives, WP financial provisions and reporting obligations framed their management of WP affairs. But both also exercised strong local control, setting a distinctive proactive imprint to their actions, allowing identification of key drivers and facilitators on their WP stories.

Neither university has felt constrained by HESA performance indicators over setting KPIs and WP targets; these were in place before the first tranche of access agreements made them mandatory. With their growing institutional commitment, both have employed block grant funding to support WP activities, with supplementation from alumni, particularly UoB, with its limited HEFCE funding-formula income from specifically recruiting 'WP' students.

Both also responded to different geographical imperatives in their WP landscapes. UWE has been heavily involved in *local* and *regional* outreach: its relative emphasis on part-time study makes it particularly attractive to locally resident students with other home- or work-centred commitments. Its greater involvement with local academies, trust schools, federations with partner colleges in the region and hosting the regional Aimhigher centre reflect and reinforce this local/regional engagement.

UoB's student catchment and operational sphere are more widespread; its involvement with the summer schools run by the Sutton Trust, a national educational charity, and the new (2009/2010) inter-university common 'compact' scheme are nationwide, while its discussion forums for WP and admissions issues are through the nationwide Russell Group of 20 larger, research-intensive universities, rather than regional consortia.

At the risk of over-generalisation, UoB's WP engagement has been driven more than UWE's by desires simultaneously to broaden access and raise academic standards, and informed by its, at-times, high public visibility in the national media. Most courses are strongly 'selecting' rather than 'recruiting', and assured of a stream of well-qualified applicants from their traditional markets. Recently, UoB has sometimes topped the UK university league table in applications-per-place: it does not *need* more high quality applications to fill its courses.

However, that UoB still moved speedily to joined-up delivery on the Dearing WP recommendations owed much to the energy and charisma of a then DVC, Professor David Evans, who skilfully led the early tentative footsteps of the WP programme. An early buy-in from senior management was also crucial in winning hearts and minds within the university. The growing role of WP research also chimes with UoB's wider self-portrayal as among the sector's research elite.

At UWE, in contrast, the case for WP support is more fundamental and self-evident. While widely recognised as one of the most successful British post-1992 universities, research has traditionally been less of a priority than at UoB, but its dependence on local recruitment and teaching-related income is stronger. Greater financial dependence on non-traditional student groups gives its WP efforts a sharper economic cutting-edge. In moving progressively to a more joined-up programme there, as in UoB, an on-campus campaign had to be won, and here too the engagement of senior management and evidence of the success of past WP practices and spending proved crucial.

Of course, everything has not always been plain sailing. Some initial unease with the WP agenda, especially at UoB, has been confronted with argument and evidence. In the uncertain times ahead, most HEIs are likely to face 'rationalisations', and WP-facing staff will not be immune, though this could increase the cost-effectiveness advantage of the UoB's applications-based, 'contexting' approach to WP, over the higher labour cost, harder-to-evaluate alternative of outreach. There may be other campus-specific challenges too. Time will tell if UWE's KPI on higher entry tariffs will harmonise with its WP agenda, while UoB will find it harder to stand against using the A^* A Level grade (consistently opposed on WP grounds) if its rivals increasingly do. Tighter management of UCAS offers and any centralisation of their management away from departments could have similar implications.

Such uncertainties aside, as we write each university has its immediate WP future strategy firmly in place and in different ways, both Bristol universities appear in good heart to confront the difficult times ahead for WP throughout the sector. So UoB will continue its emphasis on 'outstanding outreach', 'diversifying intake', 'student support' and 'monitoring and research' while at UWE the overarching future goal to continue embedding inclusive WP policy and practice throughout the student journey, from pre-entry to post-graduation employment.

Inevitably, at Bristol's universities, two sets of WP policies and practices have been forged in separate and distinctive institutional contexts. Unsurprisingly, its universities' experiences contrast significantly. Comparing them directly, as WP literatures rarely do, shows these in sharp relief. But in other respects, these experiences are remarkably similar – both are 'good news' experiences, spanning similar time periods with similar casts of leading characters and story-lines. They have recognised their differences and played to their strengths, to the benefit of their WP agendas. Finally, their collaborations here provide the chance to share experiences, discussing and promoting joint ventures in ways that otherwise would not have been glimpsed, let alone delivered. Other same-city universities could do the same.

REFERENCES

1994 Group of Universities. (2007). Enhancing the Student Experience – Policy Report. Available at http://www.1994group.ac.uk/studentexperience.php

Action on Access. (2005). Widening participation. Bradford, Action on Access.

Action on Access. (2008). Higher Education Progression Framework Guide. Ormskirk: Action on Access. Available at http://www.actiononaccess.org/?p=19_4. Accessed on June 14, 2010.

Admissions to Higher Education Steering Group (2004). Fair Admissions to HE: Recommendations for Good Practice' – the Schwartz Report. Available at http://www.admissions-review.org.uk/downloads/finalreport.pdf

Aimhigher South West. (2007). South West Summer Schools Review. Available at http://www.aimhighersw.ac.uk/progress.htm#reports

Anderson, D., Johnson, R., & Milligan, B. (2000). Access to Postgraduate Courses: Opportunities and Obstacles. Canberra: Higher Education Council, Commonwealth Department of Education, Training and Youth, Australia.

Archer, L. (2007). Diversity, equality and higher education: a critical reflection on the ab/uses of equity discourse within widening participation. *Teaching in Higher Education, 12*(5), 635–653.

Archer, L., Hutchings, M., & Ross, A. (2003). *Higher education and social class; issues of exclusion and inclusion.* London: Routledge Falmer.

Archer, W., & Davidson, S. (2008). *Graduate employability: The view of employers.* London: CIHE.

Arya, R., & Smith, R. (2005). *Living at home* ([Internal Report]). Birmingham: Aston University.

Astin, A., & Holland, J. (1961). The environmental assessment technique: A way to measure college environments. *Journal of Educational Psychology, 52*, 308–316.

Astin, A., & Panos, R. (1969). *The educational and vocational development of college students.* Washington, DC: American Council on Education.

Austin, M., & Hatt, S. (2005). "The messengers are the message": A study of the effects of employing HE student ambassadors to work with school students. *Journal of Widening Participation and Lifelong Learning, 7*(1), 22–29.

Australian Bureau of Statistics. (2009). *Education and work.* Available at http://www.abs.gov.au/ausstats/abs@.nsf/mf/6227.0. Accessed on November 12, 2010.

Bamber, J., & Tett, L. (2001). Ensuring integrative learning experiences for non-traditional students in Higher education. *Journal of Widening Participation and Lifelong Learning, 3.1*, 8–18.

Barr, R. B., & Tagg, J. (1995). From teaching to learning – A new paradigm for undergraduate education. *Change, 27*(6), 13–25.

Begičević, N., Divjak, B., & Hunjak, T. (2007). Development of AHP based model for decision making on e-learning implementation. *Journal of Information and Organization Sciences (JIOS), 31*(1), 13–24.

Biggs, J. (2005). *Teaching for quality learning at university.* Berkshire: The Society for Quality Learning at University & Open University Press.

Billingham, S. (2009). Diversity, inclusion, and the transforming student experience, Keynote address, 18th EAN Annual International Conference. York: York St John University, June 22–24. Available at http://www.ean-edu.org/index.php?view=article&catid=41%3Afuture&id=98%3A2009-annual-conference&option=com_content&Itemid=84, accessed 23/11/10

Billingham, S. (2010). *Moving from access to engagement*. Keynote address, Pathways to Education Access Conference. Cork: University College Cork and Cork Institute of Technology.

Black, J. (Ed.) (2001). *The strategic enrollment management revolution*. Washington, DC: AACRAO.

Bland, D. (2008). *Imagination at the margins: Creating bridges to re-engagement*. Paper presented to the Imaginative Education Research Group Annual Conference, Canberra, January.

Blasko, Z., Brennan, J., Little, B., & Shah, T. (2003). *Access to what: Analysis of factors determining graduate employability*. London: Centre for Higher Education Research and Information, Open University.

Blythman, M., Orr, S., Hampton, D., McLaughlin, M., & Waterworth, H. (2006). Strategic approaches to the development and management of personal tutorial systems in UK higher education. In: L. Thomas & P. Hixenbaugh (Eds), *Personal tutoring in higher education*. Stoke-on-Trent, UK: Trentham Books.

Bond, R., & Saunders, P. (1999). Routes of success: Influences on the occupational attainment of young British males. *British Journal of Sociology*, 50(2), 217–249.

Bourdieu, P., & Passeron, J. C. (1977). *Reproduction in education, society and culture*. London: Sage Publications.

Bourdieu, P., & Wacquant, L. (1992). *An invitation to reflexive sociology*. Chicago: Chicago University Press.

Bowl, M. (2003). *Non-traditional entrants to higher education 'they talk about people like me'*. Stoke-on-Trent: Trentham Books.

Bradley, D. (2008). *Review of Australian higher education*. Canberra: Commonwealth of Australia.

Bradley, D., Noonan, P., Nugent, H., & Scales, B. (2008). Review of Australian higher education: Final report. Canberra: Department of Employment, Education and Workplace Relations, Commonwealth of Australia. Available at http://www.deewr.gov.au/he_review_finalreport

Brennan, J., Mills, J., Shah, T., & Woodley, A. (2000). Lifelong learning for employment and equity: The role of part-time degrees. *Higher Education Quarterly*, 54(4), 411–418.

Brennan, J., & Shah, T. (2003). *Access to what? Converting education opportunity into employment opportunity*. London: Centre for Higher Education Research and Information, Open University.

Brown, P., & Hesketh, A. J. (2003). The social construction of graduate employability. ESRC research report. Available at http://www.regard.ac.uk/research_findings/R000239101/report.pdf

Buchler, M., Castle, J., Osman, R., & Walters, S. (2004). Equity, access and success: Adult learners in public higher education, pp. 124–156. Available at http://www.nqf.org.za/page/nqf-support/rpl/index

Burke, P. J. (2002). *Accessing education: Effectively widening participation*. Stoke-on-Trent: Trentham Books.

Burke, P. J. (2005). Access and widening participation. *British Journal of Sociology of Education*, *26*(4), 555–562.

Carleton, D. (1984). *A University for Bristol*. Bristol: University of Bristol Press.

Carnall, C. A. (1997). Creating programs of change. In: C. A. Carnall (Ed.), *Strategic change* (pp. 239–246). Oxford: Butterworths-Heinemann.

Carré, P. (1999). Motivation et rapport à la formation. In: P. Carré & P. Caspar (Eds), *Traité des Sciences et des Techniques de la formation*. Paris: Dunod.

Carré, P. (2005). *L'Apprenance, vers un nouveau rapport au savoir*. Paris: Dunod.

Caspi, A., Entner Wright, B. R., Moffitt, T. E., & Silva, P. A. (1998). Early failure in the labour market: Childhood and adolescent predictors of unemployment in the transition to adulthood. *American Sociological Review*, *63*(3), 424–451.

Catts, R., & Ozga, G. (2005). What is social capital and how might it be used in Scotland's Schools? CES Briefing No. 36, Centre for Sociology, University of Edinburgh.

Chevalier, A., & Conlon, G. (2003) Does it pay to attend a prestigious university? Centre for the Economics of Education Discussion Paper No. 33, London School of Economics, London.

Chickering, A. W., & Gamson, Z. F. (1987). *Principles of good practice for undergraduate education*. Racine, WI: Johnson Foundation.

Conference of European Ministers responsible for higher education (2009). Leuven Communiqué. Available at www.europeunit.ac.uk/sites/europe_unit2/bologna_process/decision_making/leuven_louvain_la_neuve_2009.cfm

Conlon, G. (2001). The incidence and outcomes asociated with the late attainment of qualifications in the UK. Centre for the Economics of Education Discussion Paper 13, London School of Economics, London.

Connor, H., Tvers, C., Modood, T., & Hillage J. (2004). Why the difference? A closer look at Higher Education minority ethnic students and graduates, Research Report 552, DfES Publications, London.

Conseil des Recteurs des Universités francophone de Belgique. (2009). *Annuaire statistique 2008*. Brussels: CREF.

Cooper, L. (2011). 'Activists within the Academy': The role of prior experience in adult learners' acquisition of postgraduate literacies in a post-apartheid South African university'. *Adult Education Quarterly*, *61*(1), 40–56.

Cooper, L., Majepelo, C. & Pottier, L. (2008). Report on Survey of Adult Learners at UCT, May–July. University of Cape Town, Cape Town.

Coulon, A. (1997). *Le métier d'étudiant. L'entrée dans la vie universitaire*. Paris: PUF.

Council for Industry in Higher Education (CIHE). (2004). *Glossary of CIHE employability competencies*. Gloucester: Quality Assurance Agency for Higher Education.

Crosling, G., Edwards, R., & Schroder, W. (2008). Internationalising the curriculum: The implementation experience in a Faculty of Business and Economics. *Journal of Higher Education Policy and Management*, *30*(2), 107–121.

Crosling, G., Thomas, L., & Heagney, M. (Eds). (2008). *Improving student retention in higher education*. New York: Routledge Falmer.

Croucher, K., Evans, M., & Leacy, A. (2005). *What happens next? A report on the first destinations of 2003 graduates with disabilities*. Sheffield: Association of Graduate Careers Advisory Services Disability Development Network.

Crul, M., Pasztor, A., Lelie, F., Mijs, J., & Schnell, P. (2009). *Valkuilen en springplanken in het onderwijs*. Den Haag: NICIS Institute.

Davis, T., & Murrell, P. (1993). A structural model of perceived academic, personal, and vocational gains related to college student responsibility. *Research in Higher Education*, *34*, 267–289.

DBIS (2010). Skills for Sustainable Growth, November, DBIS.

Dearden, L., McGranahan, L., & Sianesi, B. (2004). Returns to education for the 'Marginal Learner': Evidence from the BCS70. Discussion Paper No. 45, London School of Economics, Centre for the Economics of Education, London.

De Kerchove, A. M., & Lambert, J. P. (2001). Choix des études supérieures et motivations des étudiant(e)s. *Reflets et Perspectives de la vie économique*, *2001/4*, 41–55.

De Meulemeester, J.-L., & Rochat, D. (1995). Impact of individuals characteristics and sociocultural environment on academic success. *International Advances in Economic Research*, *1*(3), 278–287.

Department for Education and Science (2003). *The future of higher education*. The Stationary Office Limited, Norwich.

Department of Education and Training (2009). *Next step survey*. Available at http://education.qld.gov.au/nextstep/2009survey.html. Accessed on November 12, 2010.

Department of Education, Employment and Workplace Relations (2009a). Institution Assessment Framework Information Collection, Canberra.

Department of Education, Employment and Workplace Relations. (2009b). Transforming Australia's Higher Education System. Canberra. Available at http://www.deewr.gov.au/HigherEducation/Pages/TransformingAustraliasHESystem.aspx

Department of Education, Employment and Workplace Relations. (2010). Higher Education Support Act 2003, Other Grants Guidelines (Education) 2010. Canberra. Chapter 1: Grants to promote equality of opportunity in higher education, p. 12. Available at http://www.deewr.gov.au/HigherEducation/Programs/Equity/Documents/HEPPPGuidelines_2010.pdf

Department of Employment, Education and Training; National Board of Employment, Education and Training. (1990). A fair chance for all: National Institutional Planning for Equity in Higher Education: A discussion paper. Canberra: AGPS. Available at http://www.dest.gov.au/sectors/training_skills/publications_resources/profiles/nbeet/equity_in_higher_education.htm

DETYA (2001). The Enabling Program, a report compiled as the basis for national consultation on enabling programs using data drawn from DETYA statistics and the unpublished EIP report "The Cost Effectiveness of Enabling and Related Programs in Australian Tertiary Education" by Clarke et al., completed in 2000, Canberra.

Dika, S., & Singh, K. (2002). Applications of social capital in educational literature: A critical synthesis. *Review of Educational Research*, *72*(1), 31–60.

Dirks, K. T., Cummings, L. L., & Pierce, J. L. (1996). Psychological ownership in organizations: Conditions under which individuals promote and resist change. *Research in Organisational Change and Development*, *9*, 1–23.

DIUS (2009). Thrift report on research careers. Available at http://www.bis.gov.uk/he-debate-thrift. Accessed on May 25, 2010).

Divjak, B., Begičević, N., Grabar, D., & Boban, M. (2010). Strategy for E-learning, Faculty of Organization and Informatics – Analysis of Strategy. University of Zagreb. Available at http://www.foi.hr/CMS_home/dokumenti/strategija_eUcenje.pdf. Accessed on December 19, 2009.

Divjak, B., Vidaček-Hainš, V., & Ostroški, M. (2007). Gender issue in the field of ICT technology in higher education. VII Conference of the European Regions on Equal Opportunities, Timisioara, RO. Available at http://www.a-e-r.org/fileadmin/user_upload/MainIssues/EqualOpportunities/2007/OJ-VII-Varazdin-Vidacek.ppt. Accessed on Febbruary 10, 2010.

Dodgson, R., & Bolam, H. (2002) Student retention, support and widening participation in the North East of England. Universities for the North East. Available at www.unis4ne.ac.uk/unew/projectsadditionalfiles/wp/retention_report.pdf.

Droesbeke, J.-J., Hecquet, I., & Wattelar, C. (2001). *La population étudiante: description, évolution et perspectives.* Brussels: Editions de l'Université Libre de Bruxelles.

Duckworth, V., Gelling, C., Sheridan, B., & Shiel, C. (2010). *I teach – Journeys into teaching.* Warrington: Gate House Books.

Duckworth, V., & Taylor, K. (2008). Words are for everyone. *Research and Practice in Adult Literacy, 64,* 30–32.

Du Toit, A. (2010). Social Justice and Post apartheid Higher Education in South Africa. In: D. L. Featherman, M. Hall & M. Krislov (Eds), *The next 25 years: Affirmative action in Higher Education in the United States and South Africa* (pp. 87–109). Anne Arbor, MI: University of Michigan Press.

Educational Policy Institute. (2005). *Global higher education rankings: Affordability and accessibility in comparative perspective.* Washington: EPI.

Edwards, R., & Usher, R. (2000). *Globalisation and pedagogy: Space, place and identity.* London: Routledge.

Engle, J., & O'Brien, C. (2007). *Demography is not destiny: Increasing the graduation rates of low-income college students at large public universities.* Washington, DC: The Pell Institute for the Study of Opportunity in Higher Education.

Ensor, P. (2003). The National Qualifications Framework and Higher Education in South Africa: Some epistemological issues. *Journal of Education & Work, 16*(3), 325–346.

Entreprise des Technologies Nouvelles de l'Information et de la Communication. (2010). *Annuaire de l'enseignement de plein exercice et budget des dépenses d'enseignement 2007–2008.* Brussels: ETNIC.

Equality Act (2010). http://www.legislation.gov.uk/ukpga/2010/15/contents

Equality and Human Rights Commission (EHRC). (2010). *Making fair financial decisions: A briefing note for further and higher education institutions.* London: EHRC.

Equality Challenge Unit and Higher Education Academy. (2007–2008). Ethnicity, Gender and Degree Attainment Project – Final Report. London: ECU and York: HEA.

EUA (2008). European Universities' Charter on Lifelong Learning. Brussels: European Universities Association. Available at http://www.eua.be/fileadmin/user_upload/files/Publications/EUA_Charter_Eng_LY.pdf. Accessed on December 1, 2010.

Evans, W. (2009). *University of the West of England, Bristol – A family history.* Bristol: Redcliffe Press.

Evenbeck, S., Ross, F. E., & Kinzie, J. (2010). Developing and assessing high impact educational programs to support first year student learning and success. Paper presented at the 29th annual conference on the first-year experience. Denver, Colorado.

Featherman, D. L., Hall, M., & Krislov, M. (2010). *The next 25 years – affirmative action in Higher Education in the United States and South Africa.* Anne Arbor, MI: University of Michigan Press.

Floyd, D. L., & Arnauld, C. St. (2007). An exploratory study of Community College Baccalaureate Teacher Education Programs. Lessons Learned. *Community College Review, 35*(1), 66–84.

Forsyth, A., & Furlong, A. (2003). Access to higher education and disadvantaged young people. *British Education Research Journal, 29*(2), 205–225.

Fuller, A., & Heath, S. (2010). Educational decision-making, social networks and the new widening participation. In: M. David (Ed.), *Improving learning by widening participation in higher education.* London: Routledge.

Gamarnikow, E., & Green, A. (2000). Developing social capital: Dilemmas, possibilities and limitations in education. In: K. Arrow, S. Bowles & S. Durlauf (Eds), *Meritocracy and economic inequality* (pp. 44–61). Princeton, NJ: Princeton University Press.

Geser, G. (2007). Open educational practices and resources, OLCOS Road Map 2012, Executive Summary, (OLCOS-Transversal Action funded by the European Commission, coordinated by Veronika Hornung-Praehauser from Salzburg Research/EduMedia Group,), Salzburg. Available at http://www.olcos.org. Retrieved on March 6, 2010.

Goffman, E. (1963). *Stigma. Notes on the management of spoiled identity.* Englewood Cliffs, NJ: Prentice-Hall.

Goodstein, L. D., & Burke, W. W. (1997). Creating successful organization change. In: C.A. Carnall (Ed.), *Strategic change* (pp. 159–173). Oxford: Butterworths-Heinemann.

Gorard, S., Smith, E., May, H., Thomas, L., Adnett, N., & Slack, K. (2006). Review of widening participation research: Addressing the barriers to participation in higher education. A report to HEFCE by the University of York, Higher Education Academy and Institute for Access Studies. Bristol: HEFCE.

Government of South Australia (1990). University of South Australia Act 1990. Available at http://www.unisa.edu.au/policies/act/act.asp. Accessed on August 28, 2009.

Graham, L. (2007). Done in by discourse ... or the problem/s with labelling. In: M. Keeffe & S. Carrington (Eds), *Schools and diversity* (2nd ed., pp. 46–64). Frenchs Forest, NSW: Pearson Education Australia.

Greenbank, P. (2006). Widening participation in higher education: an examination of the factors influencing institutional policy. *Research in Post-Compulsory Education, 11*(2), 199–215.

Greenbank, P. (2007). Introducing widening participation policies in higher education: The influence of institutional culture. *Research in Post-Compulsory Education, 12*(2), 209–224.

Hall, M. (2010). Nothing is different, but everything's changed. In: D. L. Featherman, M. Hall & M. Krislov (Eds), *The next 25 years – affirmative action in higher education in the United States and South Africa* (pp. 355–369). Anne Arbor, MI: University of Michigan Press.

Halpern, D. (2006). *Social capital.* Campbridge: Polity.

Hansen, M. (2010). IUPUI academic support programs and academic success outcomes: Highlights Fall 2005–2009 Cohorts. Nonpublished report.

Harding, S. (1986). *The science question in feminism.* Ithaca: Cornell University Press.

Harrison, N. (2009) Widening participation profiles of HEIs in the south west region 2002/ 3-2007/8 unpublished report. Available at http://www.aimhighersw.ac.uk/research. html#research2010

Harrison, N., Baxter, A., & Hatt, S. (2007). From opportunity to OFFA: The implementation of discretionary bursaries and their impact on student finance, academic success and institutional attachment. *Journal of Access Policy and Practice, 5*(1), 3–21.

Harrison, N., & Peacock, N. (2009). Cultural distance, mindfulness and passive Xenophobia: Using Integrated Threat Theory to explore home higher education students' perspectives on 'internationalisation at home'. British Educational Research Journal, First published on August 26 (iFirst).

Hartley, G. (2006). Preparing for the future and reviewing the past: Improving the Achievement and Retention of Students from Low Participation Neighbourhoods. Birmingham: Aston University [Internal Report].

Harvey, L. (2003). *Enhancing employability*. London: Universities UK.

Harvey, L., & Drew, S. (2006) The first year experience: Briefing on induction. York, Higher Education Academy. Available at http://www.heacademy.ac.uk/assets/York/documents/ourwork/research/literature_reviews/first_year_experience_briefing_on_induction.pdf

Hatt, S., Baxter, A., & Tate, J. (2007). Measuring progress; an evaluative study of Aimhigher in the South West 2003–2006. *Higher Education Quarterly, 61*(3), 284–305.

Hatt, S., Baxter, A., & Tate, J. (2009). "It was definitely a turning point". A review of summer schools in the SW of England. *Journal of Access Policy and Practice, 33*(4), 333–346.

Hatt, S., Hannan, A., Baxter, A., & Harrison, N. (2005). Opportunity knocks? The impact of bursary schemes on students from low-income backgrounds. *Studies in Higher Education, 30*, 373–388.

HEPI. (2004). Postgraduate education in the United Kingdom. Available at http://www.hepi.ac.uk/466-1149/Postgraduate-Education-in-the-United-Kingdom.html. Accessed on May 25, 2010.

HEPI (2010) Postgraduate education in the UK. London: HEPI. Available at www.bl.uk/aboutus/acrossuk/highered/helibs/postgraduate_education.pdf. Accessed on May 25, 2010).

Herzfeldt, R. (2007). Cultural competence of first year undergraduates, in Aston Business School Good Practice Guide: Volume 4, pp. 23–29. Available at http://www1.aston.ac.uk/aston-business-school/research/structure/centres/helm/gpg/. Accessed on August 2, 2010.

Higgins, J. (2007). Managing meaning: The constitutive contradiction of institutional culture. *Social Dynamics, 33*(1), 107–129. Special issue focusing on Higher Education.

Higher Education Academy Business Subject Centre. (2005). Available at http://www.heaacademybusiness.ac.ukwww.heaacademybusiness.ac.uk. Retrieved from Student Employabilty Profiles.

Higher Education Authority. (2004) Achieving equity of access to higher education in Ireland: Action Plan 2005–2007, Dublin: HEA. Available at http://www.hea.ie/files/files/file/archive/corporate/2004/Access%20Action%20Plan.pdf. Accessed on June 3, 2009.

Higher Education Authority. (2008). National Plan for Equity of Access to Higher Education 2008–2013, Dublin: HEA. Available at http://www.hea.ie/files/files/file/New_pdf/National_Access_Plan_2008-2013_(English).pdf. Accessed on June 3, 2009.

Higher Education Funding Council for England (HEFCE). (1999a). Widening participation in higher education HEFCE 99/33. HEFCE, Bristol.

Higher Education Funding Council for England (HEFCE). (1999b). Report 99/24. Widening participation in higher education: Funding decisions. Bristol: Higher Education Funding Council. Available at http://www.hefce.ac.uk/Pubs/hefce/1999/99_24.htm. Accessed on August 10, 2010.

Higher Education Funding Council for England (HEFCE). (2001a) Supply and demand in higher education. Consultation 01/62. Bristol: HEFCE. Available at http://www.hefce.ac.uk/pubs/hefce/2001/01_62.htm. Accessed on August 5, 2010.

Higher Education Funding Council for England (HEFCE). (2001b). Strategies for widening participation in higher education: A guide to good practice. Bristol: HEFCE.

Higher Education Funding Council for England (HEFCE). (2003). Widening participation funded projects. End of programme report August 03/40. HEFCE, Bristol.

Higher Education Funding Council for England (HEFCE). (2004). Lifelong learning networks. HEFCE Circular letter 12/2004. HEFCE, Bristol.

Higher Education Funding Council for England (HEFCE). (2006a). Widening participation: A review by HEFCE. Available at http://www.hefce.ac.uk/widen/aimhigh/review.asp.

Higher Education Funding Council for England (HEFCE). (2006b). Widening participation: A review. Report to the Minister of State for Higher Education and Lifelong Learning from the Higher Educaiton Funding Council for England, Bristol.

Higher Education Funding Council for England (HEFCE). (2007a). Higher education outreach: Targeting disadvantaged learners HEFCE 2007/12. HEFCE, Bristol.

Higher Education Funding Council for England (HEFCE). (2007b). Young participation in higher education in the parliamentary constituencies of Birmingham Hodge Hill. Bristol South, Nottingham North and Sheffield Brightside, report to HEFCE by the University of the West of England and the University of Nottingham. Available at http://www.hefce.ac.uk/pubs/rdreports/2007/rd16_07/rd16_07.pdf. Accessed on January 2008.

Higher Education Funding Council for England (HEFCE). (2008a). Guidance for Aimhigher partnerships 2008/05. HEFCE, Bristol.

Higher Education Funding Council for England (HEFCE). (2009/2001). Request for widening participation strategic statements January 2009/01. HEFCE, Bristol. Available at http://www.hefce.ac.uk/pubs/hefce/2009/09_01/

Higher Education Funding Council for England (HEFCE). (2009). Statistics: Students and qualifiers at UK higher education institutions. Available at http://www.hesa.ac.uk/index.php?option=com_content&task=view&id=1897&Itemid=239 Accessed on December 21, 2010.

Higher Education Funding Council for England (HEFCE). (2010). Trends in young participation in higher education: Core results for England. Issues paper 2010/03. Bristol: HEFCE. Available at http://www.hefce.ac.uk/pubs/hefce/2010/10_03/10_03.pdf. Accessed on August 5, 2010

Higher Education Funding Council for England (HEFCE). (2001c). The student lifecycle. Available at http://www.hefce.ac.uk/pubs/hefce/2001/01_36.htm. Accessed on June 1, 2010

Higher Education Funding Council for England (HEFCE). (2005). Young participation in higher education. HEFCE 2005/03. Bristol: HEFCE.

Higher Education Funding Council for England (HEFCE). (2008b). http://www.hefce.ac.uk/pubs/hefce/2008/08_10/08_10.doc

Higher Education Statistics Agency (HESA). (2009). Students in Higher Education Institutions 2007/2008. Higher Education Statistics Agency. Available at http://www.hesa.ac.uk/index.php/content/view/1703/141/. Accessed on October 10, 2010.

Higson, H. E. (2009). Journey towards cultural competence: Developing University teachers EuroMed Conference, Salerno, Italy, October [available on request].

Higson, H. E. (2010). The Journey towards cultural competence: Developing innovative learning which benefits both Home and Overseas Students, Working Paper. [available on request] [Inaugural Lecture: Intercultural competence: Innovative practices to maximize student learning, 13 October 2009] Available at http://www1.aston.ac.uk/about/news/events/past-events/public-lectures-2009-2010/intercultural-competence/

Hills, J. (2003). Stakeholder perceptions of the employability of non-traditional students. London: London Metropolitan University. Available at http://www.londonmet.ac.uk/employability/projects/gem/publication/home.cfm. Accessed on May 15, 2006.

Hoare, A. G., & Aitchison, R. L. (2009). PQA: Pretty questionable assumptions. *Higher Education Review, 42*, 17–49.

Hoare, A. G., & Johnston, R. J. (2011). Widening participation through admissions policy – a British case study of school and university performance, forthcoming. *Studies in Higher Education*.

Hogarth, T., Purcell, K., & Wilson, R. (1997). *The participation of non-traditional students in Higher Education*. Warwick: Institute for Employment Research, University of Warwick.

Honeybone, A. (2002). Skills are dead! Long live skills. *Education Developer, 3*(4), 437–446.

Hoschul-Informations-System. (2000). *Eurostudent. Social and economic conditions of student life in Europe*. Hannover: HIS.

Hossler, D. (2008). The public policy landscape: Financing higher education in America. In: B. Bontrager (Ed.), *SEM and institutional success*. Washington, DC: AACRAO.

House of Commons Committee of Public Accounts Committee. (2008). Staying the course: The retention of students on higher education courses. Tenth report of session 2007–2008. London: The Stationery Office Ltd.

House of Commons Public Accounts Committee report. (2008–2009). Fourth Report of Session 2008–2009. Available at http://www.publications.parliament.uk/pa/cm200809/cmselect/cmpubacc/226/9780215526557.pdf

Huba, M. E., & Freed, J. E. (2000). *Learner-centered assessment on college campuses: Shifting the focus from teaching to learning*. Boston, MA: Allyn & Bacon.

Human Sciences Research Council. (2003). *Human resources development review: Education, employment and skills in South Africa*. Cape Town: HSRC Press.

Ippolito, K. (2007). Promoting intercultural learning in a multicultural university: Ideals and realities. *Teaching in Higher Education, 12*(5–6), 749–763.

Ismail, S. (2007). 'Did I say that?' – A follow-up study of the shifts in black and women staff experiences of institutional culture in the Health Science Faculty of the University of Cape Town. In special issue of Social Dynamics on Transformation in Higher Education. Vol. 33 Number 1, June, pp. 78–106.

Jackson, B., & Orme, W. (2007). Transformations: Librarian/faculty collaboration in first-year programs at IUPUI. In: L. Hardesty (Ed.), *The role of the library in the first college year* (Monograph No. 45, pp. 191–196). Columbia: University of South Carolina, National Resource Center for the First-Year Experience and Students in Transition.

James, R., Krause, K., & Jennings, C. (2010). The first year experience in Australian universities: Findings from 1994-2009. Available at www.cshe.unimelb.edu.au

Jansen, J. (1991). Knowledge and power in the world system: The South African case. In: J. Jansen (Ed.), *Knowledge and power in South Africa – Critical perspectives across the disciplines* (pp. 17–54). Johannesburg: Skotaville.

Jansen, J. (2010). Moving on Up? The politics, problems, and prospects of universities as gateways for social mobility in South Africa. In: D. L. Featherman, M. Hall & M. Krislov (Eds), *The next 25 years: Affirmative action in Higher Education in the United States and South Africa* (pp. 129–136). Anne Arbor, MI: University of Michigan Press.

JISC Report Scoping Study 2: Mechanisms for assessing the fairness and effectiveness of selection processes in admissions to higher education (2008), p. 44 Appendix A: Prioritised list of characteristics of fair admissions. http://www.jisc.ac.uk/media/documents/programmes/elearningcapital/fairnessstudyreport.pdf as part of the e-learning Capital programme at JISC: http://www.jisc.ac.uk/whatwedo/programmes/programme_elearning_capital/admissions/fairnessstudy.aspx

Johnson, C., Duckworth, V., McNamara, M., & Apelbaum, C. (2010). A tale of two adult learners: From adult basic education to degree completion. *National Association for Developmental Education Digest*, 5(5), 57–67.

Jonassen, D. H., & Land, S. M. (2002). *Theoretical foundations of learning environments*. Lawrence Erlbaum Associates, Mahwah, NJ. Available at http://books.google.com/books?hl=en&lr=&id=QhbBLtPudScC&oi=fnd&pg=PR3&dq=learning+environment&ots=paG8114iz&sig=hqJQOn9aoRnSiFFmjV_vlHb7CEk#PPA223,M1. Retrieved on March 20, 2008.

Jones, R. (2008a). New to widening participation? An overview of research. York: Higher Education Academy. Available at http://www.heacademy.ac.uk/resources/detail/ourwork/inclusion/wprs/WPRS_New_to_WP_complete_synthesis. Accessed on July 24, 2010.

Jones, R. (2008b). Student retention and success: Research synthesis for the higher education academy. York: Higher Education Academy. Available at http://www.heacademy.ac.uk/resources/detail/ourwork/inclusion/wprs/WPRS_retention_synthesis. Accessed on July 24, 2010.

Jones, R., & Thomas, L. (2003). The 2003 UK government higher education white paper: A critical assessment of its implications for the access and widening participation agenda. *Journal of Education Policy*, 20(5), 615–630.

Jones, R., & Thomas, L. (2005). The 2003 UK government higher education white paper: A critical assessment of its implications for the access and widening participation agenda. *Journal of Education Policy*, 20(5), 615–630.

Kahlenberg, R. D. (2010). *Rewarding strivers: Helping low-income students succeed in college.* New York: The century Foundation Press.

Kalberg, S. (1994). *Max Weber's comparative-historical sociology*. Cambridge: Polity.

Kalsbeek, D. H. (2006). Some reflections on SEM structures and strategies. *College and University Journal*, 81, 3–10.

Keep, E., & Mayhew, K. (2004). The economic and distributional implications of current policies on higher education. *Oxford Review of Economic Policy*, 20(2), 298–314.

Kelly, J. (2002, May 11). New recruits must be keen to keep on learning, say top employers. *The Financial Times*, p. 13.

Kennedy, G., Judd, T., Churchward, A., Gray, K., & Krause, K. (2008). First year students' experiences with technology: Are they really digital natives? *Australasian Journal of Educational Technology*, 24(1), 108–122.

Kiš-Glavaš, L. (2010). TEMPUS Education for Equal Opportunities at Croatian Universities – EduQuality. Available at http://www.eduquality-hr.com/. Retrieved on January 19, 2009.

Kovačić, A., Kirinić, V., & Divjak, B. (2009). Linguistic competence in tertiary-level instruction in English and its relevance for student mobility. *JIOS, 33*(1), 25–37.

Krause, K. (2006). Making connections in the first year: A key to success in an age of unreason. Keynote presented at the 19th International Conference on the First Year Experience, Toronto, Ontario, July 24–26.

Krause, K. (2010). Using student survey data to shape academic priorities and approaches. In: L. Stefani (Ed.), *The effectiveness of academic development*. London: Routledge.

Krause, K. (in press). Whole-of-university strategies for evaluating the student experience. In: M. Saunders, P. Trowler, & V. Bamber (Eds), *Reconceptualising evaluative practices in higher education*. London: Open University Press.

Krause, K., & Coates, H. (2008). Students' engagement in first-year university. *Assessment and Evaluation in Higher Education, 33*(5), 493–505.

Krause, K., & Duchesne, S. (2000). With a little help from my friends: Social interactions on campus and their role in the first year experience. Fourth Pacific Rim Conference: First Year in Higher Education – Creating Futures for a New Millennium, July 5–7, Brisbane, Australia. Available at www.fyhe.com.au/past_papers/papers/KrausePaper. doc

Krause, K., Vick, M., Boon, H., & Bland, D. (2009, unpublished report). A fair go beyond the school gate? Systemic factors affecting participation and attainment in tertiary education by Queensland students from LSES backgrounds. Brisbane: Queensland Department of Education and Training.

Kuh, G., Hayek, J., Carini, R., Ouimet, J., Gonyea, R., & Kennedy, J. (2001). NSSE technical and norms report. Bloomington: Indiana University, Center for Postsecondary Research and Planning.

Kuh, G. D. (2001). Assessing what really matters to student learning: Inside the national survey of student engagement. *Change, 33*(3), 10–17, 66.

Kuh, G. D. (2008). *High-impact educational practices: What they are, who as access to them, and why they matter*. Washington, DC: AAC&U.

Kuh, G. D. (2009). What student affairs professionals need to know about student engagement. *Journal of College Student Development, 50*(6), 683–706.

Kuh, G. D., Kinzie, J., Schuh, J. H., Whitt, E. J., & Associates. (2005). *Student success in college: Creating conditions that matter*. San Francisco, CA: Jossey-Bass.

Lang, D. W. (2009). Articulation, transfer, and student choice in a binary post-secondary system. *Higher Education, 57*, 355–371.

Lather, P. (1986). Research as praxis. *Harvard Educational Review, 56*(3), 257–277.

La Trobe University. (2009). Design for learning: Curriculum review and renewal. Melbourne. Available at http://www.latrobe.edu.au/ctlc/assets/downloads/dfl/White_Paper_Ac_Board_approved_version.pdf

La Trobe University. (2010). Design for Learning (DfL) Project. Melbourne: La Trobe University.

Law on Scientific Activity and Higher Education. Available at http://narodne-novine.nn.hr/clanci/sluzbeni/306330.html. Retrieved on December 19, 2009.

Layer, G. (2002). Developing inclusivity. *International Journal of Lifelong Learning, 21*(1), 3–12.

Layer, G. (2004). *Widening participation and employability*. York: LSTN.

Leathwood, C. (2004). A Critique of institutional inequalities in higher education (or an alternative to hypocrisy for higher educational policy). *Theory and Research in Education, 2*(1), 31–48.

Leathwood, C., & O'Connell, P. (2003). 'It's a struggle': The construction of the 'new student' in higher education. *Journal of Education Policy*, *18*(6), 597–615.

Leeds Metropolitan University. (2005). WP strategy short version. Available at http://www.leedsmet.ac.uk/metoffice/WP_Strategy_2005_-_08_final_short_version.pdf. Accessed on September 24, 2010.

Leeds Metropolitan University. (2010a). Quality, relevance & sustainability: Leeds metropolitan university strategic plan 2010–2015. Available at http://www.leedsmet.ac.uk/strategicplan/Leeds-Metropolitan_Strategic-Plan_2010-2015.pdf. Accessed on October 4.

Leeds Metropolitan University. (2010b). Equality and diversity organisation. Available at http://www.leedsmet.ac.uk/equality_diversity_old/documents/ED_Governance_Structure.pdf. Accessed on October 4.

Letseka, M. (2009). University drop-out and researching (lifelong) learning and work. In: L. Cooper & S. Walters (Eds), *Learning/work: Turning work and learning inside out*. Cape Town: HSRC Press.

Levitas, R., Fenton, S., & Guy, W. (1991). *Turned down or turned off? Choosing university, choosing Bristol*. Unpublished report. Department of Sociology, University of Bristol, Bristol.

Levitas, R., Guy, W., Fenton, S., Fenton, A., & West, N. (2006). *Declining Bristol: A report on a widening participation survey*. Unpublished report. Department of Sociology, University of Bristol, Bristol.

Little, B., Connor, H., Lebeau, Y., Pierce, D., Sinclair, E., Thomas, L., & Yarrow, K. (2003). *Vocational higher education – does it meet employers' needs?* London: Learning and Skills Development Agency.

Little, G. (1970). *The university experience: An Australian study*. Parkville: Melbourne University Press.

Little, G. (1975). *Faces on campus: A psychosocial study*. Parkville: Melbourne University Press.

Machin, S., Murphy, R., & Soobedar, Z. (2009). Differences in labour market gains from higher education participation. Research commissions by the National Equality Panel.

Maes R., & Sylin, M. (2009, April). Ébauche d'un modèle pour l'action sociale des universités à l'attention des étudiants: L'évolution de l'action sociale de l'Université libre de Bruxelles. Paper presented at the 3rd AIFRIS Conference, Tunis, Tunisia.

Maes R., Sztalberg C., & Sylin, M. (2010, May). L'expérience comme stigmate ou comme acquis? Réflexions sur les pratiques de valorisation des acquis de l'expérience en Communauté française de Belgique. Paper presented at the 26th Congress of the AIPU, Rabat, Morocco.

Mann, S. (2005). Alienation in the learning environment: A failure of community? *Studies in Higher Education*, *30*(1), 43–55.

Mason, G., Williams, G., Cramer, S., & Guile, D. (2002). *How higher education enhances the employability of graduates*. London: HEFCE.

May, H., & Bridger, K. (2010). *Developing and embedding inclusive policy and practice in higher education*. York: The Higher Education Academy.

McCulloch, A., & Thomas, L. (2011 forthcoming). Widening participation to doctoral study and research degrees: Towards a research agenda for an emergent policy issue. Higher Education Research and Development.

McInerney, D., & McInerney, V. (2006). *Educational psychology: Constructing learning* (4th ed.). Sydney: Prentice-Hall.

Metcalf, H. (1997). *Class and higher education: The participation of young people from the lower social classes*. London: CIHE.

Muller, J. (2000). What knowledge is of most worth for the millennial citizen? In: A. Kraak (Ed.), *Changing modes: New knowledge production and its implications for higher education in South Africa*. Pretoria: HSRC.

Muraskin, L., & Lee, J. (2004). Raising the graduation rates of low-income college students. Pell Institute for the Study of Opportunity in Higher Education. Indianapolis, IN: Lumina Foundation for Education.

Murray, N., & Klinger, C. M. (2011 forthcoming). Enabling education: Adding value in an enterprise culture. In M. Cooper (Ed.), *From access to success: Closing the knowledge divide: Proceedings of the 19th EAN Annual Conference*, Södertörn University, Stockholm, Sweden, June 14–16, 2010.

National Audit Office. (2002). *Improving student achievement in English higher education*. London: TSO.

National Audit Office (NAO). (2007). *Staying the course: The retention of students in higher education*. London: HMSO.

National Audit Office. (2008). Widening participation in higher education. Report by the comptroller and auditor general|hc 725 session 2007–2008|June 25. London: The Stationery Office. Available at http://www.nao.org.uk/publications/0708/widening_participation_in_high.aspx. Accessed on September 1, 2010.

National Committee of Inquiry into Higher Education. (1997a). *Higher education in the learning society (popularly known as The Dearing Report)*. London: HMSO.

National Committee of Inquiry into Higher Education. (1997b). *Higher education in the learning society summary report*. NCIHE/97/849. Norwich.

National Survey of Student Engagement (NSSE). (2010). Available at http://www.nsse.iub.edu/html/survey_instruments_2010.cfm.

NBEET. (1990). *A fair chance for all*. National and Institutional Planning for Equity in Higher Education. A Discussion Paper, 90/6. Department of Employment, Education and Workplace Relations. Available at http://www.dest.gov.au/sectors/training_skills/publications_resources/indexes/documents/90_06_pdf.htm. Accessed on October 15, 2010.

Noone, L., & Cartwright, P. (2005). Teaching 'now'-imagining the 'not yet': Possibilities and dilemmas of doing a critical pedagogy in the tertiary classroom. Paper presented at the 3rd International Conference on Imagination and Education, Coast Plaza Hotel, Vancouver, BC, Canada.

OFFA [Office for Fair Access]. (2010). What more can be done to widen access to highly selective universities? A report from Sir Martin Harris. Available at http://www.offa.org.uk/wp-content/uploads/2010/05/Sir-Martin-Harris-Fair-Access-report-web-version.pdf. Accessed on May 3, 2010.

Office national de l'Emploi. (2008). Rapport Annuel 2008. ONEM, Brussels.

Organisation for Economic Co-operation and Development. (2006). PISA Report 2006. OECD, Paris.

Ortiz, E. A., & Dehon, C. (2008). What are the factors of success at university? A case study in Belgium. *CESifo Economic Studies, 54*(2), 121–148.

O'Shea-Poon, T., Hawkins, R., Richardson, J. T. E., & Erling, E. (2010). *Improving the degree attainment of black and minority ethnic students*. Milton Keynes: The Open University.

Ozga, J., & Sukhnandan, L. (1998). Undergraduate non completion: Developing an explanatory model. *Higher Education Quarterly, 52*(3), 316–333.

Pascarella, E., & Terenzini, P. (1991). *How college affects students: Findings from twenty years of research*. San Francisco: Jossey-Bass.

Paton, K., & Surridge, P. (2005). *Student experiences of the University of Bristol: An investigation into experiences and needs.* Unpublished report. Department of Sociology, University of Bristol, Bristol.

Perry, W. (1999). *Forms of intellectual and ethical development in the college years: A scheme.* New York: Harcourt Brace.

Phillimore, J., & Koshy, P. (2010). Implications of the proposed low SES participation target for Australian University Enrolments. Adelaide: ATN. Available at http://www.atn. edu.au/newsroom/Docs/2010/ATN%20EQUITY%20REPORT%20Final%20Feb% 202010.pdf. Accessed on October 15.

Pitcher, J., & Purcell, K. (1998). Diverse expectations and access to opportunities: Is there a graduate labour market? *Higher Education Quarterly, 52*(2), 179–203.

Powney, J. (Ed.). (2002). *Successful student diversity: Case studies of practice in learning and teaching and widening participation.* HEFCE 2002/48. HEFCE, Bristol.

Prosser, M., & Trigwell, M. (1999). *Understanding learning and teaching: The experience in higher education.* Buckingham: The Society for Quality Learning at University & Open University Press.

Purcell, K., & Hogarth, T. (1999). *Graduate opportunities, social class and age: Employers' recruitment strategies in the new graduate labour market.* London: CIHE.

Quinn, J., Thomas, L., Slack, K., Casey, L., Thexton, W., & Noble, J. (2005). *From life crisis to lifelong learning: Rethinking working-class 'drop-out' from higher education.* York: Joseph Rowntree Foundation.

Ramsay, E. (2004). A new pathway for adult learners: Evaluation of a school-university access pilot. DEST, Evaluations and Investigations Program. Canberra: AGPS. Available at http://www.dest.gov.au/sectors/higher_education/publications_resources/profiles/new_ pathway_for_adult_learners.htm. Accessed on August 13, 2009.

Ramsay, E., Tranter, D., Sumner, R., & Barrett, S. (1996). Outcomes of a University's flexible admissions policies. DEST, Evaluations and Investigations Program. Canberra: AGPS.

Ramsden, P. (2003). *Learning to teach in higher education* (2nd ed.). London: RoutledgeFalmer.

Raphael Reed, L., Croudace, C., Harrison, N., Baxter, A., & Last, K. (2007). Young participation in higher education: A sociocultural study of educational engagement in Bristol South parliamentary constituency Bristol. Bristol: University of the West of England and Higher Education Funding Council for England.

Read, B., Archer, A., & Leathwood, C. (2003). Challenging cultures? Student conceptions of 'Belonging' and 'Isolation' at a Post-1992 University. *Studies in Higher Education, 28*(3), 261–277.

Reay, D. (2001). Finding or losing yourself? Working-class relationships to education. *Journal of Education Policy, 16*(4), 333–346.

Reay, D., David, M., & Ball, S. (2001). Making a difference? Institutional habituses and higher education choice. *Sociological Research Online, 5*(4). Available at htttp:// www.socresonline.org.uk/5/4/reay.html.

Reay D., David, M. E., & Ball, S. (2005). *Degrees of choice: Class, race, gender, and higher education.* Stoke on Trent, Trentham Books.

Review of the Higher Education Equity Programme (HEEP). (2004). DEST. Available at from http://www.dest.gov.au/sectors/higher_education/publications_resources/profiles/ review_higher_education_equity_programme.htm

Reynolds, D., Nichol, J., LaVelle, L., Gunraj, J., Goulbourn, J., Iji, N., Parkinson, G., Sutton, C., MacLeod, I., & Koshy, V. (2010). Aiming higher: The plymouth and peninsula tri-level model (PPM) for school/HE links. Available at http://www.hefce.ac.uk/pubs/rdreports/2010/rd07_10/

Richardson, J. T. E. (2007). *Degree attainment, ethnicity and gender: A literature review.* York: The Higher Education Academy.

Ross, F. E., & Smith, M. (2010). Collaborations for entering student success. In: S. Evenbeck, B. Jackson, M. Smith, D. Ward, & Associates (Eds), *Organizing for student success: The university college model* (Monograph No. 53, pp. 25–29). Columbia, SC: University of South Carolina, National Resource Center for the First Year Experience and Students in Transition. A Template for First-Year Seminars at IUPUI. Available at http://uc.iupui.edu/uploadedFiles/Learning_Communities/LC%20Template.pdf

Rudduck, J., & Flutter, J. (2004). *How to improve your school.* London: Continuum.

Saunders, S. (2010). Looking back. In: D. L. Featherman, M. Hall & M. Krislov (Eds), *The next 25 years – affirmative action in higher education in the United States and South Africa* (pp. 259–267). Anne Arbor, MI: University of Michigan Press.

Schwartz Report. (2004). Fair admissions to Higher Education: Recommendations for good practice. Available at http://www.admissions-review.org.uk/consultation.html

Scott, I. (2010). Who is 'getting through' in South Africa? Graduate output and the reconstruction of the formal curriculum. In: D. L. Featherman, M. Hall & M. Krislov (Eds), *The next 25 years – affirmative action in higher education in the United States and South Africa* (pp. 229–243). Anne Arbor, MI: University of Michigan Press.

Scott, P. (2004). Researching widening access: An overview. In: M. Osborne, J. Gallacher & B. Crossan (Eds), *Researching widening access to lifelong learning-issues and approaches in international research* (pp. 17–28). London: Routledge.

Shalem, Y., & Steinberg, C. (2006). Portfolio-based assessment of prior learning: A cat and mouse chase after invisible criteria. In: P. Anderson & J. Harris (Eds), *Retheorising RPL.* Leicester: NIACE Publishers.

Shaw, E., & Carter, S. (2004). *Social entrepreneurship: Theoretical antecedents and empirical analysis of entrepreneurial processes and outcomes. Frontiers of entrepreneurship research* (pp. 637–651). Wellesley: Babson College.

Shaw, J. (2009). The diversity paradox: Does student diversity enhance or challenge excellence? *Journal of Further and Higher Education, 33*(4), 321–332.

Shaw, J., Brain, K., Bridger, K., Foreman, J., & Reid, I. (2007). *Embedding widening participation and promoting student diversity: What can be learned from a business case approach?* York: Higher Education Academy.

Smith, B., MacGregor, J., Matthews, R., & Gabelnick, F. (2004). *Learning communities: Reforming undergraduate education.* San Francisco: Jossey-Bass.

Smith, C., Fisher, R., McPhail, R., & Davies, L. (2010). Good practice in assessment case study – Student assessment literacy in the bachelor of business. Available at http://www.griffith.edu.au/gihe/teaching-learning-curriculum/assessment/good-practice

Smith, J., McKnight, A., & Naylor, R. (2000). Graduate employability: Policy, and performance in higher education. *Economic Journal, 110*(464), F382–F411.

Smith, K., & Woodward, A. (2007). Action research: A vehicle for inspiring multi-literacies. Paper presented to the English Literacy Conference, Canberra, ACT, July 2007. Available at http://www.englishliteracyconference.com.au/07.php?id = 1. Accessed on December 10.

Standards for Disabled Persons for UNICA Universities. (2007). Available at http://www.unizg.hr/uredssi/images/datoteke/unica_minimalni_standardi.pdf. Accessed on December 19, 2009.

Stevenson, J., Clegg, S., & Lefever, R. (2010). The discourse of widening participation and its critics: An institutional case study. *London Review of Education, 1474–8479, 8*(2), 105–115.

Storan, J., Thomas, L., Wylie, V., & Berzins, K. (2009). Action on access WPSA meta-analysis, presented at action on access widening participation strategic assessment conference. London. Available at http://www.actiononaccess.org/resources/files/resources_John_Storan_Presentation_06_11_09[1].ppt. Accessed on June 21, 2010

Strategy for Lifelong Learning 2008–2010. (2008). Institute for the development of education. Available at http://www.iro.hr/userdocs/File/IDE_Strategy_08-10_summary.pdf. Retrieved on February 6, 2010.

Stuart, M., Lido, C., Morgan, J., & May, S. (2009). *Student diversity, extra-curricular activities and perceptions of graduate outcomes.* York: Higher Education Academy.

Stuart, M., Lido, C., Morgan, S., Solomon, L., & Akroyd, K. (2008). Widening participation to postgraduate study: Decisions, deterrents and creating success. York: Higher Education Academy. Available at http://www.heacademy.ac.uk/assets/York/documents/ourwork/inclusion/WPtoPG_Stuart.pdf. Accessed on November 25, 2010.

Supporting Professionalism in Admissions/DIUS. (2008). Fair admissions to higher education: A review of the implementation of the Schwartz report principles three years. Available at http://www.spa.ac.uk/schwartz-report-review08.html

Tate, J., Hatt, S., & Baxter, A. (2006). You can't ask a leaflet a question: Relevant information about HE for under-represented social groups. *Journal of Access Policy and Practice, 3*(2), 103–118.

The Bologna Declaration on the European Space for Higher Education: An Explanation. (1999). Confederation of EU Rectors' Conferences and the Association of European Universities (CRE). Available at http://ec.europa.eu/education/policies/educ/bologna/bologna.pdf. Retrieved on December 23, 2010. p. 5.

The Bologna Process – Towards the European Higher Education Area. (1999). From the European Commission Web Site. Available at http://ec.europa.eu/education/higher-education/doc1290_en.htm. Retrieved on December 23, 2010.

The Bologna Process – Towards the European Higher Education Area. (2007). From the Council of Europe Web Site. Available at http://www.coe.int/t/dg4/highereducation/ehea2010/bolognapedestrians_en.asp#P124_12326. Retrieved on December 23, 2010.

The Open University (OU). (2009a). *Equality and Diversity … making it happen: The open university equality scheme 2009–2012.* Milton Keynes: The Open University.

The Open University (OU). (2009b). *Widening participation strategy 2009–2012.* Milton Keynes: The Open University.

The Open University (OU). (2010). *OU futures 2010–2013.* Milton Keynes: The OU.

The Statute of the University of Zagreb. (2005). From the University of Zagreb Web Site. Available at http://www.unizg.hr/fileadmin/rektorat/dokumenti/statut/statuteng.pdf. Retrieved on December 23, 2010, p. 3.

Thomas, L. (2001). *Widening participation in post compulsory education.* London: Continuum.

Thomas, L. (2002). Student Retention in higher education: The role of institutional habitus. *Journal of Education Policy, 17*(4), 423–442.

Thomas, L. (2002b). *Building social capital to improve student's success.* Exeter: BERA.

Thomas, L. (2005). The implications of widening participation for learning and teaching. In: C. Duke & G. Layer (Eds), *Widening participation: Which way forward for English higher education?* Leicester: NIACE.

Thomas, L. (2006). CSAP publication.

Thomas, L. (2009a). A whole-institution approach to widening access and promoting student success across the student lifecycle. In: *Access to Success: Fostering Trust and Exchange between Europe and Africa*. Reader, Brussels: European Universities Association.

Thomas, L. (2009b). Mainstreaming and sustaining widening participation in institutions. Final Report to the Higher Education Funding Council for England, Ormskirk, September 2009. Available at http://www.actiononaccess.org/index.php?p = 11_2_3. Action on Access.

Thomas, L., Ashley, M., Diamond, J., Grime, K., Farrelly, N., Murtagh, L., Richards, A., & Woolhouse, C. (2010). From projects to whole school/college-higher education institution partnerships: Identifying the critical success factors under-pinning effective strategic partnerships. Accessed on http://www.hefce.ac.uk/pubs/rdreports/2010/rd07_10/rd07_10edgehill.pdf

Thomas, L. (2011). Do pre-entry interventions such as 'Aimhigher' impact on student retention and success? A review of the literature. *Higher Education Quarterly*, forthcoming.

Thomas, L., & Jones, R. (2007). *Embedding employability in the context of widening participation*. York: Higher Education Academy.

Thomas, L., May, H., Harrop, H., Houston, M., Knox, H., Lee, M. F., Osborne, M., Pudner, H., & Trotman, C. (2005). From the margins to the mainstream: Embedding widening participation in higher education. London: Universities UK/SCOP. Available at http://www.universitiesuk.ac.uk/Publications/Documents/margins_fullreport.pdf. Accessed on September 12, 2010.

Thomas, L., & Quinn, J. (2006). *First-generation entry into higher education*. Milton Keynes: SRHE/Open University Press.

Thomas, L., & May, H. (2010). *Inclusive learning and teaching in higher education*. York: Higher Education Academy.

Thomas, L., & May, H. (2011). *What works? Student retention and success programme interim publication*. London: Paul Hamlyn Foundation.

Thomas, L., Ashley, M., Diamond, J., Grime, K., Farrelly, N., Murtagh, L., Richards, A., & Woolhouse, C. (2010a). From projects to whole school/college-higher education institution partnerships: Identifying the critical success factors under-pinning effective strategic partnerships. Available at http://www.hefce.ac.uk/pubs/rdreports/2010/rd07_10/rd07_10edgehill.pdf

Thomas, L., Storan, J., Wylie, V., Berzins, K., Harley, P., Linley, R., & Rawson, A. (2010b). Review of widening participation strategic assessments 2009. Ormskirk. Available at http://www.actiononaccess.org/index.php?p=19_4. Action on Access.

Thomson, P. (2004). Unpopular voices: Listening to pupils "at risk". Paper presented at the International Networking for Educational Transformation On-line Conference on Student Voice, September 20–26, 2004. Available at http://www.cybertext.net.au/inet/focus_papers/f5_14.htm. Retrieved on September 25.

Tinto, V. (1990). Colleges as communities: Taking research on student persistence seriously. *The Review of Higher Education, 21*(2), 167–177.

Tinto, V. (1993). *Leaving college: Rethinking the causes and cures of student attrition* (2nd ed.). Chicago: University of Chicago Press.

Tinto, V. (1998). Colleges as communities: Taking research on student persistence seriously. *The Review of Higher Education, 21*(2), 167–177.

Tinto, V. (2004). Student retention and graduation: Facing the truth, living with the consequences. Occasional Paper 1. Washington, DC: The Pell Institute for the Study of Opportunity in Higher Education.

Tinto, V. (2008). Access without support is not opportunity. Keynote address at the 36th Annual Institute for Chief Academic Officers, The Council of Independent Colleges, 1 November 2008, Seattle, Washington. Available at http://www.cic.edu/conferences_ events/caos/2008_CAO_Resources/2008CAO_tinto.pdf. Accessed on August 28, 2009.

Toyne, B. (1993). Internationalizing the business administration faculty is no easy task. In: S. Cavusgil (Ed.), *Internationalizing business education: Meeting the challenge* (pp. 45–64). East Lansing: Michigan State University Press.

Trinity College Dublin (TCD). (2006a). Strategic plan update. Dublin: TCD. Available at http://www.tcd.ie/assets/pdf/TCDStrategicPlanUpdate2006.pdf. Accessed on August 11, 2010.

Trinity College Dublin. (2006b). *Report to board on the review of the student disability service.* Dublin: TCD.

Trinity College Dublin. (2009a). Strategic plan 2009–2014. Dublin: TCD. Available at https://www.tcd.ie/info/strategicplan/. Accessed on August 11, 2010.

Trinity College Dublin. (2009b). Non-traditional student statistics 2008–2009. Dublin: TCD. Available at http://www.tcd.ie/CAPSL/TIC/assets/doc/Access%20Student%20Figures_ FINAL%20for%20website.doc. Accessed on November 2, 2010.

Trinity College Dublin. (2009c). *Access plan 2009–2013.* Dublin: TCD.

Trowler, P. (1995). *Academics responding to change.* Buckingham: SRHE/Open University Press.

Trowler, P. (1998). *Academics responding to change.* Buckingham: The Society for Research into Higher Education & Open University Press.

Tysome, T. (2007). Access agenda is now back on track. *Times Higher Educational Supplemement*, pp. 6–7, July 22.

UCAS. (2002). *Paving the way.* Cheltenham: UCAS.

Ulrich, N. (2005). Monitoring and supporting mature students at Aston University. Birmingham: Aston University. [Internal Report].

UniSA. (2010). Definitions used in equity planning and policy formulation. Adelaide: University of South Australia. Available at http://www.unisa.edu.au/ltu/staff/start/ equity/definitions.asp. Accessed on October 15.

Universities Australia. (2008). Participation and equity: A review of the participation in higher education of people from low socioeconomic backgrounds and Indigenous people. Prepared for Universities Australia by the Centre for the Study of Higher Education University of Melbourne, March.

University of Bristol. (2009). Widening participation strategic assessment. Available at http://www.bristol.ac.uk/academicregistry/raa/wpur-office/strategy-documents-publications/

University of Cape Town. (2004). Policy on recognition of prior learning. Available at http://www.uct.ac.za/downloads/uct.ac.za/about/policies/rec_prior_learning.pdf

University of Cape Town. (2010). Teaching and learning report 2009–2020. Available at http://www.uct.ac.za/wervices/ip/iiu/reporting/faculties

UUK. (2009). Patterns of higher education institutions in the UK. Ninth Report. Universities UK, London. Available at http://www.universitiesuk.ac.uk/Publications/Pages/Patterns9. aspx. Accessed on August 10, 2010.

UWE (University of the West of England). (2009). Widening participation strategic assessment-unpublished submission to the Higher Education Funding Council for England, UWE, Bristol.

van Stolk, C., Tiessen, J., Clift, J., & Levitt, R. (2007). Student retention in higher education courses. International comparison. Report prepared for the National Audit Office, RAND Corporation, Cambridge. Available at http://www.nao.org.uk/publications/ nao_reports/06-07/0607616_international.pdf. Accessed on September 9, 2009.

Vidaček-Hainš, V., Appatova, V., & Prats, H. (2008). Components of effective academic learning environment: Case studies of Croatian and American students. *Proceedings of the 19th Central European International Conference on Information and Intelligent Systems*, HR, Varazdin (pp. 137–144).

Vidaček-Hainš, V., Divjak, B., & Ostroški, M. (2008). The mobility of students and the internationalization of higher education in Croatia. In: M. Cooper (Ed), *Diversity in Higher Education (Migration, Integration and Lifelong Learning)* (pp. 58–65). Papers presented at the 17th Annual Conference of the European Access Network, Technische Universität, Berlin, Germany, 30 June–2 July. Available at http://www.ean-edu.org/upload_data/EAN%20BOOK/Berlin2008confbook%5B1%5D.pdf. Retrieved on February 6, 2010.

Vidaček-Hainš, V., Divjak, B., & Horvatek, R. (2004). The importance of active students participation in communication at colleges and universities and the possible impact of achievement. International Student Retention Colloquium, Staffordshire University, Stoke-on-Trent, UK.

Vidaček-Hainš, V., Divjak, B., & Ostroški, M. (2009). *Motivation for studying and gender issue* (pp. 297–208). Vienna: DAAAM International Scientific Book 2009.

Vidaček-Hainš, V., & Horvatek, R. (2003). Country overviews: Republic of Croatia. In: L. Thomas & J. Quinn (Eds), *International Insights into widening participation: Supporting the success of under-represented groups in tertiary education* (pp. 37–42). Staffordshire, UK: The Institute for Access Studies, Staffordshire University.

Vidaček-Hainš, V., Horvatek, R., & Divjak, B. (2009). Individual approach to students in process of higher education according to their specific needs. In: M. Cooper (Ed.), *The 18th EAN Annual Conference "Changing the Culture of the Campus Towards an Inclusive Higher Education -Ten Years On"*. York, UK: York St John University.

Vidaček-Hainš, V., Kirinić, V., & Dušak, V. (2009). Computer attitudes and computer literacy levels relationships. *Informatologia*, 42(1), 30–37.

Vidaček-Hainš, V., Prats, H., & Appatova, V. (2009). Self-efficacy and components of effective learning environment in higher education: Comparison of Croatian and American students. *Proceedings of the 20th Central European International Conference on Information and Intelligent Systems*, HR, Varazdin (pp. 43–48).

Vizek-Vidović, V. (2006). TEMPUS project DUCAS-developing university counseling and advisory services. Available at http://www.tempus-ducas.info/. Retrieved on Dececember 19, 2009.

Wakeling, P., & Kyriacou, C. (2010). Widening participation from undergraduate to postgraduate research degrees. A research synthesis. ESRC and National co-ordinating centre for public engagement. Available at http://www.esrcsocietytoday.ac.uk/ESRCInfoCentre/Images/Widening%20participation%20Synthesis%20final%20repor_tcm6-36772.pdf. Accessed on November 25.

Wakeling, P. B. J. (2009a). Are ethnic minorities underrepresented in UK postgraduate study? *Higher Education Quarterly*, 63(1), 86–111.

Wakeling, P. B. J. (2009b). *Social class and access to postgraduate education in the UK: A sociological analysis*. Ph.D. thesis. University of Manchester.

Waller, R. (2006). 'I don't feel like 'a student', I feel like 'me'!': The over-simplification of mature learners' experience(s). *Research in Post-Compulsory Education*, 11, 115–130.

Walters, S. (2004). Researching access in a rapidly changing context: Experiences from higher education in South Africa. In: M. Osborne, J. Gallacher & B. Crossan (Eds), *Researching widening access to Lifelong learning-issues and approaches in international research* (pp. 29–41). London: Routledge.

Weiler, H. (1984). Knowledge and legitimation: The national and international politics of educational research. Paper for 5th World Congress of Comparative Education, Paris, July 2–6.

Wenger, E. (1998). *Communities of practice: Learning, meaning and identity.* Cambridge: Cambridge University Press.

West, A., Emmerson, C., Frayne, C., & Hind, A. (2009). Examining the impact of opportunity bursaries on the financial circumstances and attitudes of undergraduate students in England. *Higher Education Quarterly, 63*(2), 119–140.

Wilcox, P., Winn, S., & Fyvie-Gauld, M. (2005). 'It was nothing to do with the university, it was just the people': The role of social support in the first year experience of higher education. *Studies in Higher Education, 30*(6), 707–722.

Write About. (2008). *Bullying.* Warrington: Gatehouse Books.

Write About. (2009). *Inspirational people.* Warrington: Gatehouse Books.

Yeld, N. (2010). Admission policies and challenges. In: D. L. Featherman, M. Hall & M. Krislov (Eds), *The next 25 years – affirmative action in higher education in the United States and South Africa* (pp. 175–186). Anne Arbor, MI: University of Michigan Press.

Yorke, M. (2004, reissued 2006). Employability in higher education: What it is – what it is not. York: The Higher Education Academy. Available at www.heacademy.ac.uk/resources. asp?process=full_record7section=generic&id=336

Yorke, M., & Longden, B. (2008). *The first year experience of higher education in the UK.* York: Higher Education Academy.

Yorke, M., & Thomas, L. (2003). Improving the retention of students from lower socio-economic groups. *Journal of Higher Education Policy and Management, 25*(1), 63–74.

Young, M. (2008). *Bringing knowledge back in: From social constructivism to social realism in the sociology of education.* London: Routledge.

Zyngier, D. (2003). Connectedness – isn't it time that education came out from behind the classroom door and rediscovered social justice. *Social Alternatives, 22*(3), 41–49.

BIOGRAPHIES

Rashidah N. Andrews is an academic advisor in the College of Liberal Arts at Temple University, Philadelphia, Pennsylvania. She earned an Ed.M. in higher education at Harvard University's Graduate School of Education and is currently a doctoral student in educational administration at temple. Before arrival at Temple, Rashidah spent three years as project manager for the Ethnic Minorities Student Achievement Grant (EMSAG) at Halesowen College in England, one year as director of College Retention at a non-profit in Philadelphia and two years as admission counselor at her alma mater. Her research interests include access, retention and persistence of low-income, first-generation students.

Derek Bland currently teaches in undergraduate and postgraduate pre-service teacher education courses at Queensland University of Technology (QUT), Brisbane. He also coordinates two school/university collaborative projects to improve educational outcomes for 'at-risk' groups. He joined QUT in 1991 to establish a special entry and student support initiative of the university to assist people from socio-economically disadvantaged backgrounds. Before this, Derek taught secondary art and worked in the Disadvantaged Schools Program in Victoria. Derek's research interests include the role of imagination in education and the use of visual research methods with students from educationally marginalised backgrounds.

Betsy Bowerman joined the Widening Participation team at the University of Bristol as Access and Mature Students' Adviser in 2003. She is responsible for developing initiatives to raise awareness of study opportunities for adult learners and works with academic departments to develop and clarify entry routes for learners taking non-A-level qualifications. Betsy has worked in adult education for over 25 years, including 10 years as access co-ordinator at Bridgwater College. She is chair of the Higher Education Access Committee of Open College Network South West Region. She is a graduate of the University of California, Berkeley, and has postgraduate qualifications in librarianship and in education.

Linda Cooper is associate professor in the Higher and Adult Education Studies Development Unit (HAESDU), in the Centre for Higher Education

Development (CHED) at the University of Cape Town (UCT). She teaches on the adult education programmes and is chair of the Adult Learner Working Group. Her research interests have focused on learning in social movements, skills development and workplace learning, and recognition of prior learning. She has acted as education advisor to a number of trade union education initiatives and is a member of the International Advisory Committee of the Researching Work and Learning conference.

Glenda Crosling is associate professor and director of Education Quality and Innovation at Monash University Sunway Campus and is responsible at the campus level for education quality assurance and its improvement as well as innovation. She was campus leader in the 2010 Institutional Audit undertaken by the Malaysian Qualifications Agency, from which the campus was granted self-accrediting status. Before taking up her current role in January 2009, she has worked in learning and teaching in higher education with both students and academic staff for two decades. At Monash University, she has been involved in educational policy development, such as the policy and procedures, 'Values for High Quality Teaching and Learning', and played a key role in the development and implementation of a range of teaching and learning programs to enhance educational quality and student retention. She has researched and published widely in international refereed journals, books and book chapters and presented at international conferences. She is author of several books on quality teaching and learning approaches and innovation, the most recent of which was published with Liz Thomas and Margaret Heagney in 2008 by Routledge: *Improving Student Retention in Higher Education: The Role of Teaching and Learning*.

Chris Croudace took his first degree, in philosophy, at Warwick followed by postgraduate study at Cambridge. Chris then pursued a career in the further education sector before joining the University of the West of England in 1994 as the institution's access co-ordinator. He is now the University's Director of Widening Participation. In that capacity, Chris works closely with colleagues inside and outside the University to open up opportunities for people from under-represented backgrounds, families, groups and communities and positively enable such people to succeed. Chris coordinated the preparation of the University's first Widening Participation Strategic Assessment, which was submitted to HEFCE in June 2009.

Blaženka Divjak (Ph.D. in mathematics) is full professor at University of Zagreb, faculty of organization and informatics and has been vice-dean for science and international cooperation for seven years. She currently lectures mathematics at undergraduate and graduate level and project management at postgraduate level. Dr. Divjak coordinates several national and international projects. She authored and co-authored more than 60 scientific and professional papers, 6 textbooks and participated in more than 50 scientific and professional conferences. Besides mathematics, her special interest is interdisciplinary research connecting technology enhanced learning, project management and decision-making in higher education and research.

Jayne K. Drake is associate professor of English, vice-dean for academic affairs and director of the Master of Liberal Arts Program in the College of Liberal Arts at Temple University, Philadelphia, Pennsylvania. She served as president of NACADA: The Global Community for Academic Advising in 2009–2010, chaired the board of directors and held a number of leadership positions in the association. Dr. Drake travels nationally and internationally to deliver keynote addresses and conducts workshops on a number of advising-related topics and serves as a consultant to colleges and universities regarding the development and reorganisation of advising services.

Vicky Duckworth is senior lecturer in Post Compulsory Education and Training (PCET), course leader for full-time provision and associate fellow for the Centre for Learning and Identity Studies (CLIS) at Edge Hill University. She is interested in practitioner and collaborative research methods, action research and linking research and practice. She is particularly interested in issues of violence, basic skills, empowerment and egalitarian and critical approaches to teaching and learning. She is author, co-author and editor of several books which include promoting Widening Participation in teacher training, critical approaches to curriculum design and contemporary issues in Lifelong Learning. Currently she is co-editing two books, which include creative approaches to teaching and learning and leadership across the educational sector. Further to this she is co-authoring a research book for Open University Press.

Scott E. Evenbeck, founding president of New Community College of the City University of New York (CUNY), served from 1997 to 2010 as founding dean of University College and professor of psychology, Indiana University Purdue University Indianapolis (IUPUI). Evenbeck serves as a Policy Center Advisor in the Foundations of Excellence in the First College Year and as a board member of the American Conference of Academic Deans. He completed his A.B. degree at Indiana University Bloomington and his M.A. and Ph.D. at the University of North Carolina at Chapel Hill.

Kerry Ferguson was appointed in 1997 to the position of dean (equity and access) at La Trobe University, Melbourne, Australia, and in 1999 appointed pro vice chancellor (equity and access). In 2005, her role expanded and she was appointed to the position of pro vice chancellor (equity and student services). Her portfolio includes responsibility for student services, student equity, equal opportunity including equal opportunity for women in the workplace, indigenous education, counselling services, careers and employment services, student complaints, student engagement and enrichment and the University Ombudsman. Her previous experience has spanned 20 years with the faculty of health sciences at La Trobe University. She has held various academic positions after her previous career as an occupational therapist with psychiatric services. She has been the head of the School of Occupational Therapy, deputy dean and dean of the Faculty of Health Sciences at La Trobe University. She continues to be a clinical member of the Australian Family Therapists Association. She is committed to the quality provision of student services, to redressing disadvantage in the higher education field and to student engagement at all levels in universities.

Michelle Gammo-Felton is the Widening Participation Manager for the Liverpool Institute for Performing Arts. She was a widening participation student herself when she first studied at Lancaster University. After completing her degree, she went on to work at Lancaster University for several years in student recruitment and then on to Westminster University working on widening access projects. It was here that she became interested in WP, and in 2008, she completed a master's in social justice and education at the Institute of Education, University of London. She has been at LIPA since April 2008.

Michelle Garvey is the inclusive curriculum development officer in Trinity College Dublin (TCD) where she has been working on Trinity Inclusive Curriculum (TIC) since October 2008. Before commencing work on TIC, Michelle worked in various positions in TCD, the University of Sheffield and Sheffield College of Further Education including philosophy tutor and peer mentor and as administrator on a back to education programme. Michelle has worked as a qualified guidance counsellor, with an M.Ed. from TCD. She also has a B.A. (hons) from TCD and an MPhil from the University of Sheffield, both in philosophy.

Janet Graham was appointed as the first Director of the Supporting Professionalism in Admissions (SPA) Programme in May 2006 and leads a small team of five providing advice and support to universities and colleges on a range of strategy, policy and good practice issues in admissions. She is leading SPA's work on contextual data and has worked on SPA's applicant experience strategy, feedback, admissions tests, admissions policies and many other areas, bringing SPA's work and fair admissions to the attention of leaders in HE. Janet was previously head of the University of Cambridge Admissions Office, worked at the University of Leicester as Director of Admissions and Student Recruitment and, in the 1980s, at Leicester Polytechnic in various posts including Head of Admissions. Janet was a member of the HE sector-led Delivery Partnership and Professor Steven Schwartz's task group that published the *Fair Admissions to Higher Education* report in 2004.

Marit Greek, associate professor, Centre for Educational Research and Development, has multicultural pedagogy as her subject area. From 1979 until 1995, she was a part of the academic staff at The Faculty of Nursing, where she for a period was dean. She has since 1995 been working with diversity in higher education, concentrating on how to prepare the academic staff to meet the cultural and linguistic diversity and how the the educational organisation can cope with the increasing change in the student population change. Greek has been responsible for supervising Norwegian second language students at OUC and has conducted research on developmental work this field. Her concern has been to create an inclusive and including learning environment, to contribute to pedagogical approaches that encourages and appreciates diversity and to exploit the resources represented by a diverse student population.

Margaret Hart began her professional life as a local authority social worker in Greater Manchester in the late 1970s. She moved to work in the voluntary sector, where she managed a community-based support service for children with disabilities and then took up senior management roles at regional and national level in two of the UK's largest children's charities. Alongside this, she became involved with the Open University (OU) both as a student and as a tutor. In 2003, Margaret changed direction and moved to work for the OU on a full-time basis. As head of Widening Participation, she holds a lead role in developing widening participation strategy and inclusive practice and has also led the development of the Community Partnerships Programme, which creates opportunities for higher education in highly targeted locations. These developments owe much to the understanding gained in her 'first career' of the needs of people living in disadvantaged communities and of community development approaches. She is a firm believer that social justice must be approached holistically and that success in widening participation requires strong co-ordination with social policy beyond higher education, active engagement of locally based partner organisations in outreach activity and an action learning approach to institutional transformation.

Sue Hatt has had a long and varied career in higher education. She worked at the University of the West of England, Bristol, firstly as an Economics lecturer and then as the regional manager for the South West region's Aimhigher programme. She held various posts within the institution and the sector, and her responsibilities have included maintaining and developing franchise and access links, smoothing the transition for first-year students, developing teaching and learning within a changing institutional environment. She was a QAA subject reviewer for Economics in England and Scotland. Her research interests include the evaluation of widening participation policy and practice, the student experience of higher education and gender, education and the labour market. She has published books and articles on these topics.

Sandra Hill is a senior lecturer in the Business School of the University of the West of Scotland. Although an experienced business studies lecturer, her research interests turned to education recently when she participated in the Doctor of Education programme at Stirling University. Her Ed.D. thesis examined the role of social capital in enhancing employability of business graduates, and she is now involved in examining how the educational experience can be enhanced through the programme design and delivery to provide greater opportunities for students to develop social capital relevant to employability.

Tony Hoare became a lecturer in Bristol in 1976, in geography, his undergraduate degree and Ph.D. subject previously as a student at Cambridge. Among his research interests is that of the UK's higher education sector, including its varied social and geographical patterns of student recruitment. This was stimulated by his serving as departmental admissions tutor and membership of a number of related university committees, including, latterly, widening participation. He became the University's inaugural director of Widening Participation research in 2006, tasked with providing an empirical research underpinning to the University's WP policies and practices. To further this, he established a joint WP research group between the two Bristol universities, which he still chairs.

Renata Horvatek graduated in philosophy and comparative literature at the University of Zagreb. She holds the position of international relations officer in the Faculty of Organization and Informatics at the University of Zagreb, and her main responsibilities are coordinating ERASMUS agreements and exchanges of students and teachers, coordinating outreach activities and public relations. Her interests are educational opportunities for under-represented groups of students and policy research that enables widening participation. She is currently a Hubert H. Humphrey fellow at the Pennsylvania State University in USA.

Amanda Ingleby has 10 years of experience in the field of widening participation, which has been recognised through an Aston University Excellence Award. She has extensive experience of setting up, leading and evaluating partnership outreach and widening participation projects and is currently the Strategic Adviser for Widening Participation. In her current role, Amanda is engaged in learning and teaching research within Aston University's Centre for Learning Innovation and Professional Practice (CLIPP). Amanda has held various professional development and teaching positions and has specific responsibility for HE quality assessment preparation and is co-author of Practical Pointers for Quality Assessment (1997).

Salma Ismail is a senior lecturer in the Higher and Adult Education Studies Development Unit (HAESDU), in the Centre for Higher Education Development (CHED) at the University of Cape Town (UCT). She teaches on the adult education programmes and is an active member on UCT's Transformation Committees and the Adult Learner Working Group. Her research interests have focused on adults learning in informal contexts such as in development and social movements, recognition of prior learning, the interactions between curricula including pedagogical practices and changing student needs and expectations. Salma's work in academic staff development has been in equity research and institutional transformation.

Steve Kendall is director of Widening Participation and Associate Dean of Partnerships at the University of Bedfordshire. In his senior management role, he provides leadership and vision to the University in respect of its mission to be a pre-eminent access university. He is a frequent contributor to national and international conferences. Recent work includes a contribution to the HEFCE-funded HEI school links project 'Bringing the Tapestry Together'. As chair of the Aimhigher Regional Group of Partnerships (East of England), and Area Director for Bedfordshire, Steve is significantly involved with current Aimhigher developments, issues and concerns. (Aimhigher is a national initiative enabling partnerships of HEIs, further education colleges and schools to work together to improve aspiration, attainment and progression from among those who are under-represented in higher education).

Christopher M. Klinger is the former director of the University of South Australia (UniSA) Foundation Studies access programme. He is also the chairperson of Adults Learning Mathematics, an International Research Forum (ALM), and an editor for the ALM International Journal. Committed to the notion that higher education should be accessible to everyone who aspires to it, not just school leavers, Chris has been involved with access education for a decade and a half, helping over 2500 non-traditional students gain entry to undergraduate degree programmes. He is co-author (with Zeegers, Egege and Deller-Evans) of *Essential Skills for Science and Technology* (Oxford University Press, 2007).

Kerri-Lee D. Krause is chair in higher education, director of the Griffith Institute for Higher Education and dean (student outcomes) at Griffith University, Brisbane, Australia. Her role connects the student experience and outcomes with support for academic staff and curriculum development. Her research expertise spans broadly across higher education policy areas, with a focus on the quality and changing nature of the student experience, the changing nature of academic work and the implications of these changes for policy and practice. She regularly provides advice to the sector on enhancing institutional quality, along with strategies for managing the changing student and academic staff experience in higher education.

Renaud Maes is counsellor for acknowledgment of prior experiential learning at the continuing education centre of the Université libre de Bruxelles and scientific associate of the research unit 'Psychology of Organisations (UPO)'.

Neil L. Murray is currently senior lecturer in applied linguistics and senior consultant English language proficiency at the University of South Australia. He has 25 years' experience managing and teaching on access programmes in Japan, the United Kingdom and Australia and holds degrees in applied linguistics from the universities of Cambridge and London. Currently, researching the intersection of widening participation and language and literacy, he is author of numerous articles in applied linguistics and access education and co-author of *Contemporary Topics* (Longman), *Inside Track: Writing Dissertations and Theses* (Longman) and *Writing up your University Assignments and Research Projects* (McGraw-Hill).

Tony O'Shea-Poon's early career was in human resources in the banking sector, until he saw the error of his ways and began to search for a more meaningful life. He obtained a B.A. in international studies through the

Open University and in 1998 began working in the field of equality and human rights, going on to take an M.A. in human rights at Birkbeck, University of London. He has worked on health inequalities for a primary care trust and spent many happy years wearing numerous hats in the voluntary sector, first as co-ordinator of a youth charity and then as equalities officer in an organisation for lesbian, gay, bisexual and transgender people. As head of equality and diversity at the Open University, where he has worked since 2005, he leads on the development and implementation of the equality scheme, driven by the University's social justice mission, the public sector equality duties and the business case for diversity. He chairs the Equality and Diversity Management Group. He is also the chair of Shika Tamaa Support Services, a HIV support and education charity and a training associate for Q:alliance, a lesbian, gay, bisexual and transgender charity.

Frank E. Ross, founding associate provost for student success at University of North Texas at Dallas, is the chief student affairs officer responsible for all student services and enrollment management functions. He previously served as assistant vice chancellor for student life and learning at Indiana University Purdue University Indianapolis (IUPUI). He completed his B.S. degree at Ball State University; M.A.E. degree at Western Kentucky University; M.A. degree from Ball State University and his Ph.D. at Indiana University.

Sabine Severiens has devoted most of her research life to diversity and inequality in education. Her main studies were a four-year longitudinal study on women in engineering education, a three-year study on ethnic minority students in higher education and a study on dropout of ethnic minority students in teacher education. Most recently, together with a group of researchers joined in the Consortium of Research on Urban Talent, she conducted a study on diversity and the transition between secondary and higher education. Before she started working at Risbo (www.risbo.nl/uk) in 2001, she worked for 10 years at a teacher training institute (University of Amsterdam). This is where she conducted her Ph.D. research on inequality in secondary education. Since 2005, Sabine has been director of Risbo. In this job, she combined her research activities with managerial tasks. In 2009, she was appointed professor of education by the Erasmus University Rotterdam, with a focus on diversity.

Dan Shaffer is one of three senior project officers for the Supporting Professionalism in Admissions (SPA) programme. Before joining SPA in December 2008, Dan held the post of Assistant Registrar at Aston University for over four years, responsible for admissions, enrolment, examinations and teaching facilities. Before Aston University, Dan spent over eight years in admissions at the University of Central England (now Birmingham City University), and spent two years as a part-time visiting lecturer in psychology alongside his admissions duties. While at both institutions, Dan was responsible for developing policy and good practice in higher education recruitment and welfare activities as well as gaining practical knowledge of the student experience beyond admissions and contributing to national discussions on good practice. Dan's current research for SPA includes leading on the applicant experience strategy, admissions' consideration of disability and on good practice in offer-making and managing student intake numbers.

Brian Spittle is in his 23rd year of administration at DePaul University. In his current role as assistant vice-president for enrolment management and marketing, he oversees the Center for Access and Attainment, which includes the university's federally funded TRIO programs for low-income and first-generation students along with community outreach activities and partnerships with Chicago schools and educational organisations. He is also an adjunct faculty member in the Department of Educational Policy Studies and Research at DePaul. Brian is a member of a number of advisory groups including the Steering Committee for the Consortium on Chicago School Research and the College and University Task Force for IB Americas. Brian received a bachelor of arts in politics from Nottingham University and a master's degree in political science from McMaster University in Canada. He has a Ph.D. in social and philosophical foundations of education from the University of Buffalo, New York.

Jacqueline Stevenson is a reader in Widening Participation at Leeds Metropolitan University. Much of her recent work has centred on issues around race, ethnicity and social class in relation to access to higher education and educational achievement. She has researched extensively with refugees and asylum seekers, members of ethnic minority communities, offenders and ex-offenders, young people leaving public care, those who are long-term unemployed, substance misusers and people who are homeless. Her research is primarily qualitative in focus and she has a particular interest in narrative research including story-telling and narrative inquiry.

Michel Sylin is professor at the Université libre de Bruxelles and head of the research unit 'Psychology of Organisations (UPO)' at the ULB.

Cécile Sztalberg is head of the continuing education centre at the Université libre de Bruxelles.

James Tate's background is in philosophy, which he studied as a mature student returning to education. He has taught philosophy for the University of Dundee, Keele University, the Open University and the University of the West of England, Bristol. He has worked in widening participation since 2000, firstly at the University of Exeter and subsequently at the University of the West of England in the Aimhigher programme. He has been involved in a number of publications as a part of the Aimhigher regional team in the South West.

Liz Thomas is director and chair of the Widening Participation Research Centre at Edge Hill University. She is also senior adviser for Widening Participation at the Higher Education Academy and lead adviser working with Institutions for Action on Access, the national widening participation co-ordination team for England. Liz is currently directing the What works? Student retention and success programme on behalf of the Higher Education Funding Council for England and the Paul Hamlyn Foundation. Liz is committed to using research to improve policy and practice, and she is renowned internationally for her research on widening participation and student success. She has undertaken research, consultancy and keynote addresses in Europe, the United States and Australia. Liz is author and editor of nine books on widening participation, including *Improving Student Retention in Higher Education: The Role of Teaching and Learning* (2008, RoutledgeFalmer). She is also editor of the journal *Widening Participation and Lifelong Learning*.

Violeta Vidaček-Hainš is an assistant professor at the University of Zagreb, Faculty of Organization and Informatics Varazdin. She has a Ph.D. from the University of Zagreb, Faculty of Organization and Informatics. She is coordinator for students with disabilities at the Faculty of Organization and Informatics. Her research fields of interest are (i) comparative studies and factors of effective learning environment in the higher education; (ii) interpersonal communication skills and (iii) students with disabilities. She has published more than 30 research papers and made presentations at many international conferences in Europe and the United States.

Richard Waller is director of Lifelong Learning in the Department of Education at the University of the West of England, Bristol. Originally trained as a sociologist, he has taught widely in further and higher education since 1994. He also worked as an access adviser in the University of Bristol's Widening Participation office before leaving to undertake full-time doctoral studies in 2001. Richard's research interests focus broadly on issues of social justice, particularly the intersection of education, social class and identity. He has published widely on this area, including numerous journal articles and book chapters from his Ph.D. on the experiences of adults returning to formal education as mature students.

Rick Wolff is a researcher at Risbo/Erasmus University Rotterdam. His research focuses on ethnic minority students in Dutch Higher Education. He has published on national and institutional enrolment figures and dropout and completion rates of ethnic minority students (compared to ethnic white students), compared higher education experiences of ethnic minority students and ethnic minority dropout students and studied the impact of parental education and ethnic background on study success. He has worked on studies on the learning environment of ethnic minority students in higher education and on teacher training programs (primary education teaching). Currently he is finishing his Ph.D. project on ethnic minority students in Dutch Higher Education.

Wâtte Zijlstra studied business administration at Erasmus University in Rotterdam. Since 2001, he has worked for The Hague University as a senior advisor in communication and marketing and as a lecturer for the master's programme on International Communication Management. Wâtte Zijlstra has undertaken several research studies into student satisfaction, employee satisfaction and student enrolment. Over the last two years, Wâtte has conducted research into the causes of academic achievement of the bachelor students as project manager of the 'Monitor Information Team Academic Achievement' at The Hague University. Wâtte also participates in COST (Consortium of Research on Urban Talent), a partnership of several researchers engaged in research in talent development of youngsters aged 12–24 years living in the urban areas of The Netherlands.